FIGHTING NAPOLEON

Also by Gareth Glover and Published by Frontline Books

The American Sharpe
The Adventures of an American Officer of the 95th Rifles in the Peninsular
and Waterloo Campaigns

The Waterloo Archive
Volume I: British Sources

The Waterloo Archive
Volume II: German Sources

The Waterloo Archive
Volume III: British Sources

The Waterloo Archive
Volume IV: British Sources

The Waterloo Archive
Volume V: German Sources

The Waterloo Archive
Volume VI: British Sources

An Eloquent Soldier
The Peninsular War Journals of Lieutenant Charles Crowe of the
Inniskillings, 1812–1814

Wellington's Voice
The Candid Letters of Lieutenant Colonel John Fremantle, Coldstream
Guards, 1808–1837

From Corunna to Waterloo
The Letters and Journals of Two Napoleonic Hussars, 1801–1816

Waterloo: The Defeat of Napoleon's Imperial Guard
Henry Clinton, the 2nd Division and the End of a 200-year-old Controversy

FIGHTING NAPOLEON

The Recollections of
Lieutenant John Hildebrand 35th Foot
in the Mediterranean and
Waterloo Campaigns

Gareth Glover

Frontline Books

FIGHTING NAPOLEON
The Recollections of Lieutenant John Hildebrand 35th Foot in the Mediterranean and Waterloo Campaigns

This edition published in 2016 by Frontline Books,
an imprint of Pen & Sword Books Ltd,
47 Church Street, Barnsley, S. Yorkshire, S70 2AS

ISBN: 978-1-47388-684-1

CIP data records for this title are available from the British Library

For more information on our books, please visit
www.frontline-books.com
email info@frontline-books.com
or write to us at the above address.

Printed and bound by CPI Group (UK) Ltd, Croydon, CR0 4YY
Typeset in 10.5/13.5 point Palatino

Contents

List of Maps

Foreword

Over the last decade or so, I have had the privilege of publishing a large number of previously unknown memoirs of soldiers who fought in the Napoleonic wars, some of which are very extensive, whilst some are incredibly short indeed. But, I can honestly say, that every one of them has imparted at least one snippet of new information that has challenged my understanding of the subject, or was previously completely unknown to me.

Although we may think we now have a very good appreciation and knowledge of this period in history, much is still to be learnt. Unfortunately, many of these memoirs skirt over the commonplace, the norm, the everyday, because they were generally written contemporaneously and often only for a private family audience, who had no need or desire to be told about what was for them just ordinary life experiences.

That is precisely the problem regarding these letters and journals from 200 years ago, they often miss out the minor detail, which actually to both military and social historians is a veritable gold mine, in enabling us to understand better their everyday lives. It is this very basic detail which we quite often lack and for which we strive.

It is of course important to me as a military historian to understand the grand strategies, the movements of troops on campaign and on the battlefield and the weapons and uniforms they used. But just as significant and as important, if not more so, is the quest to understand their basic lives as humans thrown into, that unnatural state, war, and how they coped with it.

In the last decade, much of my work on this original source material has unsurprisingly been concentrated on the two best known and well-studied theatres of operations of the original 'Great War', as Victorians referred to the twenty-three years of world war against France and Napoleon. These of course are the Peninsular War (Spain, Portugal & Southern France 1808-14) and the Waterloo campaign of 1815. Consequently, over the last five years my search has been focussed very much on the Waterloo campaign, hardly surprising given the prominence of its 200th Anniversary in 2015 and the associated media attention.

Paradoxically, this anniversary and the subsequent ephemeral, perhaps superficial and fleeting world interest, has actually spawned a great drive to seek for a better understanding of every aspect of the campaign. I do not think that I over exaggerate the situation, by stating that the history of the battle and those that fought it has progressed farther in the last ten years than it had in the previous 150.

Although the quest for new material on these campaigns is certainly not at an end, it is understandable that many will wish to expand their horizons beyond those Belgian fields. Within the unbelievably fascinating and complicated period encompassing the all-embracing title 'The Napoleonic Wars' are still many other theatres of operations where our knowledge and understanding is often very poor and incomplete.

I have therefore chosen to extend my work initially into the realms of the Mediterranean theatre. Many may be aware of some of the major events that occurred in this area of operations, which included the Siege of Toulon, Napoleon's invasion of Egypt, Nelson's great victory at the Nile, the Battle of Maida and perhaps may also have a fleeting knowledge of the operations on the east coast of Spain.

But besides these individual actions, the Mediterranean is presumed to be a mere backwater, insignificant in comparison with the main events on continental Europe. But this is to belittle a major theatre of operations which was active throughout the entire duration of the war and had a marked bearing on the overall war effort in many profound ways. Indeed, in a more modern equivalent, it is similar to the entire Allied operations in North Africa and Italy from 1940-44 being reduced to nothing more than the battles of El Alamein, Tobruk and Monte Casino.

In fact, both of these campaigns, although 130 years apart, have suffered from the same problem, being completely overshadowed by the fighting in Western and Central Europe. There is simply a lack of knowledge of the constantly fluctuating fortunes of the protagonists and a basic lack of understanding of the greater strategic threat to either protagonist of losing control of the Mediterranean. It is high time that this was remedied.

As a part of this focus, I have sought new memoirs from soldiers and sailors who fought in this theatre, being one where the expansive coastlines and numerous strategically placed islands led to a much greater level of cooperation between the services, with joint operations actually becoming very much the norm.

This memoir by Lieutenant John Hildebrand, whose family had hailed from Saxony in Germany only two generations before, is one such, and is actually a real gem.

Not only is it a rarity because of the theatre it describes, but it is also a first for this famous regiment. The 35th Foot and subsequent Royal Sussex Regiment is rightly famous for its exploits; the regiment was involved in the massacre that spawned the famous book *Last of the Mohicans*; it was at the capture of Quebec; the Battle of Bunker Hill; Maida; the unsuccessful expedition to save Gordon of Khartoum; the first Battle of Ypres – where it became informally known by the Germans as 'The Iron Regiment'; Dunkirk; El Alamein; Monte Cassino and Arnhem, to name but a few.

But until now, no memoir from anyone serving in the two battalions of this distinguished regiment during the Napoleonic Wars has ever been published and it is high time that this situation was rectified.[1]

But beyond its rarity value, the real reason why the memoir is now being published is that it is genuinely written in such a pacey and exciting style, whilst it also pulls no punches and gives a real 'warts and all' view of the life of a subaltern officer at this time.

Indeed, his memoir reads more like those we associate with an independently minded young Royal Navy officer of this period, who often seem to have acted first and thought about the consequences later, than the more usually restrained and controlled responses of a young army officer, who was heavily constrained in his actions by the presence of senior officers and a more rigid adherence to the military code.

It would seem that these young army officers serving in the Adriatic, being granted more freedom and often working without close supervision, caught the same bug as the 'gung-ho' naval officers on the

---

[1] The author is aware of Major John Slessor's letters being published in Alethea Hayter's *The Backbone*, but these only amount to snippets of his letters, which is a shame, as they are very instructive.

station, who were always on the lookout for an adventure, whether at sea or on land.

Small ship actions, cutting out operations and small scale landings, were almost everyday occurrences and this spirit of adventure was clearly adopted by many of the young army officers on this station, who had been thrust into positions of some importance and influence at a very young age.

So I invite you to join John Hildebrand in his various far-from-mundane and often humorous adventures in Malta, Sicily, Lagosta, Ragusa (now Dubrovnik), Italy and Corfu.

Yet even then, John was not finished. He returned home in 1814, thinking that his life of active service was probably over forever. Instead, within six months, John found himself in Belgium, as part of Wellington's Army during the Waterloo campaign and was subsequently involved in the march on Paris and the storming of the fortresses of Cambrai and Peronne.

By this time, he really had seen enough of war and as with many ex-army officers from time immemorial, he followed the tradition of becoming a vicar, in which capacity he saw out the remainder of his very long and happy life.

Written at the end of his life, his memory clearly maintained its sharpness, as the author has found very few serious mistakes in his recording of incidents which had occurred some sixty years before, but clearly came to his recall, so vividly does he paint the scenes.

Perhaps, understandably, a few dates or the sequence of events he describes seem to differ slightly from the known records, in these instances I have highlighted and discussed them, but in many cases John's accounts actually seems the more plausible.

Some historians have previously cast doubts over the authenticity of these accounts because of these few discrepancies, but apart from a few insignificant errors in correctly dating events the author has found very little to seriously question their validity. In fact, I am very confident that it will soon become a favourite of many who care to read it. Indeed, it is such a good read I really cannot fully understand why it has lain virtually ignored for so long.

Gareth Glover
Cardiff 2016

Acknowledgements

Any work of this complexity owes a word of thanks to many individuals, not least John Grehan, who was a staunch advocate of a book on this theatre of the Napoleonic Wars.

I must also offer my grateful thanks to Matthew Jones, Assistant County Archivist at the West Sussex Record Office, for his kind permission to publish Hildebrand's journal (Reference RSR Mss 1/47) and for providing copies of letters from Hildebrand's Italian and Croatian contacts (Reference RSR Mss 1/48), which help greatly in establishing the truth of his claims in the journal.

I cannot also omit my very grateful thanks to a number of members of the Napoleon Series Discussion Forum, who helped me greatly in finding a number of pieces of very obscure evidence regarding John Hildebrand and his family and also on some of the people and events mentioned in his journal. I specifically mention Ron McGuigan who never ceases to amaze me with what he can uncover on the most obscure subject, Robert Burnham, Tom Holberg and Robert Woo. Without their expert help this book would not be anywhere near so complete and I thank them wholeheartedly for it.

I must also not fail to thank my mother Margaret, for providing me with the initial transcript of the journal, saving me many hours of work, this really is becoming a family concern.

My thanks also to George Weston, treasurer of Kibworth History Society, who kindly provided information on Hildebrand's final years and photographs of his burial stone.

But finally, I must add my heartfelt thanks to my darling wife Mary, who has always encouraged and supported my passion without question. But this book is in fact the first to be completed since she agreed to support me fully, in what was a 'unanimous' joint decision, for me to end full time work and to try to make a living following my dream, as a full time Napoleonic historian, consultant and battlefield guide. If that isn't true love what is?

Chapter 1

John Hildebrand and His Family

John Biggs Hildebrand was born on 29 March 1794 at Berwick-upon-Tweed, the first son of Heinrich Hildebrand and Elizabeth Biggs. The Hildebrand family originally hailed from Saxony in Germany and had originally settled in Western Ireland around 1760 where they quickly developed a large portfolio of property around Westport.

John's father Heinrich had anglicised his name to Henry and married Elizabeth Biggs in Bath on 29 December 1788. The couple had two daughters (Elizabeth in 1789 and Charlotte in 1791) before our John appeared in early 1794 when his father was apparently a surveyor by profession at Berwick.

Soon after John's birth, Henry joined the Essex Fencibles as a Cornet on 14 October 1794 and then transferred as a Lieutenant and Adjutant into the Sussex Fencibles on 19 November 1796 vice George Hildebrand deceased (probably a distant relative).

The Fencibles were volunteer troops raised at times of crisis, such as the American War of Independence and the French Revolutionary Wars, to carry out garrison and patrol duties, releasing the professional regiments for foreign service. The men were unpaid but the officers were professionals and were paid a salary. Fencibles had both infantry and cavalry units, though Henry continued to be throughout his short military career, a cavalryman.

In March 1799, the Army List shows Henry with the Sussex Fencibles at Hamilton Barracks near Glasgow, which our John mentions. Henry omits to state that he also got a brother here, Henry Thomas, who was born in the December of that year.

On 1 March 1800, Henry resigned from his post as Adjutant. In 1802, with the short-lived Peace of Amiens, the Fencibles were disbanded and officers were given the opportunity to transfer into the regular Army (if there was a position available) or retire. Henry resigned his position and is recorded in 1803 as a surveyor in Berwick once again.

Our John was to see another six siblings born between 1799 and 1806; George, James, Anne, Jane, William and Matilda. The family all seem to have been blessed with longevity, his father Henry living until the age of seventy, dying in 1836. His mother lived until 1858, dying at the ripe old age of eighty-eight.

Growing up in various military barracks clearly gave our John a hankering for the Army, which he duly joined as an Ensign in the 35th (Sussex) Regiment of Foot without purchase on 16 September 1809. This may well indicate some family influence through his father who had been in the Sussex Fencibles.

John was probably very lucky to have just missed the Walcheren Expedition which had a devastating effect on the Army, with thousands dying from malaria, and many more suffering for many years afterwards from recurring bouts of fever.

But he was lucky enough to enjoy active service in the Mediterranean from 1810 until 1814, in garrison at Malta and Sicily before latterly being involved in the various operations to capture all of the numerous small islands that constitute the Greek Ionian Islands. This brought him to the attention of Lieutenant Colonel Robertson, who commanded the force in these islands and who worked tirelessly, if not always harmoniously, with the Royal Navy squadron in these waters under Admiral Fremantle and Captain Sir William Hoste, who actively encouraged these joint service operations to clear these islands of their French garrisons.[1]

John was still an extremely junior officer, when suddenly and very unexpectedly, he was given command of the small island of Lagosta by Robertson. Despite his own trepidations, our John took on his unlooked-for command, with great seriousness and was resolute in all matters which arose, even when challenged by the arguments over claims of supremacy within the local Greek clergy.

John gained his lieutenancy in the 35th, again without purchase, on 23 September 1813. But then, his moment in history dawned, and he

---

[1] Major John Slessor remarked 'Admiral Fremantle commands the Navy, Colonel Robertson the Army, but I regret to say they do not pull together, a circumstance much to be lamented and at the same time very injurious to the service' Reference Alethea Hayter, *The Backbone*, p.252.

did not hesitate to grab the opportunity. When asked to supply a small contingent of his troops to help support the local Croat insurgents in their attempts to blockade the great fortress of Ragusa (modern day Dubrovnik), he jumped at the chance. As a young officer, and clearly a bit of a hot-head, he leapt in with both feet and only later considered his actions and their potential consequences.

John left his small contingent as a reserve on the Dalmatian coast and moved forward with the insurgents to take a look at Ragusa and its defences whilst in disguise, not contemplating for one moment that capture by the French, something that he actually only narrowly escaped, would have led to his immediate execution as a spy.

He then determined to command the insurgents in close blockade of the fortress for a number of months, leaving his detachment on the coast with little knowledge of his whereabouts. He was again, on a number of occasions, very close to being killed as the insurgents sought to keep the large French garrison blockaded, in an attempt to starve them into submission.

Eventually, after many months of blockade, Austrian regular forces arrived and John does not hide his frustration as he was forced to watch the French garrison capitulate to this newly arrived force, whilst Captain Hoste and the Royal Navy gained all of the glory of the capitulation by signing the official surrender. But his view of operations was necessarily restricted from his post directly under the guns of the French garrison and his understanding of the contributions of others was perhaps less than clear or fairly portrayed.

He does, however, recognise that his small insurgent band was diplomatically offered the privilege of leading the occupation forces into the fortress in recognition of their valiant struggle against all odds. Eventually, the capitulation of Ragusa released John, and we soon find him independently landing on the Italian coast in an effort to catch up with Colonel Robertson and his men on their epic march across Italy to Genoa. However, recalled to his post, he was finally part of the hurried expedition to capture the Island of Corfu before peace was finally declared.

With the war ending in 1814, John returned to England on sick leave, imagining that his active military life was over and that he could now expect a life of garrisoning the far flung corners of Britain's overseas colonies for the remainder of his career, something which he certainly did not relish.

However, fate was then to throw another curved ball, with the return of Napoleon to the throne of France and war breaking out once again. Before long John found himself marching across Belgium and France as the Waterloo campaign dramatically burst into life and he was fully involved in the consequent march on Paris.

It would appear that his brother George also joined the 35th alongside him in 1815, but he did not serve at Waterloo and was forced to go on half pay with the reduction of the Army in 1817.

But having seen so much excitement and having felt such exhilaration under fire, the idea of enduring decades in boring garrisons around the world, failed to enthral him and a life in the clergy called him instead.

John did not write his memoirs until he was seventy-five, these were clearly only ever intended for the enjoyment of his immediate family but he actually died before he was able to finish them completely. Thankfully, John had completed all but a few appendices and these lively, irreverent memoirs which he has left us, are both instructive and a joy to read, concerning a period of our history that time has nearly forgotten.

Chapter 2

Reporting for Duty

John Hildebrand was born in a time of war indeed he was hardly to know a world without conflict before he was twenty-five years old. Only the year before he was born, Louis XVI and his wife Marie Antoinette had been led to the guillotine and the crowned heads of Europe began to resist the far-reaching tentacles of that fearsome and dangerous new creed stretching out from France – Revolution.

Britain had joined that war against the revolutionaries, but had little success in its military operations during the remaining few years of the eighteenth century, beyond a few naval victories, some advances in India, and the capture of a number of spice islands in the Caribbean. Too often however the Army had failed badly in its operations and the one sent to Holland in 1799 was certainly no exception; the campaign being famous now for spawning a nursery rhyme and teaching a young officer, who was later to become better known to the world as the Duke of Wellington, how not to fight a campaign.

But then things began to improve, with the Army learning from these failures and developing better tactics. It expelled General Bonaparte's army from Egypt in 1801 and defeated a French army in Italy in 1806, whilst it also saw continued successes in India, the Cape of Good Hope and the Caribbean.

John grew up in various military barracks in a pseudo military life and he would have undoubtedly been acutely aware of the news of the latest victories of both the Navy and the Army. He clearly developed a hankering to join the Army himself as soon as he could.

In 1808, Arthur Wellesley, had landed a British army on the mainland of Europe for the first time in a decade, with an actual view of staying there and committing it to a long term strategy.

5

In 1809 John joined the 2nd Battalion of the 35th (Sussex) Regiment, he would have been granted one month to complete purchasing his uniform and equipment. His uniform consisted of a black felt shako, a red jacket with orange regimental facings on the cuffs and collar on the short-tailed jacket; a crimson sash tied around the waist; grey trousers; boots and gaiters and, of course, he was armed with a 1796 pattern infantry officer's sword. His hair would now be cut short, the hated 'queue' having only recently been abolished. Officer's ranks were denoted by the epaulettes, two for a field officer (major or above), one on the right shoulder only denoting a captain, and one on the left shoulder only for a subaltern. He would have then joined the regimental depot at Chichester where he would have been expected to learn the basic infantry manoeuvres and drills.

Both battalions of the 35th Foot had been stationed in the Mediterranean for the last few years, mostly in garrison on the Island of Sicily. The 2/35th had been sent out to the Mediterranean in 1806 to join the 1st Battalion at Melazzo. By this time, the 1st Battalion had already made a name for itself at the Battle of Maida in Italy earlier that year. Both battalions then formed jointly the garrison of Messina, protecting the island from invasion from the nearby French-held mainland.

Both battalions also proceeded to Egypt in 1807 for what turned out to be a short and disastrous campaign and then returned again to Sicily. On their return to Sicily, the losses in the 1st Battalion were made up from the 2nd Battalion and the latter had then returned to England before being sent on the 'Grand Expedition' to Walcheren, in an attempt to destroy the French fleet holed up in Antwerp. The battalion was involved in the Siege of Flushing, losing a number of men to enemy fire. It was another inglorious disaster with the army losing about 100 men in conflict and over 5,000 succumbing to malaria and leaving thousands more often debilitated from frequent relapses for the rest of their life. John was not to know it then, but he was lucky just to avoid being sent there. His memoir opens with a brief summary of his early years:

> I was born in 1794[1] a time of great and anxious political and military excitement. My earliest recollections are of warlike matters: my

---

[1] He was actually born on 29 March 1794 at Berwick on Tweed. He was the son of Heinrich Hildebrand and Elizabeth (nee Biggs).

being mounted in buckskins in military uniform at six years of age on a tiny Shetland pony in a barrack yard at Hamilton in Scotland; one of a squad of Lilliputian soldiers, principally officers' sons, duly equipped and mounted, parading under the Adjutant's quarters awaiting our pay (2d a week, or something like it) [as] embryo warriors. Indeed, in that age everyone was imbued with ardent, entirely engrossing military propensities, excited to the extreme by loyalty to good old King George III, and hatred and defiance of [all] Frenchmen. Every man was a soldier of some sort: in the regular Army, the Militia and Volunteer Corps of innumerable degrees and appellations. All but [for] a miserable minority of rebellious, but from their activity, dangerous miscreants; breathing loyalty to their king and country and defiance of France, then threatening us with invasion. I well remember the enthusiastic crowds filling the streets of Beverly in Yorkshire (then a cavalry quarter) on the evening of the Jubilee when King George completed the 50th year of his reign[2] Nothing could exceed the enthusiasm then exhibited and young as I was, it was never to be forgotten; such was the impression it made on youthful mind and affections.

England was then one vast camp, military preparations meeting one in every direction, every wagon, cart, and every degree and description of vehicle duly marked, numbered and registered, so as to be easily collected for the conveyance of troops to any point of the threatened invasion. The schoolboys in the streets and all boys playing at mock fights, invariably representing English and French, the latter, of course, always vanquished, but, in the enthusiasm of the moment often, leading to hard blows and sharp results. My old heart, even now, feels warmed at the retrospection; it no doubt, led to my fascination for and [a] determined pursuit of a soldier's life. Nor was there less enthusiasm in the national female breast with regard to loyalty and courage; Spartan mothers.

Thus much for the exciting circumstances which roused the impatient military spirit within me at a very early age and continued increasing until at the age of 15 (a year earlier than the usual regulation period) I was, to my inexpressible delight, unexpectedly

---

[2] At the time of this Jubilee in 1811, John Hildebrand was clearly on active service and he must therefore be confusing it with some earlier royal occasion, possibly the 40th year of his reign in October 1800 or the King's Seventieth birthday in June 1808?

gazetted to an Ensigncy in the 35th Regiment of Foot[3], the 1st
Battalion of which had been in the Mediterranean for some years
and [had] seen much and varied service in Egypt and at the battle of
Maida in Calabria, and was then engaged in subduing the Greek
Islands[4]. The 2nd Battalion, 1,000 strong[5], had gone on the Walcheren
Expedition, the [depot] being fixed at Chichester, then the most
convenient quarter, from its proximity to Portsmouth, for the
assembly of troops to reinforce that unfortunate expedition, and for
the reception of the returning wounded and sick [which were] daily
arriving. Thither I was ordered by the Horse Guards to report
myself, to be sent forward with the first detachment to join the
expedition, which we were daily and most impatiently expecting.

But it so happened that things had turned out disastrously and
the losses both in the field and by sickness [were] so considerable,
without any prospect of ultimate success, that the question then was
only how to withdraw our troops with the best grace and the least
dishonour we could, and no further reinforcements to our regiment
were forwarded, to my extreme disappointment, at first. But the sad
sights of the daily returning sick, their miserable sufferings and
wretched plight from the effects of the fever and ague, very soon
cooled all such ardour and made me more than acquiesce patiently
in remaining where I was.

Chichester Barracks[6] is well known and I believe is at present
exactly as it was in 1809, although built of wood, which I suppose, like
the ever-darned stockings, have been renewed again and again, yet
still the same! Indeed, from long experience, since, I am come to the
conclusion that wood[en] buildings, well saturated, when in a perfectly
dry state, with glass and tar renewed at times after, will last forever.

I cannot look back on that depot, my first military love, even now,
without the thrilling [feeling] of early delight and the enjoyments of

---

[3] John became an ensign without purchase vice John Denny on 16 September 1809.
[4] The 1/35th had been landed at Naples in 1805 and initially formed the garrison of Melazzo
fortress.
[5] In 1808, the 2/35th returned to England from the Mediterranean and then participated in
the disastrous Walcheren campaign. The 2nd Battalion then remained in England until late
1813, when they landed in Holland and participated in the failed assault on Bergen op Zoom
but were then involved in the Waterloo campaign in 1815.
[6] A tented barracks was set up in 1795 and upgraded to wooden huts in 1803. It was renamed
Rousillon Barracks in 1958 before it was later largely demolished.

my introduction into [the] freedom and aspirations of a soldier's life.

The first few weeks at the depot were absorbed in drills, guards, &c and the fill-up of idle life, trifling, but then to me, most enjoyable pastimes. We had a few (and really unusually handsome) ladies, so kind, considerate and condescending, that their attentions rendered everything to one so young delightful beyond measure. Nothing to do, only to bide the return of the battalion, then daily expected from the disastrous, discomfited expedition. Yet, when it did return, how sad but how glorious it appeared! With its colours and caps so torn with musket-balls, the men all almost sallow and diseased with that terrible Walcheren fever, the outward effects of which gave them an unnaturally swollen stomach and a melancholy and sunken visage. Yet those fine fellows who had borne so much sickness and privation so nobly and had highly distinguished themselves in the field, as their well riddled caps and clothes testified, when they marched into the barrack yard and were halted in line, stood erect, with countenances still retaining their natural determined defiant expression. There appeared no quailing, no depression, beyond the individual instances of the immediate temporary sufferers of the moment, which no spirit of manly determination could subdue.

Out of a battalion of 800 men (it had been 1,000 shortly before, when it embarked) not 500 were then fit for duty; all alternately prostrated, every 2nd or 3rd day, in fever and ague, and that for many months afterwards. In the intervening days they were *tolerably* equal to duty. Many had died, and few ever *entirely* shook off the effects of that dire disease; I know some of the officers died of it many years afterwards. And, then, several were left on the field, killed by the enemy and many [others] returned to be cured of their wounds, or to die. Among the latter was Colonel Pettit[7], who had been wounded by one of his own sentries at Flushing, mistaking him, from his having gone out beyond the lines and perhaps not having received or heard the reply to his challenge. He died and now lies in Deal chapel yard, a gallant and brave soldier, none better, and no one more esteemed and looked up to as a good and valuable soldier.

And this seems to be a fair opportunity of noticing the origin and professional rise of another distinguished officer, still happily

---

[7] Lieutenant Colonel Peter Petit died at Deal 2 September 1809.

surviving, then a captain of the light company of the regiment. He had commanded gallantly, ably and in a most distinguished manner, 4 companies in a reconnaissance before Antwerp. Attacked by a much superior force of the enemy, and with great skill and judgment, after a successful resistance, having formed square, [he] effected his retreat. General Taylor[8], [was for] many years Military Secretary at the Horse Guards, who had accepted a command in this expedition, was on the field at the time, witnessed and admired him and never lost sight afterwards of the gallant Captain Arthur, who advanced rapidly in the service and was afterwards a distinguished Governor General of Bombay &c.[9]

With the return of the 2nd Battalion from Walcheren and the unfortunate loss of their battalion commander to the fever, his replacement was Lieutenant Colonel Caesar Arnett, who seems to have proved to be an unpopular change. John was clearly less than enamoured with his new commander and his ways, and it would seem that poor inspection reports at this period were laid directly at his door.

It is however difficult now to judge how fair these comments are, as many regiments devastated by Walcheren fever took a number of years to recover to a point where they were deemed of a standard to proceed on active service and even those sent to Spain seem to have been prone to weakness on the march. But, John was also evidently a man of action who did not relish a life of garrison duty at home and was clearly looking for any opportunity to lead a more active military career. He therefore took the first opportunity to step forward when the opportunity came to accompany a major reinforcement for the 1st Battalion, still stationed in the Mediterranean and was en route almost immediately.

The return of the battalion brought about great changes. A very young lieutenant colonel had the command[10]. He was connected with a great Army agent of clothiers, with considerable interest and

---

[8] Lieutenant General Sir Herbert Taylor was Military Secretary from 1820-27.

[9] Sir George Arthur, Bart, was then a Captain in the 35th Foot, born near Plymouth in 1785, he was Governor of British Honduras (1814-22), Van Diemen's Land (1823-36), Upper Canada (1837-41) and Bombay (1842-46); he died in 1854.

[10] Lieutenant Colonel Caesar Arnett replaced Lieutenant Colonel Petit in command of 2nd Battalion. He and his wife were lost in a shipwreck in 1819.

much money, [but] very much disliked, and something more. By the ardent and service loving officers, who very soon perceived, or thought they perceived, a want of military energy and desire to get the regiment into good service order for the Peninsula, then the first and highest ambition of the corps, and that the repeated reports of Inspecting Generals were unfavourable to their state of discipline and consequently to their being sent to Spain and they suspected not without design.

This brought about discontent and if not a spirit of opposition to the Lieutenant Colonel concerned, [then] something very like it. High mettled temperaments, ill brooking [at] being kept back from the field of glory and honour, broke out in ill disguised disgust and resentment. In short the commanding officer, being moreover, not a little of a martinet, was not only disliked but suspected from what had been seen of him, on former active service, of anything but a military inclination to command the regiment.

Parties were formed, from [an] uncontrollable feeling [rather] more than design; one (a very small one) *for* the commander, the other against. The regiment became uncomfortable and, as a matter of course, disorganized, and was kept at home as being at the yearly Inspections repeatedly reported [as] unfit for active service. I dwell on this point because it led to my seizing the first chance I had to get away to the 1st Battalion, to try my luck there.

One evening, at Mess, it was announced by the commanding officer that a call was made on the battalion for 300 volunteers to join the 1st Battalion in the Mediterranean. The men were soon got [together], most of them of the very best, at Morning Parade. Indeed had it been permitted, very few would have declined. The duty roster of the officers was consulted for the '1st for Foreign Service' and I found I was so far down, that I had no choice; but having accidentally heard that one of the subs, in consequence of a domestic calamity, would rather not leave England then, I instantly went to him late at night to ask him to exchange with me, and succeeded in obtaining both his and the commanding officer's consent. We had short notice and marched for Portsmouth to embark very early the next morning, under the command of Captain T. Tisdall[11] and I *was*

---

[11] Captain Thomas Tisdall.

11

delighted. I was really in ecstasy (remember [that] I was only 15, with little self restraint and no discretion to make me pause).

We marched early and although only half grown, [I was] strong for my age and full of zeal, I bore it well, indeed [I] did not feel any inconvenience or fatigue of a long and laborious march.

Chapter 3

Passage to Malta

The detachment that sailed is recorded as numbering 2 captains, ten subalterns and 300 men.[1] Troop transport ships could only sail safely in convoy, to avoid being attacked by French privateers or even Barbary pirates. Such transport ships were only furnished to a basic level, there would be no luxurious voyage here. It should not be forgotten that some wives and even children travelled with the men and privacy for them was virtually non-existent. But such had to be endured for some three months in these cramped, smelly vessels and it was endured apparently with great fortitude by all.

Finally, after a little excitement when an officer of the regiment was arrested for debt, the convoy was ready to proceed and the weather became favourable.

But within days, serious storms struck and the fleet was forced to turn to seek shelter in the coves of Cornwall and Devon. At the second attempt, they travelled rapidly, without incident, to Gibraltar, passing the isthmus on which the City of Cadiz stands on route. This city, was then in the early throws of a siege by French forces which lasted eventually for some two and a half years. They dropped off some supplies here and then continued on their route, calling at Gibraltar and then proceeding to Malta, a journey prolonged interminably by constant light airs or even no wind at all as they struggled to sail across the Mediterranean.

At the Downs we found assembled a numerous fleet, of all sizes, (excepting large ones, which were not then in fashion) or use. It was

---

[1] Historical Memoir of the 35th, p.110.

said, and I believe it, [that] there were at least 500 sail at Spithead waiting to start with the convoy that was being prepared, without which no mercantile vessel in those days, dare venture out of harbour, or [even] our roads. The lot of our detachment under Captain Tisdall fell to two transports of about 300 or 400 tons each; the cabins very small and accommodation of the scantiest order. In these vessels we were to stow ourselves and our men. One, the headquarter ship, had a little better accommodation than the other, in the shape of a 'state cabin' of 6 feet by 6, or very little, if any, more, which was appropriated to our commanding officer for the voyage. [He was] an old sub, worn out in physical and mental powers, but a kind-hearted, good, jovial fellow, with a fine, handsome, high-spirited (in no minor degree) wife; luckily [with] no children, and I should say from appearance [that] there had never been a chance of them since his marriage. As every word and move could be distinctly heard, although not seen, this was anything but *privacy* to them, or comfortable or agreeable to us; and I mention it (and the circumstances matrimonial in the other transport, which I will try to describe) for the comfort and consolation of such ladies and gentlemen of similar rank who may be, in these days, embarked in the comparatively magnificent accommodation of ships [fitted] with modern improvements. I have, already, partly described the *Headquarters* ship, its state cabin and limited accommodation, but *how* limited I can scarcely make intelligible to modern experience in such matters. The state cabin, diminutive as it was, leaving only a space for 6 small narrow fixed berths which were to accommodate 6 or 7 bachelor officers, I forget which.

But this was magnificent compared with the second and smaller transport in which I was; two married officers with their wives (luckily no children yet), separated from each other and from the cabin of the bachelors by carpets hung up in a very rough way fitted for the nonce[2], as best they could and forming a very imperfect and incomplete screen from sight and none from conversation. But I will not dwell on this, our uncomfortable state, which lasted above three months, and [shall] only remark [on] the wonderful patience and

---

[2] His meaning here of the word 'nonce' is the very traditional use as meaning 'now' or 'for the immediate'.

forbearance with which it was borne by the ladies and I may add their husbands. I suppose that such could not now occur or be borne.

I then resolved never to marry as a sub, at least in these rough times; after a war of so many years, everything seemed out of joint and certainly there was not much refinement.

While lying at Spithead waiting, as we did, 3 or 4 weeks, for our signal to sail, I was one morning in my berth, when the cabin was assailed by several rough-looking and boisterous fellows and instantly a lieutenant who slept in the berth above me (he was older than officers of his rank generally) sprang out on them with a cutlass[3]. He, it seemed, had expected them and kept it ready for the purpose and attempted to cut them down; but was skilfully disarmed and subdued by men who came prepared for it and evidently understood their business. They were Sherriff's officers come to arrest at the suit [at law] of a tailor and carried him off to a sponging-house[4], where he was obliged to remain till he had communicated with the regiment at Chichester, when 3 or 4 brother officers, but not specially his friends (for he had been a very short time in the corps having exchanged from another) came down, paid the money and set him free. And it is solely for this [reason] that I have mentioned the circumstances, I mean the prompt and generous aid thus afforded by not very rich men to a brother officer in difficulty; [shows] the *esprit de corps* I am happy to say [is so] general in the Army.

At last the signal was made, really, to get under way and sail (we had, I suppose, by way of practice, done so two or three times before and [then] anchored again) and off we went. It was early in March and with so large a fleet of all sizes and kinds [of] merchant ships, transports, &c, it was no easy or rapid matter, notwithstanding the previous experiments, explanations, orders &c, from the commodore of the convoy. A fair breeze down Channel soon cleared us of it and seemed clear for a rapid run to Gibraltar; but the wind

---

[3] This would appear to describe Lieutenant James Semphill who had previously served in the same rank in the 96th Foot and 4th Garrison Battalion. He died in 1811.

[4] A Sponging house – a bailiff's or other house in which debtors are put before being taken to jail, or until they compromise with their creditors. At these houses extortionate charges were commonly made for food, lodging, etc.

veered round suddenly to the south and it blew a storm, which drove us back to port at Falmouth, which we were fortunate enough to reach [safely]. Here we were detained by [poor] weather, I think, a week or more, and I enjoyed it much. The hills or mountains around afforded delightful exercise, exceedingly so to my feeling and excited by the absolute start for foreign service and foreign lands. We sailed again and this time, with a fair wind, plentiful although moderate (just enough to keep all sails full) but not unmanageable. The commodore, in the line of battle ship majestically [sailed] ahead, two fine frigates and a brig or two I believe, [stood] on the outskirts, directing our movements, overhauling everything asail, protecting us as a shepherd would a flock of sheep. Before every night [fell] a signal was made to shorten sail and sometimes to *lie to* for slow sailors [to catch up], of which we had many, and [to] collect all together snug for the night. On the 4th or 5th day we reached Cadiz, the siege of which was then going on; the bombardment of which was to us a fine and glorious sight.[5] And having thrown in supplies, [we] proceeded to Gibraltar, which we reached on the 7th or 8th day from England. After having been driven by the current and becalmed for several hours between Algeciras and the Rock, the Spanish gunboats from the former place playing on us, with a heavy fire all the time, but without doing serious injury, or killing any men [we arrived safely]. This I notice because it was my first exposure to fire and therefore not without much pleasurable excitement [having been] impressed strongly on my memory.[6]

We were kept here a few days, the French being then rather active in the neighbourhood and then once more renewed our voyage.

As I do not mean this as an exact and statistical account of the military operations I witnessed in the Mediterranean, varied and exciting as some of them were, for which, indeed, (in consequence of the loss on two subsequent occasions I experienced of such notes and memoranda as I had made at intervals, as I had opportunities) I am without the means. I shall merely mention, once [and] for all,

---

[5] Marshal Soult besieged the City of Cadiz for over two years without success.
[6] As Spain had been in open revolt against France for at least a year at this time, it is unlikely that they were Spanish boats attempting to capture the merchant vessels off Gibraltar, being more likely to be French crews.

that I only pretend to give my reminiscence of what I have from memory, a clear and distinct recollection, with any little new or strange matters of interest or gossip, or more serious observations, as struck me, as they occurred, with sufficient force to fix them in my memory, after a lapse of 56 years. Of which (however it may surprise many younger heads) I have [a] recurring abundance. The part of the 'Great War'[7] on which I am now entering is but little known by general readers. At the time the events occurred, long before steam and accelerated postage, newspapers were rarely met with especially on distant stations, and comparatively with the gigantic struggle in the Peninsula, [were] little thought of. Important as they really were in themselves and calculated to afford ample scope, by their extent and variety, for the development of military energy and resolution; perhaps much more so, for individual officers in the most humble rank, than those of separate commands, experienced in the same grades, in all the absorbing and important movements, actions and battles of the great army under Lord and afterwards Duke of Wellington.

It frequently occurred that even very young and junior officers were thrown, without much or any previous notice or preparation, on their [own] resources in difficult, strange positions, which could not fail to sharpen the intellects and improve the ready resources of those who had energy and capacity to seize on them. With this I cease such remark, trusting that, in the following narrative, a full illustration of them will be found. Besides the intense excitement and enjoyment of such a life of enterprise, the experience gained in many ways could hardly fail of producing improvement of mind as well as vigour of body, self reliance and confidence, fitting for the duties and exigencies of after life, whether military or civil. My object is not to write a book for the public, but merely as an amusement in my old age and to revive, as far as may be, the memory of my varied and active experience in the 8 eventful years from 1809 to 1817, of such matters as then appeared strange or worthy of remark and which certainly contributed much to my enjoyment and perhaps to my improvement.

---

[7] It should be remembered that until 1918 the appellation 'The Great War' had been used to identify the Napoleonic Wars which lasted almost without interruption for twenty-three years, from 1792-1815 and in all corners of the globe.

This is not intended for a personal narrative of my adventures, such as they were, [not] supposing them to have been either meritorious or singular, but merely to dot down, as far as my recollection will serve me, what I saw in the course of my early days, and what has ever since been a daily source of amusement and enjoyment to my own mind (too deeply engraved and exciting to be erased) for the amusement of myself and children. At the same time I cannot but think that an honest straightforward account of the life I led in the Army, without [an] attempt at romance or the slightest exaggeration or departure from the simple truth, in such varied scenes, might not only amuse, but afford some materials for reflection in the minds of some young officers of the age I then was, and give some hints for ready perception of what should be done in similar circumstances if it should happen that this is ever printed or thought worthy of publication.

Now to proceed. We had a lazy and tedious passage from Gibraltar to Malta, constantly becalmed and once or twice carried by the currents to [within] an unpleasant proximity to the Barbary and African coasts, at that time swarming with Algerine rovers[8], on the active lookout and ready to pounce on any unfortunate vessel within their reach and insufficiently armed to resist their audacious and unexpected attacks. These Rovers, as they were called, drove a large and successful trade in this way, notwithstanding the never-ceasing vigilance of our inimitable cruisers: there was no steam then to make them independent of wind and weather, especially of calms. It may be easily supposed how uncomfortable was our state, especially the poor ladies shut up in their stifling small cabins, and the hardly less[er] misery of the bachelors. One morning very early, we to our intense delight [were] awoke by the steward coming into our cabin and announcing that Malta was in sight. Of course we all rushed on deck and saw it plainly as it appeared at no great distance.

---

[8] Piracy carried out in the name of the Beys of Algiers or Tunis was a constant menace during the war. In 1816, having dealt with the French war, the Navy turned on the Algerian pirates and destroyed them.

Chapter 4

Malta 1810

The small but strategically important island of Malta had previously formed part of the Kingdom of Sicily for nearly 400 years until, in 1530, Charles V of Spain gave the island to the Knights of St John, charging them to hold it against the rampaging hordes of the Ottoman Empire, which were seriously threatening to overrun Central Europe at this time.

The great Sultan Suleiman the Magnificent besieged Malta for six months in 1565, but his 40,000 troops failed to capture the island despite it being defended by only 9,000 troops, many of whom were little more than untrained men from the local populace. This has become known in Malta as the 'Great Siege'. With winter gales setting in, Suleiman ordered the siege lifted and the knights continued to oversee the island, whilst building up its defences, to face any future invasions. But the Ottomans never did return and the Knights of St John ruled the island for nearly 270 years without challenge.

But, then came Napoleon. His fleet sailed to Malta on its route to invade Egypt in 1798 and requested permission to water the fleet. Grand Master Hompesch refused permission in an attempt to remain neutral, but this only enraged Napoleon, who duly sent a division of infantry ashore which attacked Valetta from the landward side, where its defences were weakest. Hompesch rapidly agreed to a capitulation, clearly the knights of the ancient order of St John, were no longer of the same calibre as those who had faced Suleiman.

Napoleon left a sizeable garrison on Malta when he sailed on for Egypt and whilst he had been there he had ordered a number of positive reforms, such as reforming the institutions of government and finance; the abolition of feudal rights; the abolition of slavery; he freed all of the Turkish slaves; and reorganised the system of public education.

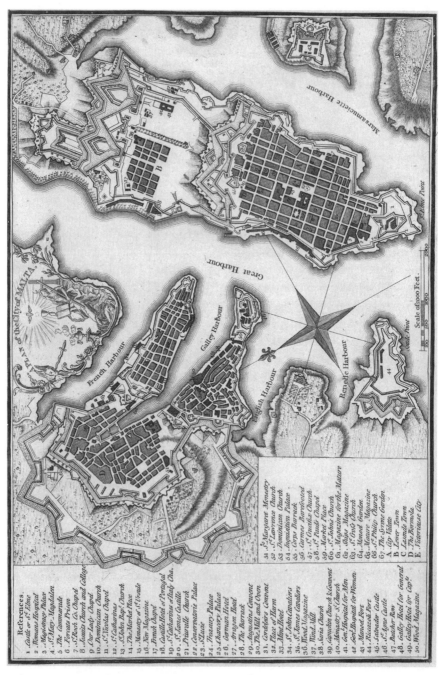

Above: A map of Valetta Harbour published by I. Stockdale, Piccadilly, 1800.

All of these reforms were enthusiastically accepted by the populace, who had grown tired of the rule of the knights. But this changed rapidly when the devout Maltese saw the French soldiers closing the convents and stealing church treasures. Soon the island was in rebellion and the French commander, General Claude-Henri de Vaubois, ordered his 3,000 troops into Valetta, which was now effectively besieged by the Maltese. After a number of failed attempts to take Valetta that caused heavy losses, the Maltese requested help from the British.

With the defeat of the French fleet at the Battle of the Nile, Admiral Nelson ordered a complete blockade of the island in 1799 with a mostly Portuguese squadron, causing the French garrison to suffer severe food shortages. In time British and Neapolitan troops also landed on Malta to continue to confine the garrison in Valetta itself. A relief supply convoy sent from Toulon in early 1800 was intercepted and destroyed, although occasionally odd ships did manage to break the blockade. The failed attempt by the *Guillaume Tell*, one of the few French survivors from the Battle of the Nile, to sail from Valetta with a large number of soldiers onboard bound for Toulon, was the final straw. The French garrison valiantly continued for nearly another six months, but the end was now inevitable. By the summer of 1800, up to 100 Frenchmen were dying daily and on 4 September they finally surrendered to the British.

In 1802, it was agreed within the terms of the Peace of Amiens that Britain would hand over Malta to the Emperor of Russia who was titular head of the Knights of St John. However, seeing that Napoleon was not keeping up his end of the bargain, Britain refused to hand over Malta. It had taken too much effort to capture and was too strategically important to forego if war was inevitable again, which it was. War broke out again the following year.

The convoy arrived at Malta and John's detachment was landed to await favourable winds and onward transportation to the Ionian Islands, where the 35th were then stationed, although the prospect of peacefully garrisoning these Greek islands drew little enthusiasm from John, who dreamt of seeing some real action.

The first action John did see was not exactly what he wished for or dreamt of; being the only officer left onboard his transport he was called on to sort out his detachment, who to a man, on their first day in Malta, after months cooped up in the squalid transport, went mad with the cheap liquor and caused a terrible scene, which even led to a Board of

Enquiry. Luckily John's actions that day were approved by the board and he survived his first real test.

On 20 May 1809, a fleet had proceeded with a small force of troops, including the light company of the 35th, from Sicily to capture the Islands of Procida and Ischia near Capri on the Italian coast, which they did with relative ease, capturing the French garrisons of around 700 men and over 100 cannon.

In September 1809, the 1st Battalion 35th had then been stirred again from its inertia in garrison at Melazzo in Sicily and embarked as part of Brigadier General John Oswald's[1] expedition to capture the Ionian Islands from the French. The 1,600 troops arrived off the Island of Zante on 1 October and with the town in British hands, the French garrison in the castle high above the town soon capitulated and the island fell.

On 3 October the troops re-embarked and moved on to Cephalonia[2], whose tiny garrison capitulated immediately. From here, a number of minor operations were launched, one company of the battalion led by Major Clarke, landed on the Island of Cerigo[3], and having dragged some cannon up to a height overlooking the fort, forced the garrison to surrender with minimal loss.

But amidst these successes, other issues could not be ignored, and on 30 September, it is recorded that Private Edward McGratt of the 35th was shot for attempted mutiny. In 1810, the regiment had wintered at Zante, but one more, much harder nut, remained to crack in the Ionian Isles, Santa Maura[4]. This island was larger and held a French garrison numbering over 1,000 men. General Oswald led a new expedition on 21 March 1810 consisting of 1st Battalion and some locally raised troops, including the Royal Corsican Rangers and the Greek Light Infantry.

The troops starting to land on the island that same evening caused the French garrison to abandon the town and concentrate their forces at the castle, situated on a nearby long, narrow isthmus

A number of direct assaults were required to drive the French from their fortifications on the isthmus and to allow a regular close siege of the fortress to commence. On 7 April Major Clarke was killed whilst in

---

[1] Oswald was a lieutenant colonel in the 35th, but detached from the regiment as a brigadier general.
[2] Today more often known as the Island of Kefalonia.
[3] Cerigo is more normally now known as Kythira.
[4] Santa Maura is now known as the Island of Lefkada.

the trenches preparing the batteries.

The batteries opened on the 8th and Lieutenant Colonel Lorenzo Moore led a successful attack on a redoubt, very close to the ramparts, where a second parallel was immediately commenced, which caused the garrison to surrender, realising that their situation was now hopeless.

Apart from Major Clarke, the only casualties in the regiment amounted to a sergeant and two men killed and Brigadier Oswald and five men wounded. There is no doubt that the services of the 1st Battalion 35th had been instrumental in the capture of the Ionian Islands and the men of the battalion were scattered amongst the islands as the chief part of its garrison.

But news finally arrived, that John and his party were not to join the battalion in the Greek isles, but to join a force being brought together at Sicily, for which they sailed immediately.

No one now could imagine the Malta of that day. It was the centre and emporium of all the trade of the shores of the Mediterranean and [of] all the seas connected with it, besides being the rendezvous of the ships of the [Royal] Navy in those seas. In short every mercantile transaction, every movement of the Navy and Army for that quarter must pass through Malta. In those days there was no steamship, nor any means but patience, of escaping that harbour and proceeding to their destination, until the elements and wind permitted it. Hence the port was at times crowded to a very inconvenient degree and a corresponding degree of hustle and bustle, when a change of wind or weather offered an opening. Our destination was to join the 1st Battalion in the Greek Islands, hoping that would soon lead to more exciting and active service; for the capture of the Ionian Islands having been recently completed, the garrisons in them had relapsed into the usual apathy of such quarters and were anything but desirable for a permanency to young and ardent spirits. Therefore, our detachment heard with delight that our voyage must be arrested there for a time and that we must, as soon as arrangements could be made, proceed to join the Army, then under Sir John Stuart in Sicily[5].

[5] Lieutenant General Sir John Stuart, Count of Maida, commanded the Mediterranean theatre until 1810 when he went home because of ill health, he died at Clifton in 1815.

But I should mention that I had my first trial of self-possession and firmness here. On the day that our transports cast anchor, in the 'great harbour' of Valetta, all the officers excepting myself, with their wives, hastened ashore with impatience to relieve themselves of the long, long, unpleasant and irksome restraints and miseries of the ship. Leaving me in sole charge as the youngest and therefore having the last choice of such indulgence; and the care of such a ship not at all above the charge of such a boy. But they had scarcely gone out of the ship, when, sitting in the cabin, I was visited by the Master, as the commanders of such ships and all mercantile ships were called, in considerable alarm and excitement, informing me that the soldiers (almost all young recruits and demoralised by the voyage and the long, inevitable relaxation of discipline on ship board) had been swimming ashore, bringing off wine and spirits and were all going up to the wine shops along the quay, stark naked, more or less intoxicated, and he was afraid to show himself on deck. I was, of course, considerably alarmed at this account of my charge and starting up as quickly as possible to the deck, was indeed both alarmed and disgusted at seeing, at the instant, the gangways surrounded by our men, none of them sober, who were waiting for some fellows swimming towards the ship, each with two canteens strapped round them from the neck, who were assisted up the side of the deck, perfectly naked and dripping; their canteens being instantly seized by the eager expectants.

I instinctively rushed forward and endeavoured to seize the swimmers by their canteen straps, but having no hold of their wet and slippery skins, they at once freed themselves to the great and vociferous enjoyment of the others, who with derisive and contemptuous shouts began to throw coals at me. It became a very serious matter and I was, for an instant, at a loss what to do. But, without hesitation, I rushed down to the cabin, seized my pistols, which were loaded and returned to the deck (the Master and crew had concealed themselves below and could not by any persuasion be induced to side with and help me). Placing my back against the bulk head of the companion stairs, I swore I would shoot the first man I could catch with wine or [who] threw coal at me. At the same time, I contrived to make a signal of distress which, being unusual, soon brought several boats from the ships of war lying around, who, bringing some marines, soon managed to quell the riot and place

24

the culprits in restraint. I never have since been able to account for the drunken and at one time, reckless men not having fired at me; for every man had sixty rounds of ball cartridges. It was this that overawed the Master and crew.

I must be pardoned this lengthy account of what, perhaps, many might think a very little matter; but which was my first trial of the kind and certainly for some time, threatened a rather disastrous result. And so it was considered, by the Court of Enquiry held on it next day, who highly approved of my conduct. We were landed and placed in a convent, a very usual barrack of that day and of which Malta seemed full; and as guard duty was then very heavy in the garrison, allowing only 2, sometimes only 1 night in bed, the Fort Adjutant placed us immediately on his roster and I mounted guard next morning over 500 French prisoners in a large convent. I had this duty several times after, not a very pleasant one. For besides the larger number confined in one building, on three tiers of long and large floors (in the centre of the top one of which was the Officer's guard-room). They were a mixture such as the French Army was then composed of, of all nations almost, of Europe, but chiefly then, Italians and French, stretched in confusion at full length, on the floor and amusing themselves with their noisy games, and with their usual disgusting hunting [of] each other's heads, the usual and never failing resource when not otherwise occupied. At no time [were they] much inclined to cleanliness (and much addicted to garlic and fleas), the compulsory sojourn among them for 24 hours at a time was anything but agreeable. But all was new to me and youth and professional zeal make many things tolerable, and indeed hardly considered as worth a consideration, which at other times and [in] other circumstances would appear real hardships.

Chapter 5

Sicily 1810

The Island of Sicily had stood as a beacon of hope against Napoleon's all conquering forces which had captured all of mainland Italy but had been unable to cross the narrow straits and take the Island of Sicily. Ever since Norman times, the southern portion of Italy below Naples and the neighbouring Island of Sicily had been generally governed as one Kingdom, although the ruling family had fluctuated between the Aragonese kings of Spain and the Hapsburg emperors of Austria. Eventually this was formalised at the Treaty of Vienna in 1738, which established that the Kingdom of Sicily was to be governed as a subordinate but separate branch of the Spanish domains. Hence in 1759 when Charles VII of Naples (mainland Sicily) who was also Charles V of Sicily, became King Charles III of Spain; he immediately appointed his third son, Ferdinand I of the Kingdom of the Two Sicilies.

Ferdinand, known locally as 'Re Nasone' (King Big Nose) was married to Maria Carolina, daughter of the Austrian Empress Marie Theresa and sister of Marie Antoinette. Ferdinand was a fun loving sportsman who was happy going out hunting every day, whereas Marie wished very much to be an enlightened but absolute monarch and it is very clear who actually wore the trousers in this relationship. With her trusted favourite, an Englishman named John Acton, Marie looked to expand and improve her navy and hence influence in the Mediterranean; and Sicilian troops were involved in the allied attempt to hold Toulon against the French revolutionaries.

A failed attempt to drive a French force out of Rome, caused the French to invade; and a brief but extremely bloody revolution occurred on mainland Sicily when the royal family was forced to flee to Palermo and the French declared the Parthenopean Republic. But within six

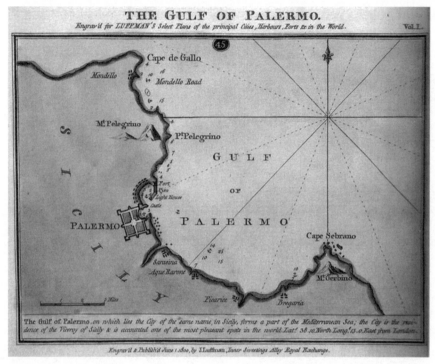

Above: A map of the Gulf of Palermo, published by J. Luffman, June 1800.

---

months a bloody counter-revolution, aided by Lord Nelson and his fleet, evicted the French troops and their revolutionary sympathisers and the survivors were soon shipped to France.

Things had then remained relatively quiet in southern Italy until 1806 when Napoleon ordered a French army to invade mainland Sicily and the royal family were forced to retire into the Island of Sicily once again. Napoleon then appointed his elder brother Joseph, King of Naples and Sicily, declaring Ferdinand's reign at an end.

However, Ferdinand still ruled Sicily and there the remains of his army was strongly bolstered by British troops, and the waters around the island were constantly patrolled by the ships of the British Royal Navy, in order to prevent the French army crossing the narrow straits of Messina. Despite this the Neapolitan Island of Capri did fall to the French in 1808 and Napoleon also made Marshal Joachim Murat King of Naples and his brother Joseph became King of Spain.

The British Minister in Sicily Lord William Bentinck, who actually acted as both politician and military commander, applied pressure to reform the constitution of Sicily and Ferdinand largely returned to his hunting whilst Queen Maria was forced into exile in Austria, leaving their son Francis as de facto ruler although he did not officially become Francis I until 1825.

In the summer of 1810 King Murat had an army of nearly 40,000 men, consisting of 18,000 French troops, 17,000 Neapolitans troops and 5,000 Neapolitan Guards with a fleet of nearly 400 small ships ready to act as transports. These troops were stationed around Reggio, ready to strike across the Straits of Messina to attack Sicily at a moment's notice.

As many British troops had been thinned from the island's garrison to land on the East coast of Spain in an effort to support Wellington's operations in the Iberian Peninsula, urgent orders were made to draw in any available men and John and his party seem to have been part of this movement.

On 17 September 1810 strong winds drove the patrolling British warships into port and Murat attempted to launch an invasion against Sicily. Three thousand five hundred Neapolitan troops are reported to have crossed successfully, landing at Scaletta. But no other troops followed, the French troops commanded by General Grenier apparently refusing, saying that they had no orders to proceed. By the following day the Neapolitan troops had to re-embark and abandon the attempt leaving behind 1,000 dead or prisoners.

Although it was a serious attempt, the alarm was sounded before the Neapolitans had landed more than 1,000 men, as Hildebrand asserts. The remainder were prevented from landing by the fire of the 21st Foot and two cannon they had placed on the beach; the landing attempt then being abandoned. At dawn, the troops that had landed were surrounded and, with no hope of escape, they immediately surrendered to the 21st Foot.[1]

In fact, John's time here seems to have been spent very uncomfortably at Fort St Salvadore guarding political prisoners and suffering greatly from maggots. His only source of diversion being the incessant small-scale naval actions he watched in the Straits with great interest. Occasionally he got the opportunity to get a little closer to the action, sometimes too close for comfort! But by October, it was clear that the

[1] *History of the 21st Foot* by Cannon.

threat was over, as the bad weather came in and Murat's force broke up for winter quarters.

John and his men were not unhappy to be ordered back to the island of Malta that November, where they were again forced to await transport to the Greek islands in an attempt to join the battalion for a second time.

After about 3 weeks we were delighted to receive the order to embark for Sicily, where an army of about 12 or14 thousand men was assembled under General Sir John Stuart; then threatened with an attack from Murat who commanded an army, I believe, of 40,000 men, along the coast of Calabria, from Scylla to beyond Reggio, on the opposite shore of the Faro of Messina. Sir John Stuart had commanded our army in Calabria and gained the splendid Battle of Maida, but overwhelmed by numbers had been obliged to retreat to Sicily. The last glorious exploit being the obstinate and skilful defence of Scylla under the then, Colonel, afterwards General G[eorge]. D. Robertson[2], who defended it to the last moment, and then, when no longer tenable, cleverly withdrew the remainder of his garrison, by night, without discovery or loss.

Colonel Robertson's conduct and skill in this defence obtained for him glorious renown and placed him in the first rank of enterprising commanders in the army. After 2 or 3 days of slow progress, we arrived at Messina, having touched at Syracuse and Catania and found Sir John Stuart's army in camp from the northern point of the Faro along the coast as far as Taormina (embracing the citadel and town of Messina). Most of the convents and monasteries of the latter place being occupied by our troops as barracks; those along the straits of the Faro being under canvas and the citadel strongly garrisoned. Fort St Salvadore[3], an old and important fort at the extremity of the tongue of land or peninsula forming the harbour and extending from the citadel which stands on this narrow tongue, was destined to [be] our [point of] occupation, the strength of our detachment of 300 men being just fitted to it.

[2] Colonel George Duncan Robertson, had risen to the rank of major in the 35th Foot and was then given command in 1807 of the Sicilian Regiment as a lieutenant colonel.

[3] Fort St Salvatore is at Messina.

This fort is very old, and had been occupied by the Crusaders, Richard Coeur de Lion, having taken up his residence in it with his queen for some time as a stronghold and retreat in case of disaster.[4] In these days of travel and matchless gazetteers, any attempt at [a] description would be out of place, but in 1810 it was not so well known: I shall, however, briefly remark that Fort St Salvadore was in a wretched state of repair, only [but] for the outer walls, which were entire, I might say in ruin. As a barrack it was most comfortless and could hardly keep out the wind and rain, but taking it as a campaigning refuge, we were but too happy to have it for our quarters.

One circumstance, however, I must mention, both because it exemplifies the ruinous state I have described and because it really caused me, for 3 or 4 days, much discomfort and uneasiness. I slept on the usual bed of that country, 3 boards placed on two trestles, on which was placed my mattress. Of course, being in light marching order, I had no curtains. The ceiling, if such might be called, of my only room was formed of loose and ill-joined rough boards. I kept several sporting dogs and not being very nice or particular as to my apartment, they had the full run of it and occasionally I suppose brought in a bone. My habit was to stay at our room, which afforded me somewhat more comfort and besides agreeable company, made me little anxious to go to my uncomfortable bed very early, and when I retired I at once got into it, and of course, youth like, was soon sound asleep, not awaking all night until called in the morning for parade. One morning, as soon as I opened my eyes, to my horror I perceived all the upper part of my breast and body covered with large white maggots ¾ of an inch long at least and [as] thick in proportion. Springing out of bed in a fright, I summoned my soldier servant, naturally supposing it was through some neglect or carelessness and with the impetuosity of a boy, at once berated him

---

[4] Richard the Lionheart was in Sicily in 1190 A.D. at the same period that Tancred became King of Sicily. The Queen referred to was Queen Joanna, spouse of the recently deceased King William II of Sicily and Tancred was refusing to honour her inheritance. Unfortunately for Tancred, Joanna was Richard's sister and he was determined to see her rightfully restored to her inheritance. This disagreement led to Richard's knights half destroying Messina before Tancred relented.

soundly. He would take no blame himself, but referred to my numerous dogs and with strict injunctions to have all cleared away and to take care it did not occur again, I set out for the day, not returning as [was] usual, but for a few minutes to dress for dinner, until bed time again. All recollection of maggots had left me in the excitement of a battle of gun-boats I had witnessed for several hours in the strait [immediately] under the fort. I stayed rather later than usual at Mess and got into bed and slept as usual, until called. The moment I awoke I perceived and felt the same horrid mass about my throat, mouth and chest as the day before. I flew into a rage, summoned the man and at once accused him of not having cleaned away the maggots &c, &c, but with the same replies from him, which did not set me quite at ease and it was on my mind a great part of the day. But, going to bed as usual, after having looked (I fear but carelessly) at the sheets, which my man assured me he had just examined, off to sleep I went again. But next morning I was astonished, disgusted and alarmed at finding myself again in the same plight! What could I think? It was always about my mouth and neck. I felt sick and remembering that Herod was eaten up by a disease of self-bred worms, I could not but suppose that they all proceeded during the night, *from my own mouth*; and I at once fell into despair, no longer blaming my old servant, but fully persuaded it was as I have suggested. It never occurred to me, in my haste and fright, to examine the ceiling above, which, had I been older and less hasty, would probably have been the case. All at once, my old servant thought of going to the floor above, which from its ruinous state neither he nor I had done before; and just above the head of my bed he discovered a large dead rat, lying more than half-decayed, between the crevice of the boards, solving and explaining to my infinite relief and comfort the whole matter.

To explain the dilapidation of our quarters it was said that the fort had been seized on and occupied by the English and other nations so often in the course of [the] centuries that the Sicilian government hardly looked on it as their own and therefore would stand [against] any amount of urging or threatening rather than expend a shilling on repairs; so it was we found it and being but birds of passage, this time it gave us but little trouble. But there is another, and after it's recurring to my memory very many times, in a period of now, above 50 years, still a more distressing recollection of that fort; it is this. We garrisoned it for our own use and convenience; but as it had been used, from time immemorial, by the Sicilian government as a state prison for political and [also] often for an unpardonable class of offenders. It was their general, perhaps universal, place of confinement in bad cases, i.e. for the worst of felons sentenced to perpetual confinement, *without pity* (as supposed to be deserving none) or hope of being pardoned or ever regaining their liberty; these wretches were all confined in the bomb proofs of this fort and never could I forget the horror I felt when first on guard and visiting my sentries, at witnessing their wretched misery. In these bombproofs the wet trickled down every part of the walls, both above and around them in an almost continual stream, they lay on the wet ground with hardly a vestige of straw, and that as wet as it could be, their hair matted and tangled and of course without a vestige of cleanliness, and this from year to year without amelioration or change!! It is impossible to exaggerate such misery or to think without horror, even at this distance of time, without shuddering and questioning oneself, could these things be? And yet, from what I then saw and could learn, and from my observation and knowledge of the people, I cannot doubt that so it has continued ever since and does so now. It might occur, how could this be permitted and continued in a fort garrisoned by an English garrison? But in delivering it over to us, the right of imprisonment &c were reserved, they retained the same jailers and the same Provost Marshal, who visited them whenever they pleased and *our* sentries had only the honour of keeping guard over them and in one case, I learned, from some oversight or carelessness I suppose, actually performed the office of preventing the wretches sleeping beyond ½ an hour at a time, by calling each name at that interval; which, however, I believe and hope they from custom answered mechanically in their sleep and therefore without the dreadful suffering such barbarity would imply and was intended. I was told that one, at least, of these unfortunates had been in that confinement 30 years! that he had murdered several persons &c, &c: even so, the punishment was worse than death.

Our stay at Fort St Salvadore was one of continual excitement almost *every day*. When weather permitted, there was a regular sea fight in the channel just under the ramparts; I fear to mention the number of gunboats engaged on both sides, there were so many.

When the sea breeze set in, as it did regularly at about 10 o'clock A.M., they met in mid-channel and pounded each other with long 18 pounders all day till the wind died away in the evening and whenever any one of the boats was hit and crippled there was a regular scramble, one side striving to protect and get it off to its own side, the other bidding strong to capture or prevent it.

The distance across, however, in few places exceeding 2 or 3 miles, made retreat so easy that a capture seldom happened, or the gunboat sunk. The crew of each, on our side, consisted of a capitano and from 30 to 40 men, principally Neapolitans, altogether a formidable force and in my opinion, they fought at all times in a spirited, bold manner, eager and ready to expose themselves on all occasions.

As the gunboats were very many, some hundreds and it required some British officers to lead and command them, generally if not always, they were army officers. Occasionally when the wind was strong, a line of battle ship, or two, with some frigates and brigs from the port led on and took part in the engagement, keeping in, as much as possible, to the opposite shore and sweeping the coast with their broadsides, destroying the batteries and everything within reach in their progress, for 3 or 4 miles; returning to anchor in and about the harbour in the evening when the sea breeze died away.

What I have been describing, occurred almost daily from the time we joined Sir John Stuart's Army early in June till late in October or November, when it was broke up by the retreat of the French Army under Murat.[5] That army had lain encamped, a very short distance from the shore; and with our glasses we could see their parades and movements with great clearness, as they could equally perceive ours. Murat was very often seen distinguished by [his] lofty figure and splendid dress, surrounded by a numerous and splendid staff. His headquarters was at Reggio, very near. It may seem strange that two such armies and under such distinguished commanders, should have remained so many months within sight of each other and no serious or effectual attack be made on either side, but we had to defend Sicily with a very inferior force, but so strongly posted, with so many men of war and gunboats, that the French never dared a

[5] Marshal Joachim Murat, was installed by Napoleon as King of Naples in 1808, a position he retained until 1815.

serious attack. Twice only, as far as I am aware, did they make any show of attempting a landing and these were so miserable and ill conducted, that they were captured instantly they reached our shore. Indeed, it was said, and I believe it, [that] these attempts were only made to test the *practicability* of a landing and composed of the worthless refuse of the army; a small number, about 1,500 men each. I witnessed one of these miserable expeditions, which appeared so contemptible that I could not understand it. The whole force was captured the moment they landed by the 21st Regiment[6] and the outlying pickets, on one of which I was that night. They reached the shore as the day broke, on a fine clear morning and before 7 o'clock they were all [made] prisoners, without firing a shot. In fact a successful landing in our face was impracticable, with our vigilance and such an army. I am the more particular in describing these transactions, because they never have been sufficiently known in England, excepting of course, at the Horse Guards. From 1809 to 1814, the whole military and war interest was centred in Spain and many dashing and important movements took place during that time, in other quarters, which were little known or noticed.

In those days of slow packet-service and few newspapers, many important services escaped entirely the public ear, or excited but little attention, excepting as related to the death struggle then carrying on in Spain. And many a dashing deed which in these days would merit and be rewarded with high distinction and public celebrity, then passed entirely without and their authors and actors have passed away into oblivion and to the grave without the reward even of public notice. But as all these things transacted must be on record *somewhere* and might be disinterred, their truth and importance might yet be made matter of history.

Even that great general Sir John Stuart, the hero of Maida, is now hardly remembered or known, having suffered eclipse by the exciting and absorbing glory of the period.

These gunboats ought to be in some degree described, for they are quite unlike and inferior to those of the present day. They were of 2 kinds, one with a heavy 18lb iron gun in the bow, the other a 12lb also iron; consequently, both of great weight.

---

[6] The 21st (Royal North British) Fusiliers.

Sometimes a lighter brass gun, which had been captured from the enemy, was either added to or substituted for these heavier pieces. But the boat was always heavy and cumbersome, the former carrying about, or always, 40 men; the latter a smaller number, but both propelled by oars and heavy lumbering sails, and accomplishing in speed, the gunboat, i.e. the larger [one], about 3 miles an hour in calm waters, the smaller, called a scampavia,[7] i.e. runway or swift boat, about 5 miles on the average. They were half or ¾ decked so as to afford cover for the men, but consequently so low in head room as to afford nothing more and ventilation for health was but little studied and in that climate and with the habits of the crew (fleas, &c, had full swing) little comfort could be sought below deck. Yet in many expeditions with them, taking, of course, as the commandant, the capitano's or best berth, I was often glad to avail myself of it and arose in the morning at sunrise and while it was rising (in that hemisphere an indescribable and glorious sight) relieved myself as I could of the discomfort by such ablutions as the circumstances and state of the water would permit. I can remember many such mornings of real enjoyment, looking out anxiously, &c, for anything. Each of the crew had a cutlass, which I always found [with] him, when called on, willing and ready to use, and those who could added a brace of pistols to their armament, which I am not sure [whether] our government supplied. Such was the gunboat of that day, and on that occasion and with which the respective opposite shores swarmed. I never saw any others in the Mediterranean, nor in the Adriatic, in which I saw much active service in them and had several under my command.

I have obtruded this description because I suspect that it will be difficult in these and future days to form any conception of them, or of the service in which they were so useful and effectual.

We remained from June till November in St Salvadore, when Murat withdrew his army and Sir John Stuart could dispense with our services, and then [we] were sent to Malta, where we remained, undergoing of course a good many guards and garrison duties, for 3 or 4 weeks, when we again embarked, at last to join our 1st battalion in the Greek Islands.

---

[7] A long, low war galley, used by the Neapolitans and Sicilians in the early part of the nineteenth century.

Chapter 6

The Ionian Islands 1811

The Ionian Isles off the Greek mainland were traditionally called the Heptanese or Seven Islands, being comprised of seven major islands and numerous minor ones.

The islands have had many owners, including the Greeks and Romans, the Byzantine Empire, the Venetians and the Turks (although Corfu was the only Greek Island that the Ottoman Empire failed to conquer) before they all were restored to Venetian control at the end of the 15th Century.

In 1797, Napoleon conquered Venice and, by the subsequent Treaty of Campo Formio, these islands passed into French hands. However, the following year the Russian Admiral Ushakov expelled the French and a joint Russo/Ottoman Septinsular Republic was formed. The islands, however, were again ceded to France at the meeting of the Emperors Napoleon and Alexander at Tilsit in 1807.

In 1809 Cephalonia, Cerigo and Zante fell to the British, followed by Lefkada in 1810. Finally, the detachment which had sailed to join the 1st Battalion of the 35th around November 1809, eventually met up with the rest of the battalion in May 1811[1], no less than eighteen months later.

John soon became used to the rounds of garrison duty, which covered Ithaca, Santa Maura and Zante in turns, making the tedium of forming a garrison perhaps a little less monotonous.

---

[1] The History of the regiment records the arrival of the detachment on 7 May 1811, *History of the 35th*, p.110.

We there found the entire capture of them [the Ionian Islands] had been completed[2] and landing at Zante[3], we became at once, part of the garrison.

As was the universal custom at that time, the civil government followed and was merged into the military command and its offices filled up at the senior officer's discretion; following the example of the two powers which had preceded us in these islands, each by conquest, viz the Russian and next the French, from whom we captured them. Accordingly, we found Major Slessor[4], 2nd in command of the 1st Battalion 35th Regiment, an old and experienced officer, of great tact and a first rate linguist, at the head of the *Civil* government of the Island of Zante, installed as 'Capo de Governo'; and a better choice in every respect could not easily have been made. The garrison then consisted of the above named battalion, 1,000 or 1,200 strong old veterans, lately returned from Egypt to the attack on and capture of the Greek Islands; and some of the other regiments, or portions of them, of Foreign Auxiliary Corps, of which the British Government, at that time and for some years before had availed themselves; largely to complete the forces requisite to meet the necessary contingencies of that active and warlike time in all parts of Europe; but especially then on the shores of the Mediterranean and to supply reinforcements to the Army in Spain. They had been largely employed in the army of Sir John Stuart, in Calabria and as we have seen, in the defence of Sicily.

In these distant times it may not be superfluous to mention some of those corps, which were then regularly incorporated, and the officers, permanently provided for by future ½ pay and pensions, in the British Army. Some few of whom, who still survive and live comfortably and well in their own countries and are even now on the ½ half-pay list of the army; especially those of the 'King's German Legion', a large and valuable body, then acknowledged to be among and equal to the very best soldiers of our service.

Anyone having access to the old Army Lists of that period, will be able to form some idea of the formidable extent of these foreign corps, in fact altogether a large and important army.

---

[2] Virtually all but the more northerly Island of Corfu had been captured.

[3] Zante is more often known as Zakynthos.

[4] Major John Slessor.

Above: A map of Malta and the Ionian Islands published by John Arrowsmith, London, 1842.

Their officers, especially those of Germany and the Corsican Rangers, with indeed those of most others, were not generally very young men; but many above middle age. These latter were mostly unfortunate noblemen and their kindred who had been driven from their homes and country by the sad and disastrous war with Napoleon; and most of them, having served in the army in some way, were but too glad to take service in the British Army, in positions and ranks often much below what they might have attained to in their own, but affording the means of living. An ensign of 40, or even older, years of age was no very unusual thing to meet with: the captains were generally so, gentlemen, good soldiers, always ready for any undertaking and although bearing a contrast with our much more youthful officers, and therefore perhaps not quite so ardent and active: steady, brave, experienced and *always to be relied on* in any duties committed to them. We had portions of several of these corps in Zante and other Ionian Islands. My recollection does not serve me with the minute particulars, but there were several, the German Legion which I have mentioned, the 'Corsican Rangers', 'Dillon's'[5] (from some part of Germany, I believe), 'De Meuron's' (French)[6], &c, &c. Altogether a very *mixed* force; intermixed, I suppose, as a matter of precaution as well as convenience, where implicit confidence could not safely be placed, to entrust in the same nations with an equal and perhaps preponderating (numerically) strength, in our garrisons. In fact, in our various services and the consequent contact or close proximity to so many nations, then former allies and friends, it often happened that our foreign auxiliaries, from exposure to the temptations of old comrades and connexions [*sic*], too often showed a disposition (even in some cases commissioned officers) to desert to the enemy, inducing the necessity of much additional precaution and unpleasant suspicion: a thing the British officer could hardly be brought to understand or entertain. But on the whole it may have had not a bad effect on ourselves, in keeping us alive and watchful, and teaching the young and inexperienced the necessity of keeping wide awake at all times, and be always on guard with regard to them.

I must not quit this subject without alluding to that blunder and expensive one of the day, the 'Greek Light Infantry', a *whim*, I believe, originating from the enthusiastic feelings of the Prince

---

[5] Dillon's Regiment was a unit in British pay; at this time. It consisted mainly of French émigré officers with Spanish and Sicilian soldiers. It was later formed into a single battalion with de Roll's Regiment.

[6] De Meuron's Regiment actually consisted of Swiss troops in British pay.

Regent, who had participated in the mistaken great expectations, of such men as Lord Byron[7], of the regeneration of the Greek nation and renewal of its renown, if duly fostered and encouraged, roused and excited very generally by our recent conquest of the Ionian Islands, the first and in those regions then considered valuable exploit of our army just returned from Egypt, in 1806. The Prince took up the cause with great zeal, and the 1st Battalion of the Greek Light Infantry[8] Corps was raised, a fine looking body of men but, as it turned out, *utterly useless* as soldiers and worse; so troublesome and unruly in discipline that, however hard the duties of the different garrisons of Zante, Santa Maura, Cephalonia, &c, no commanding officer could ever be persuaded to have that corps, if he could possibly avoid it; and as, after the addition of a 2nd Battalion[9], it formed a force of 2,000 men, it was not only a large and useless expense to the country, but by filling up the place of a more desirable reinforcement, was a constant and vexatious annoyance, hampering the chief in command and other senior officers. I believe they were never brought to face the enemy excepting at the attack on the citadel of Santa Maura when under Major Church[10] and several English captains (who were all wounded) and others who had served gallantly in the English army, and had each taken a step of promotion in the corps, they behaved so ill and caused such confusion and disappointment that they were never tried again. The only and constant effort after that was to place them out of the way. I offer this account and criticism with reluctance, as recent events[11] have proved that modern Greeks fully bear out its truth and, in the

---

[7] The great poet Lord Byron sided with the Greeks in their attempts to free themselves from the Ottoman Empire, sailing to Greece to support them and sinking some £4,000 of his own money into refitting the Greek fleet. Despite having no prior military background, Byron got fully involved with the preparations for an attack on Lepanto, but died, possibly of sepsis, in 1824 before the attack could take place.

[8] The 1st Regiment of Greek Light Infantry was a single battalion regiment raised in 1810 from Greek and Albanian soldiers with Greek/British officers.

[9] Actually it was raised as the 2nd Greek Light Infantry Regiment in 1813.

[10] Major Richard Church of the Royal Corsican Rangers had formed and commanded the 1st Greek Light Infantry Regiment.

[11] This shows that John Hildebrand wrote this memoir just before he died in 1868, this would appear to explain why it is unfortunately unfinished.

surrender of these valuable conquests and strong holds, the Ionian Islands, to them[12], it is hard for one who saw so much of them to restrain his indignation and reprobation of such a wanton national sacrifice, with a sure conviction that a time will come when the step will be bitterly rued and retraced, if that may be, at great expense of much treasure and many valuable gallant lives.

But with regard to the raising of the 2nd Battalion of Greek Light Infantry, I feel myself called on to notice the excitement it aroused in military circles of that day. The 1st Battalion was notoriously a failure, and worse and there was no better material whence to draw the 2nd. Much speculation and many influences were set in action, to decide on the *patronage*, especially of the higher grades. It had been generally taken, in a way, quite for granted that the Major (Church) of the 1st should get a step and become as he ought Lieutenant Colonel of the 2nd new levy, but, from rumours from home and at the Horse Guards, such was understood not to be the case; and Major Church started quietly, by the first packet, to see after it. I believe it had been destined, and with supposed authority, for a different man; but Church, who was a fine manly-looking officer, presented himself at the Prince's levee in a most magnificently embroidered and ornamented picturesque uniform of the corps, made at Zante and which so became his manly figure as to astound the prince; delighted him beyond measure; and Church left the room with the appointment of Lieutenant Colonel. He has since advanced from step to step in his distinguished career, and is now, if alive, I believe, a prince and field marshal in the Russian Empire, with all its rank and privileges.[13]

From headquarters at Zante, monthly detachments were sent to reinforce the other island garrisons at Santa Maura, Ithaca[14], &c and

---

[12] Britain had retained a protectorate over the Ionian Islands after 1815. However, by the Treaty of London of 1864, the islands were ceded to Greece but Britain retained the use of Corfu port.

[13] General Sir Richard Church, born at Cork in 1785, of Quaker parentage, who, having served with distinction in both the British and Neapolitan services, was made a C.B. in 1815 and K.C.H. in 1822. In 1827, he was appointed Generalissimo of the insurgent Greeks, whose success was due largely to his strategy. He lived afterwards in Athens, where he died in 1873. I can find no evidence that he ever held a Russian rank.

[14] Or more commonly known now as Ithaka.

in February 1811[15] I was ordered to accompany that of the latter. It was not an agreeable duty, to leave headquarters mess &c and therefore was shunned when it could be. Besides that, Santa Maura was an unhealthy quarter compared with Zante, subject to low fevers and ague, but, from whatever cause, these changes were regularly kept up so that everyone had his turn. We were embarked as usual in a transport, with a detachment to Ithaca, to be landed there on our way, and had the usual beautiful weather and scenery among the islands; nothing could exceed it. Our master, as we then called them, of the transport was a young man with all the outward appearance of a sailor, but very little experience, the son of the owner, and therefore placed in such a trust too early, who took things easy in every way, made himself disagreeable to the officers and failed in acquiring their confidence in his qualifications.

The weather was so lovely and calm that inexperienced men could not imagine a dangerous change. When we reached Ithaca it was evening, all sails, even to studded sails, set and not a breath of air; we were entirely land locked among the islands. At the usual hour all retired to rest without [a] care or fear.

I walked the deck with some others till a late hour and then followed the rest to bed, and was very soon fast asleep in my berth, remaining completely insensible of sounds or disturbance of any kind; when about 4 o'clock I was startled by the ship heeling over to the larboard side, that of my berth, and an immense large sea which pitched on me completely blocking up the door and rendering exit impossible. At the same time the wind roaring in such a way as those who have not experienced a 'White Squall' in the Mediterranean cannot imagine. And the shouting of the captain and crew, with the intense cries and lamentations of women and children, adding to the horror, I did all I could to arise and force my escape, but 'twas impossible, the large chest and other things could not be removed by me and after struggling in the greatest alarm, as long as I could, I was obliged, from sheer exhaustion, to fall back and lie still, having brought myself to the conclusion that, even if I could get out, as the ship seemed ready to go down, it was as well to lie still and be

---

[15] This is clearly an error for February 1812 as he did not reach the Ionian islands until May 1811.

drowned in my berth as elsewhere. But after some minutes, another lurch having taken place, I tried again, struggled for life and contrived to squeeze myself through and reach the deck in my shirt, as all there were, when I found the most indescribable confusion. The captain (or master) in his shirt, storming and ordering all kinds of things which could not be done, or heard, the women and children, as women and children must be on such occasions and even the old veterans, many of them on their knees imploring God's mercy.

The ship was lying entirely on her side, close to a lee rock of I believe about 200 feet and within a very few yards of a point which, if weathered, would have saved us, every sail, studded and all, still on her, for not one of them could be taken in, and but for that and the good and trusty masts, on that rock of impossible ascent or escape, we must have gone. But she shot ahead of it within a yard!!

However, 'a miss is as good as a mile', we did escape and the next day landed our men in Ithaca and we, the officers, set out to 'see the Lions'[16]. And indeed there is much worth seeing and admiring at Ithaca; the wonderful caves on that rock, barren as of old, can never be forgotten by anyone who has been through them: I have seen many caves in various countries but none so beautiful and surprising as them. The stalactite columns of those caves are truly splendid and wonderful and in my humble and unscientific opinion, they or others of the same kind must have suggested the grandeur of what is called the gothic style of architecture, roof and bulky pillars. But where, and of what kind, Ulysses' *Palace* was[17], is hard to be imagined and if things are as they were then, Penelope's lot must indeed have been trying and recluse [*sic*] and her charms unimaginably transcendent to have given her occasion to persevere in such lengthened and faithful resistance to her lovers. But altogether a visit to picturesque Ithaca will well repay the trouble of a visit. Leaving the relief to the garrison, we proceeded to Santa Maura, a much larger and important island, with a citadel and fortifications on a peninsula, which gave our

[16] A term for seeing the 'sights'.

[17] Some Greek archaeologists have recently claimed to have discovered the remains of the Palace of Ullyses (or Odysseus in Greek) on Ithaca, but many others claim that he was a purely fictional character.

troops some trouble to take at the capture of the island, an unhealthy and dirty quarter. Here we found Lieutenant Colonel Lowe[18] (afterwards the well-known Sir Hudson) in command with his regiment the 'Corsican Rangers'[19] in the citadel. As he became so celebrated in after years, I may just mention that I joined his command and regimental mess and saw a good deal of him during my detachment duty; and, as far as a very young subaltern could know his great commanding officer, was on pretty familiar terms with him. But his manners and habits were extremely retired, and not encouraging. I remember his usual habit, at mess, after dinner was to go to sleep, or appear to do so, which did not endear him much to the younger members, at least those who could not feel assured that he was sound asleep as he appeared; and altogether it was a disagreeable and wearisome duty, refreshed, almost only, by the excellent shooting to which I was always devoted, when I had opportunity to indulge; and that was really magnificent both in the island and on the continent, which could be reached almost at all times, without much difficulty, by wading on foot.

At the period of expiration of our detachment duty at Santa Maura, we returned to Zante, expecting the tiresome life of garrison duty with all its disagreeable, for some time to come. When, suddenly an order was received by our commanding officer to send 300 men volunteers from the 35th Regiment and the Foreign Auxiliaries to join a force under Colonel G.D. Robertson, the distinguished gallant and skilful defender of Scylla, who was about to undertake an expedition to the Island of Lissa, in the Adriatic, which I volunteered for, altogether 600 men of all arms. This was undertaken by order of the commander in chief at Malta and the ships with the different detachments were to rendezvous at the splendid harbour of Cephalonia, then a very minor command, of a company or two depending on Zante.

---

[18] Lieutenant Colonel Hudson Lowe commanded the Royal Corsican Rangers and from 1809-12, he was installed as Governor of Cephalonia and Ithaca and later Santa Maura.

[19] The original regiment of Royal Corsican Rangers had been raised by Captain Hudson Lowe in 1800, but it had disbanded with the Peace of Amiens in 1802. A new regiment was raised in 1803 when war resumed mainly comprising Corsicans, but supplemented by Sicilians and Sardinians.

Chapter 7

Lissa 1812

After being on the islands for a year John was desperate to gain some more active employment, when he was suddenly ordered to join an expedition to capture the Island of Lissa in May 1812. The Royal Navy had regularly used the excellent natural harbour on Lissa for a number of years, but without a land force stationed there, the islands were always under the threat of invasion by the French who had until now left it in the hands of a very unprofessional local militia who wisely chose not to antagonise the Royal Navy by attempting to curtail their use of the harbour.

The Navy was very keen on persuading the Army to send a force to garrison the island and the copious correspondence both to London and local Army commanders emphasised the many great advantages to the war effort of holding Lissa securely. Their reasoning included some very tenuous ones, such as, the overall denial of absolutely anything to the French and to help maintain lines of communication with their allies; to more specific claims, such as, denying them the undoubted ship building capability; to disrupt the enemy's lines of communication; procurement of both supplies and facilities for the repair and construction of ships and the ability it gave to ferment revolt against the French on the nearby mainland. It also gave the British a forward base, allowing ships to remain on station in the Adriatic for much longer periods, instead of constantly returning to Malta to replenish, a three month round trip.

It may also have had something to do with a French raid on 22 October 1810 when three frigates commanded by Admiral Bernard Dubourdieu with 500 troops on board landed on Lissa. Dubourdieu claimed sixty-two vessels were burned, forty-three of which were laden and ten privateers;

whilst restoring ten French ships. However other sources claim a more realistic six ships destroyed and a number of storehouses. The islanders were fearful of another attack without a garrison.

Nevertheless, Lissa remained a low priority for the Army for a number of years whilst Sicily was under such a serious threat but, by 1812, the Army was prepared to countenance placing a small garrison there.

In February 1812, Lord Bentinck wrote home that he had appointed Lieutenant Colonel Robertson of the Sicilian Regiment to the command of Lissa and was going to give him 600 troops with which to accomplish its conquest. The expedition collected at Cephalonia, from where it was to sail on transport ships protected by HMS *Imogen*. The troops ordered to take part consisted of about 200 men of the 35th; 200 Corsican Rangers; 100 men of Roll's Regiment and 100 of the Calabrian Free Corps with a detachment of thirty artillerymen and one engineer officer.

After three failed attempts to sail because of bad weather, the little fleet set off on 25 May and was met off Lissa by a squadron consisting of *Eagle* of seventy-four guns, *Apollo* and *Alceste* frigates and the *Weazle* brig.

The troops landed on Lissa the following day unopposed, in fact the local population was very glad to see them. Immediately on arrival the position of new forts and storehouses was agreed with the engineer Captain Henryson, and a large programme of construction began in earnest.

The infantry had to survive under canvas for the first few nights before Henryson and his ten sappers had constructed temporary shelters for them all. Once settled in, the occasional opportunity to cooperate with the Navy in supplying small numbers of troops in small ship operations and particularly in landings designed to destroy French defences along the coastline, helped to stem the inevitable boredom. It also helped to foster an air of cooperation between the different forces and seems to have infused an enterprising attitude into the Army officers like their Navy counterparts.

A number of Croatian militia deserted and made their way to Lissa, Colonel Robertson gained permission to form a corps from these men to be known as the 'Illyrian Light Infantry'[1] but it does not seem to have

---

[1] Fremantle Papers 38/6/21.

grown into much of a unit. In fact, Robertson soon found it easier to supply passage for these deserters to join the Austrian Army under General Nugent in Northern Italy.

I never saw a finer or more capacious harbour than Cephalonia, which at that time was little accounted of, or at least not much used by us; afterwards its advantage became more apparent, and it levelled Zante in importance. Here we lost a fine and much esteemed subaltern officer, while lying at anchor which we did for 3 or 4 weeks, waiting for Colonel R[obertson] and his headquarters. He arose well to all appearance, but complaining of headache, took breakfast and half an hour after, while conversing with myself and others, fell back and died without a struggle, of apoplexy, a sad and striking lesson to us all in our thoughtless career[2]. He was much liked and lamented; we buried him at Argostoli, the capital of the island, and as well as I can recollect, R[oman] C[atholic] with all its ceremonies; for we thought little of such things in those days on foreign service, indeed we were indifferent to them. We had no chaplain. I had not seen one since I left England, a mere boy, nor did I for several years after, excepting now and then meeting a Naval chaplain on board ships of war at dinner, and once or twice in our united service expeditions, in the Adriatic, by chance.

It was otherwise in the Navy. Almost every captain of a frigate had his chaplain, generally his intimate companion and friend, appointed by himself and paid by the government; and in line of battle ships there were, I believe, permanent chaplains, regularly appointed as such, but selected by the admiral. At any rate, I seldom saw a ship without one and he the friend and constant companion of the captain. A great and indescribable advantage over the army; for, excepting in large and important stations, such as Malta, Messina &c, we seldom or never saw the clergyman; and when we did, not one calculated to command our respect or affection. It must be confessed, they were generally not of the stamp and character of

---

[2] There are few obvious candidates for this subaltern officer in the records. However, given the date of early 1812, the most likely candidate is Lieutenant John French 35th Foot who is recorded as having died (cause unspecified) in January 1812. The British Cemetery at Argostoli unfortunately does not have a full record of burials and many gravestones are missing.

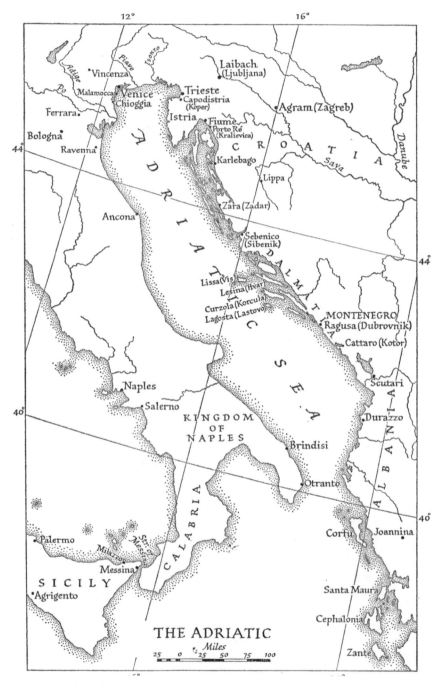

Above: A map of the Adriatic.

those of present day; in fact there was then hardly a *semblance* of religion in our army on *foreign stations*.

This was not reckless disregard of it; but an utter ignorance of its requirements or advantages, which, when we consider the very early age of those who entered the army, myself barely 15 and then with no more instruction than could have been gleaned at school so early, and even the best of our common schools took but little pains in such matters. It is not to be wondered at, however lamentable, that so many in our Christian armies should be in really heathen darkness, beyond the very first elements and forms of Christianity and therefore insensible of it and its sad and fearful consequences. Happily, not so in the Navy; owing I doubt not to each ship having *generally*, its chaplain. I hardly ever saw a ship without some, if not several, officers of real piety and sound knowledge of religious matters, the influence of whom descended throughout all grades.

I did not mean to draw this or any other comparison between the two services; but being on the subject I cannot refrain from giving vent to the result of reflections of many years, and offer my thanksgiving that matters in the army (which must have originated in the neglect of high authority in this respect) are now satisfactorily and beneficially altered. I never saw it, but that, when even only the *forms* and regularity of devotion were *reverently* observed, it had a good and beneficial effect on all within their influence.[3]

We, now having assembled the transports of our force, once more proceeded towards Lissa. In the month of March[4], in the Adriatic, it is generally fine and equable weather and such we found it but slow sailing until we reached our destination.

Having lost twice, my memorandums and dates, few enough that I then thought worth the trouble, on the changes and very active service I was afterwards engaged in, I cannot now fix on the precise days or periods of our movements; but our arrival at Lissa must have been early in March 1811[5]. We found it an island like all others around it, almost without culture, excepting in patches here and there and immediately about the villages, and having all the

---

[3] It should be borne in mind that this passage was written many years later in life when he himself was a clergyman.

[4] It was May not March when the expedition took place.

[5] Again, he is wrong. This should read May 1812.

appearance of what we would call a moor in England. The inhabitant Dalmatians or Venetians very rough specimens of civilization, excepting in the highest class, of whom were some, descended I believe, from Venetian or Italian origin, who affected some refinement and indeed were entitled to their assumption, although living in a primitive and in a poor and most unassuming style. They were evidently very poor in property but had not lost the distinctions of grade and conventional ceremony and pride.

The island had been hardly recognized by us nationally, till the year 1810, and its beautiful and spacious harbour only used as a roadstead or naval rendezvous, to watch and cripple the intercourse and trade of the coast of the Adriatic, especially of Venice, Trieste, Fiume[6] and Zara with all the neighbouring minor creeks and little harbours, used by the French, and their depending provinces, in their sneeking but not unimportant coasting trade carried on by small vessels, trabacoles[7] i.e. half-decked or open boats with lateen sails, creeping along the shore, suited to such service. To check which was the principal object in occupying Lissa by our government; and it effectually answered the purpose. The little French convoys of gunboats being no longer a reliable protection from our cruisers always at hand and ready to pounce on them.

On the [blank] day of March 1811 was fought the celebrated naval action of Lissa[8], in its immediate neighbourhood, which, by the distinguished conduct of Captain Gordon[9] in capturing with a very inferior force the first line of battle ship *Ramillies*[10], which had been built and afterwards blocked for some years in the harbour of Venice, and had at last ventured out to meet its fate, and Hoste who commanded, brought the island into notice and themselves into the

---

6 Now Rijeca in Croatia.

7 A ship of moderate size, with two or three masts and squaresails, used on the Adriatic.

8 On March 13th, 1811, off Lissa, Captain, afterwards Admiral Sir William Hoste, with four frigates, annihilated a French-Venetian squadron of six frigates and a number of lesser ships. I believe this episode has caused John to mistakenly date his time at Lissa to the same year.

9 Captain James Gordon R.N. commanded *HMS Active* of 38 guns.

10 Hildebrand is in error here, as Captain Gordon captured the stronger Venetian frigate *Corona* to complete the victory of Lissa. The French did not own a ship named *Ramillies*. I believe that the Venetian first rate taken refers to the capture of the *Rivoli* by HMS *Victorious* in 1812.

highest [grade] of the list of highly distinguished officers and commanders.

The harbour of Lissa was then entirely unprotected by fortifications or forts, the remedy of which, however, was immediately set about under the direction of a captain of Royal Engineers; but when finished were found to be so commanded by the neighbouring heights that it was necessary to add several Martello Towers, which certainly restored the required protection (none on the land side) to a great degree. The harbour was surmounted by heights, arising in the form of a semi-circle sloping up from the edge of the shore to a considerable height; and therefore commanding the town and harbour and but for the Martello Towers the entrance of the port and anchorage.[11]

Barracks adequate to the garrison appointed and other necessary buildings were run up hastily, and indeed in a manner which showed that they were not intended for permanent occupation. In the mean time the troops were put under canvas and here I may mention, as an example of the boisterous storms to which the Adriatic climate is exposed, that on the third or fourth night after we landed, in beautiful and calm weather, without a symptom of disturbed atmosphere, I went to my camp bed in my bell tent at 11 o'clock at night, and at 4 in the morning, having slept in the mean time as soundly as health and youth usually ensures, I was awoke by the cold and drenching state of my bed clothes, discovering that I was entirely without a vestige of covering or shelter of any kind, exposed to a down-pouring [of] rain and violent wind, under which I must have continued to sleep for some considerable time, my tent and upper bed clothes having been lifted up and swept away to a considerable distance by the storm. But we were soon under the temporary roofs provided by our engineer, and enjoyed ourselves in them with all the buoyancy and spirits of youth and novelty. In fact we began to feel that we had entered on *service* and had got into the line of seeing or doing something. Very soon after our landing here and being settled down in barracks, we perceived that service was really *active* here. Several expeditions, for cutting out convoys &c, were undertaken by the

---

[11] The fortifications planned and built by Captain John Henryson had always envisaged the building of the three Martello towers. They were not an afterthought as John believed.

Navy, in the most important of which they generally had recourse to Colonel R[obertson]'s force, who was nothing loath to such aid. It is so long ago and being quite without notes or memos of this period, I cannot enter into particulars of these undertakings, exciting and interesting as they were at the time. But of *one* I have a clear recollection, although the names of both ships and captains have, I am ashamed to say, escaped me. One evening at mess, we were informed that the frigate or perhaps two in the port were about sending out one of these expeditions to capture a valuable convoy of merchant coasters, on a rather more extensive scale than usual.

I instantly repaired to the frigate, and requested to be allowed to join it as a volunteer (I had not then learned the restraints of duty and discipline in such matters and acted from my own impulse) but was peremptorily refused, as I ought to have known I must be in such an unauthorised attempt. The next *evening*, the usual time for such attempts, the frigate's boats were got ready and alongside, duly manned and equipped, under two lieutenants; I witnessed the preparations and the eagerness with which the young middies then (before examinations &c became the necessary custom) *swarmed*, so to say, on the decks of [the] men of war, to accompany it. I found afterwards that several *little boys* who had been forbidden, had smuggled themselves into the boats, rolled up their small bodies in the sails and using every subterfuge they could think of to escape detection, many succeeded. A finer set of gallant daring boys it was impossible to imagine, ready for anything and fearing nothing (indeed the younger ones, having no experience did not know to what dangers they might be exposed). It turned out, however, a sad affair.

The French through their spies had had due notice of their intention and all particulars and were so well prepared by musketry and batteries, around their convoy, that the attack entirely failed, and the boats returned the next evening to Lissa, with almost every officer more or less wounded, and the loss of some men killed. It was a melancholy sight to see those young and ardent boys and youths thus so laid prostrate under pain, suffering in some cases loss of limbs, and I had reason to be thankful that authority and discretion, superior to my own, had prevented my being among them. Defeat and disaster soon reconcile one to the disappointment of hopes of glory which might have been acquired. We had several expeditions of this kind, for which, in fact, the fortifying and establishing of the station had been designed, and which it most effectually served. A secure and good harbour to resort to, on necessity, and where to await occasions that might occur, placed the Navy in command of the entire coast.

Sometimes, on more serious and important attacks a brig of war or two or even a frigate would take the command and lead, and then, generally, some soldiers, from our old veterans, were added, when, I heard more than one Naval captain say, they, by their disciplined and experienced courage and coolness, always proved most useful and valuable in landing to attack batteries. Indeed, nothing could be more satisfactory and harmonious than the union of the two services, or more complete than the success which had planned and thus brought them together. Aboard and on shore, there was always the same unison, mutual confidence and zeal for the service, to which all were devoted. Thus all went on quietly and pleasantly, only varied by the daily occurrences of passing, or *rumours* of passing convoys of the enemy's boats &c; always a subject of much interest to both arms. And several were the captures made, enlivening the tedium of garrison life on an island, and to the Navy in particular a more substantial source of supply to their purses. In those days they had a more ready and effectual way of reaching the just rewards of their daring and activity than at present. When a capture of country boats was made, a board of naval officers was formed to examine the prizes, 'adjudicate', and decide that they were not sea-worthy (in most cases, perhaps in all, plainly, strictly correct) not capable of undertaking the long passage to Malta which was the headquarters of the Admiralty court, in those seas. Then there was nothing to be done but realise, by sale of the boats and the appropriation of whatever money could be found in them (and sometimes this amounted to some thousands of dollars, the produce of their mercantile speculations and sales in their expeditions) and at once to *divide*, strictly according to the rules and rights of the service, by the purser over the capstan.

Nothing could, under the circumstances, be fairer than this. Every man got his share of what he was entitled to at once, and without the interminable delays of Naval Agents, and the serious diminutions of their manipulations and legal abstractions; so much better than *now* were such things managed by sensible, honest, straightforward and perhaps, comparatively unskilful men. Who can, in these days, reckon on what he knows he has hardly earned and entitled himself to, by his courage and success, in the way of prize money? Or even when to expect it, in any reasonable time (even in his life time) however long he may have been spared to his family? I myself waited *for years* for the prize money of a small capture in the Adriatic and at Waterloo; and when it reached me, in each case, so diminished and short of what we had reason to expect, that it was of little use. The fees and prize agents had the best of it.

Chapter 8

Attack on Lagosta[1] 1813

During 1812, the British became aware that the forces holding the remaining French islands had diminished to the point that there were virtually no Frenchmen left. The islands were held by small detachments (between 30 and 100) of local Croatian Militia units with a smattering of Italians. The French forces were being sucked into the main army as news of the disaster in Russia became known.

It became clear to Admiral Thomas Fremantle, commanding in the Adriatic, that mopping up these islands would not prove too onerous a task if he could enlist Army support and this would remove a number of bases for French privateers, which remained a continual menace. Fremantle therefore put aside his irritation with Colonel Robertson and his pedantic Army ways; to gain agreement for joint operations against the remaining islands.

Their first target was the Island of Lagosta, which lies some thirty-five miles from Lissa. John was to perform the role of Adjutant in this expedition. In a forward reconnaissance, the engineer officer, Captain Henryson, rated the fort on Lagosta to be strong enough to withstand an attack for one to two months. However, the 300 troops transported from Lissa, including two companies of the 35th, landed on Lagosta on 29 January 1813[2] and apparently took the island with little fuss. The French garrison had immediately retired into a large fortification built on a hill which overlooked the town. From here the garrison maintained a heavy fire. The official history then states that, in a swift advance,

---

[1] Now known as the Island of Lastovo.
[2] The history of the 35th wrongly states that this occurred on 21 January.

Captain Francis May of the 35th, with only forty men, rushed a fortified battery at the foot of the hill, which was quickly overrun, the cannon spiked and a large food store destroyed. Dismayed by such a rapid success and with Colonel Robertson offering easy terms to bring things to a swift conclusion, the garrison of around 140 men surrendered.

John's version, however indicates that a more embarrassing initial check was suffered, followed by a hurried and painful retreat and re-embarkation; with success only coming on the following day after a more aggressive assault. This version has the ring of truth about it and I believe it may be a more authentic version.

The majority of this force then moved on to capture the Island of Curzola,[3] which fell on 3 February after a minor engagement. Having left a small garrison on Lagosta, a force of 160 men, bolstered by a force of seventy sailors and fifty Marines from the ships, landed at Port Buffalo. At daybreak the following day, Major Slessor of the 35th led a detachment to successfully capture a fortified building near the town despite heavy musketry fire. The *Apollo* then bombarded the shore batteries, quickly silencing them. When Major Slessor then sent in a proposal for the women and children to evacuate the town before the ship began bombarding it, the small garrison, who had no real fortifications to retire into, capitulated.

John did not proceed with the expedition to Curzola, as it appears that he was very unexpectedly (even to himself) given the command of the Island of Lagosta. Such an offer, to a junior ensign was extremely unusual, but he does seem to have been persuaded to take it. This was not however without precedent. Major Slessor had been appointed Governor of Zante in 1810 by Brigadier General Oswald, who then commanded on the station, despite there being a number of more senior officers in the force who could have been given the prestigious office.

> But now I come to a period of my narrative which obliges me to enter more fully into my own particular share in the transactions, I must describe a more active service. All at once, and without the least hint or warning (for such were the necessary condition and observance of the kind of service in which we were then engaged)

---

[3] Now more normally known as Korcula.

we were informed by the Adjutant that Colonel R[obertson] was about undertaking, in conjunction with the Navy, an expedition, but wither and for what purpose, or its proposed strength, no information [was known]. The very secrecy and mystery added much, if it were possible, to our enthusiasm of active operations which we were well assured, under Colonel Robertson, would be of a serious and distinguished character. It was to consist of an army force [of] 300 men, two frigates and the proportional accompaniment of artillery &c, and to my astonishment and joy that *I* was to be the Adjutant of the expedition; an office which I knew would be coveted by more than one of my superior officers. Indeed, all were much my superiors in the force under Colonel R[obertson], I knew very little of the colonel personally, he was always kind and civil when we met, which was generally, excepting on duty, out shooting on the mountains. He had never asked me to visit his quarters, and although kind and friendly, kept me I thought, at a little more than due distance; but he was naturally and by habit a reserved man, what, one would say, a strict and cautious commanding officer. Therefore, this mark of distinction was the more surprising and flattering to my military pride and ambition.

All was got ready and arranged forthwith and the next evening (for in all such cases on that station, under such distinguished officers of both services, despatch was the word, prompt and ready at all times) we embarked in two frigates, the '*Apollo*'[4] and (I believe but cannot clearly remember) [the] '*Alcmene*'[5], but I am sure that the respective captains were Taylor and Graham; the former a distinguished and estimable captain, drowned a few years after, in attempting to land at Rimini in the Papal States[6]; and a brig, I think the '*Weasel*', Captain Black[7]. Altogether, with the soldiers and the crew of these ships, a very formidable force, and with experienced men and officers in command. We sailed just before dark (I find by an official letter) on the 28th or 29th January 1813, and proceeded all night, not knowing or even guessing whither; but, to us the

---

[4] HMS *Apollo* of thirty-eight guns, Captain Taylor R.N.
[5] The other ship involved in the attack on Lagosta was the *Esperanza* privateer.
[6] Captain Bridges Taylor drowned in a boating accident off Brindisi.
[7] HMS *Weazle* of eighteen guns commanded by Captain James Black.

57

young, especially in a state of anxious excitement, not easily realized now, even in recollection.

At day break next morning, we found ourselves in a remote harbour of a desolate looking coast, but the hills, with which it was closely surrounded, well clothed with fine fir and pine trees and well covered with the underwood of that country, arbutus, myrtle, &c &c, mountainous and desolate enough.

We knew nothing of where we were or what we had to do, excepting that gathering from the circumstances of the preparations and our leader's character, we had no doubt of having [our] work cut out in the way of fighting, and taking the enemy by surprise. We learned *afterwards* that our landing place was 'Porto Rosso'[8] at the N.W. of the island of Lagosta.

The next morning at daylight, we were ordered into our boats to disembark, a cold and bleak morning. But as all were in high expectation and spirits, this was done with alacrity and speed as far as practicable, under the circumstances, and at an early hour we were all paraded on the shore. Told off to our stations and the line of march arranged and communicated to the officers, the crews of the naval force (all equipped with various arms) I think, being placed in the advance of the line after the flank companies, as a matter of course: and on we marched, directed by guides ready and appointed for the service. The leader, Antonio Questich, if I remember his name right, a fine brave young man, enterprising and resolute and daring enough for any undertaking, and one whom I had afterwards, opportunities enough to test and prove as such. It appeared that he was under the sure impression that from his information and arrangements we should be able to come on the enemy unprepared and attack and take the fort of Lagosta by surprise. But it did not turn out so; they had also their spies, and when we reached [to within] a mile of the fort situated on the pinnacle of one of the many precipitous and high hills of volcanic formations which the Island is full, we were saluted by a heavy discharge of round-shot and shells, besides musketry from the batteries on the surrounding hills in our immediate neighbourhood, which caused the colonel to call a halt and place his men under the

---

[8] Porto Rosso is now known as Skrivena Luka in the south-east corner of the island.

best shelter he could conveniently find beyond the observation of the enemy.

Colonel R[obertson] was an old and experienced soldier, of the highest order, but was perhaps a little too cautious of *responsibility*, and most reluctant to risk the lives of his soldiers when it could possibly, with consistency and duty, be avoided; a feeling of which younger, but not more daring officers, were not always so observant. He therefore called a halt during which, for perhaps an hour, we were well peppered by shot and shell from the fort, but the distance was too great to disturb or injure us much. It was not, however, an agreeable situation, for men would by far prefer moving on to any attack rather than standing without motion or excitement under fire especially of shell. So Major Slessor of the 35th, second in command of the land force, a gallant and experienced officer, rode up to me and proposed that he should volunteer and I should accompany him, to assault and take the outer batteries (not the fortress) which were annoying us and thus open the road to attack the fortress itself. I was glad to fall into his proposal, for I did not like standing there under fire.

But his proposal was rejected by the chiefs, unwilling to run such risk of losing lives. The Naval men were terribly disappointed at the check we had received and at not being allowed to rush on. But wiser and more responsible heads decided otherwise, and after a halt and some time devoted to consideration and reflection, it was decided to our chagrin and bitter disappointment, that we should retrace our steps and re-embark!!

I shall never forget this retreat. The poor sailors, dispirited by disappointment and disgust, with feet with thin shoes sore and cut by the rocky road they had trod so far (six miles of the very roughest of rocks) besides the unaccustomed weight of musket and 60 rounds of ammunition with accoutrements, were completely knocked up at the outset and throwing into the bushes as they past all encumbrances, soon became a confused and discontented mass, without order or discipline. The soldiers, who from discipline and being used to hard marches bore it better and brought up the rear, but not the less disappointed and chagrined. I had command of the rear guard with some of the best and steadiest men, most of them on whom I could thoroughly depend in every way and to whom I could look and trust in my own raw inexperience for support and the resources which nothing but experience can give, so that I was in no difficulty to meet and repel the pursuit of the enemy, which they warmly, and in the exuberance of their triumph at our repulse, kept pressing on us, but without avail, until towards dusk, when we reached the port whence we had started and where the frigates still lay at anchor.

We were ordered immediately to prepare to re-embark, but without the slightest hurry or disorder. As soon as the sailors saw their ships they returned to discipline and order, deliberately got the boats ready, and seemed quite at home in providing for the safe conduct and comfort of the soldiers, who it must be confessed, were not a little tired and dispirited.

As commanding the rear guard, I of course, remained on the shore until all the boats but the last had put off, expecting and intending to follow up with the last. And I was just about getting into it with a few of my men, when Captain May[9], an old and gallant officer, a Swiss, and a thorough[ly] experienced soldier, placed his hand on my shoulder and said, 'H, you are not to go aboard, but remain here with your company, to maintain this landing place until relieved!'

I was tired out, like the rest, had looked forward to rest and enjoyment on board, with no slight anticipated pleasure when this announcement was made, and my first impulse was to turn and I was ready to reply 'Why May, we have just retreated and those woods are no doubt occupied by the men who have followed us up, who will of course, try to drive me into the sea'. But in an instant it occurred to me that the captain was the very man to have coolly replied 'Well, go on board and *I* will stay here. Do you take the remaining men on board and I will report what is done.'

But (and I have since thought it one of the luckiest self-restraints of my life), *I said not a word*; but as soon as the captain had departed, I called around me the best and most experienced of my men, told them that my orders were to keep that landing and that I was of course determined to do so. That as they knew, the woods around contained many of the enemy and therefore it behoved us to be

---

[9] Captain Francis May, 35th Foot, had initially served with the York Light Infantry Volunteers. He died in 1817.

strictly on the watch in every direction &c and gave them my instructions how to carry this out and [to] act on an emergency. That we had reason to think we should be attacked there was no doubt; but by making fires, and a good deal of bustle here and there, it would be supposed we were too well prepared and vigilant to be safely disturbed. They did *not* advance, and the daylight found us preparing for any orders we might receive. Having no idea what the intentions of our chief were, or what we were to do. So thus, my first serious service ended, so far in defeat and mortification stronger than I can describe.

At day-break next morning, the force of the day before, but refreshed and recruited in mind and body and the sailors' feet much recovered and better shod for the work, reassembled on the landing place and with a relish for the service sharpened by the previous check. More determined than ever, once more we set out in advance; nothing doubting that we should now succeed, whatever the obstacles, to our heart's content. On we trudged, over the old road of rocks and imperfect pathway, until we came about 10 in the morning, in sight of the fortress; when instead of halting or turning aside, we marched straight up the ascent to the rising table land on a level with or commanding the fort, at about the distance of ¾ of a mile or something less. Here we halted and were saluted with a brisk fire of cannon shot and shells, so well directed as to become rather inconvenient; and many of the *younger* soldiers, when the round shot now and then for the first time took them in a straight line and made the tops of the bayonets and muskets rattle, 'ducked' to the sound; which so irritated the colonel that he rode out in front and gave them a sharp lecture on the folly of ducking to the sound of a shot which must then have [already] passed them; and as he was speaking, one went close to his head, when he merely ran his finger along his forehead, saying 'tis only a round shot, my men, you must not mind them again' with a cool confidence which, from experience, was only a matter of course to him, and at once illustrated his lecture and we had little more of it from that time.

Our two field pieces and a small howitzer were then placed in position and opened on the fort, not a very formidable display, and the men drawn up in line and told off for the attack, all of which was under the immediate eye of the garrison of the fort, which truly, perched on such a pinnacle and having no apparent road to it but up a long and exceedingly steep corkscrew path, looked formidable enough, and *if properly defended*, must have caused us much trouble and loss and with doubtful result, and as the firing increased in fierceness and intensity, it was therefore looked on as a serious but not disheartening matter.

But it was not to be settled so easily; and after [the] due consideration of our colonel and naval captains, we were ordered to bivouac for the night where we stood. It was not intended that we should a 2nd time retreat, but should storm, and we hoped [to] take it the next morning. Before daylight, we were in position, awaiting anxiously orders to advance. But as I had not expected or prepared covering for such an event (I had only a thin coat) on the summit of an exposed high hill and a bora (or as it is otherwise called Tramontana[10], a furious and penetrating piercing wind, descending from the Dalmatian Alps and blowing sometimes 3 or 4 days) blowing on us. I shall never forget the misery of that night, lying down on the bare ground, or rather bed of rocks and so exposed. I fortunately had a soldier's canteen full of rum which I placed as my pillow, and had of sheer necessity, to keep life in me, to have frequent constant recourse to and I verily believe that rum saved my life that night. So I can never hear with patience of drinking cold water being the fit thing [to do] in such circumstances.

The fort being duly summoned without effect, all preparations made and due directions given, and we commenced preparations for a nearer attack. All at once, after all their blustering and never ceasing cannonade, a flag of truce was displayed and a party commanded by an officer descended to arrange terms of capitulation, which was soon done, we, in the mean time halting, in our position. The colonel and Captain Taylor meeting the French a little in advance, the result was that 3 officers under command of an old veteran lieutenant and 125 rank and file, with due compliment of non-commissioned officers and a rather strong party of artillerymen, laid down their arms as prisoners of war – to be sent by us on parole to the Island of Lessina[11] and serve no longer in the

---

[10] The tramontana, or tramontano, is a cold wind from the north, tinged with frigid air from the Alps and northern Apennines, and can blow at up to force eight in strength.

[11] Lessina is now known as Hvar.

French army during the war. We took immediate possession of the fort; but the troops did not move from our position. Immediately the colonel communicated to us assembled around him, explained what he had done and that he intended without delay to pursue his advantages by attacking and he hoped capturing the larger and more important Island of Curzola[12], about 8 or 10 miles off nearer the mainland. He sat himself down without further remark on a soldier's knapsack (it was a clear beautiful and bracing air, such as I never met with but in that climate) and called for the acting sergeant-major, told him to give him a sheet of paper, ink &c which he spread on a drum head and wrote a letter on it. And then, without previous hint, told me to my utter astonishment, and at first to my dismay at the charge intended to be laid on me, that he had decided on leaving *me* in sole charge of the Island of Lagosta, which he said, I expect to be attacked in a short time, and which you must defend, 'it is an important advanced post'.

This was on the 30th January 1813, when I was but 19 years of age; and no wonder I was *dismayed* at such a charge. I have a most lively recollection of my feelings at the time; it is impossible ever to forget that moment. My instant impulse was to beg the colonel, with tears in my eyes I endeavoured to conceal from shame, not to leave me such a responsibility. I was overwhelmed with the suddenness of the communication and saw how little I had done to prepare myself for it. I begged and entreated that he would appoint some older and experienced officer instead and so warmly did I plead, that I felt he might misapprehend my feelings and I said 'Colonel, do not misunderstand me, you tell me this island will probably be attacked and that I am to defend it; I do not feel myself equal to such an understanding, but do not suppose that I wish to avoid the defence. If you leave me with a senior officer *in command* I beg it as a favour to be left with him and will do my best to carry out his arrangements; but *pray* do not leave me *in command!*' The colonel, a taciturn man of few words at all times, was evidently irritated at my persevering importunity and at last said emphatically, 'Sir, you do not appear to appreciate the compliment I am paying you and the trust I have in you, *you* must remain in command and if need be, defend the island.

[12] Also known today as Korcula.

I cannot as you request, leave another officer with you; for you are the junior officer under my command, therefore he would and must command you, which is not my intention. So sergeant, give me the paper' and forthwith he wrote on the *knapsack* [on] *paper and on the drum head in the field* the following letter; the original of which I have now lying before me, with all [the] other documents alluded to in this narrative, always at command for the inspection of anybody.

> To Lt Hildebrand
> 35th Regt.
> Lagosta, 30th January 1813
>
> Sir,
> Having judged it necessary to occupy the Island of Lagosta and put a garrison in the fort, consisting of 1 lieutenant, 5 sergeants, 1 drummer and 44 rank and file, together with a bombardier and 3 gunners, you are appointed to the command of the garrison. You are to show the utmost vigilance and alertness in the defence of this island; from the nature of the country the militia of the island (N.B. above 300 men) will be of greatest use to you. You are therefore to endeavour to gain their affections and to have them organised in the best possible manner. You are to respect their laws and customs and particularly their religious ones. You will correspond with me by every opportunity that offers. You are to keep the garrison under the strictest discipline. Provisions for three months will be placed in the fort and a sufficient sum of money left [to] you. You are to endeavour to get intelligence of all the enemy's movements and have in recollection that they are only a few miles distant from you. In addition to your means of defence, two gunboats [later increased to 4[13]] will be left with you.
>
> I have the honour to be,
> Sir,
> Your most obedient Servant
> G.D. Robertson
> Lt Col

[13] A note by Hildebrand.

P.S. You are to make yourself particularly acquainted with the nature of the country viz. positions, water, &c.

He then turning around, with an encouraging and kindly expression of countenance, added 'You know you must keep a good look out and your glass does not seem a very powerful one', and then unbuckling the straps of that he had on, said 'I will give you mine, I have another on board' and taking it off, he *put it over my shoulders*. Every officer, then on service and I suppose now, carried a telescope, but very inferior generally to those now in use.

He then shook my hand and added 'Now I leave you in sole command'. But I had not even then given up my endeavour to get him to leave with me another officer and urged him on the score of the impossibility of meeting all the *duties* that would be required of me, and at the same time attend to the means of defence and get the militia in proper order and discipline. Here he gave way, in a certain degree and before we parted he said 'Well, there is something in that, I will when I return to Lissa, send an officer to assist you for one month (which promise he fulfilled as soon as possible); but remember he is not to take the command'.

The colonel with the troops, immediately marched to the port without entering the town and having inspected only the fort and its defences, proceeded to Curzola, a larger and more important and beautiful and fertile island nearer the main land, with a fortress, where the French had a garrison of 150 men, with due complement of officers, artillery &c. It had been stronger formerly, but like Lagosta and all the posts on that coast, had been lately reduced in consequence of the drafts required by their main French army, then on its retreat from Russia.

Chapter 9

Commandant of Lagosta 1813

John's new kingdom measured about nine miles long by three-and-a-half miles wide with steep cliffs rising from the deep waters surrounding it. It was thickly forested with Holm Oaks and Pinewoods and lightly populated. The climate was warm even in winter and generally sunny, but this led to issues with water supplies which were usually drawn from wells.

He took his role seriously, inspecting his island command from end to end, not forgetting to take his rifle and gun dog. But soon rumblings in the local militia, arguments over seniority in the local clergy, and ships being sunk for insurance scams or to avoid lengthy quarantine, filled his time and stretched his patience.

John claims (not unsurprisingly) that those officers deputised to assist him, although more senior in the Army, did so with very bad grace. Lieutenant Butler had hoped to gain the honour himself and made his position abundantly clear, thankfully for John, Butler's period on the island was of very short duration. But then John was nearly captured at sea, in a very embarrassing incident, all of his own making.

Later a Captain Barbier of De Roll's Regiment was sent to assist him, but John claims that Robertson had made it clear that he was to act as commandant, no matter the rank of any other officers that arrived there. The status of commandant, even if junior in rank to other officers on the same station, was normal; but clearly, his lowly rank made this very unusual and it is clear that Barbier did not see his position in the same light.

This was compounded by the Navy officers on station, who certainly seem to have dealt with Barbier rather than with John Hildebrand; this, though, was perhaps largely down to the fact that John left this post on an unauthorised expedition soon after, which undoubtedly caused much of this confusion.

With Napoleon being driven rapidly out of Germany, Francis, Emperor of Austria, his father in law, declared war on France on 12 August 1813. This caused the very unhappy inhabitants of Croatia to break out in revolt, forming bodies of partisans who looked to free their country from French rule but were not particularly keen to simply replace this with the old Austrian regime. However, when an army of 70,000 Austrians was sent into northern Italy under the command of General Joseph Hiller with the specific role of reclaiming Italy and Illyria for the Emperor, it was clear that this would lead to tensions.

But I must return to my own island and situation, which at my age and with my little experience was on its first aspect most perplexing and full of anxieties and apprehensions. But I had not long to deliberate what I should do and prepared for it. *Two days* after I was called on to hear and decide on a very important and most strange and unexpected difficulty. The circumstances were these.

I have said that the militia of the island (which had been in a way organized and disciplined as *National Guards*, by the French, amounting to some 300 or 350 men) were my principal support to look to in case of [the] expected early attack and consequently that according to Colonel R[obertson]'s instructions in my appointment it was my duty to watch carefully and 'endeavour to gain their affections and have them organised in the best possible manner'. But in a day or two, I discovered that there was some cause of disturbance among them and on enquiry found that it was a religious feud that had arisen in the island as to the claims of two ecclesiastical dignitaries, rivals, as to which was to be the head man now that, by the capture of the island they had been completely severed from intercourse with and the authority of their bishop, who resided at and was Bishop of Ragusa. It was then, in the severity of the laws of Napoleon, death to any one there keeping up any intercourse with any other under the dominion of the English Government; thence the dispute between the Vicar General and this Paroco General of Lagosta (in which there were 17 beneficed and other priests, requiring superintendence) *who* was to be chief. It

67

disturbed the minds of the people and strong parties were formed to support either side.

As proof of these clerical difficulties, a letter was retained in his files and is inserted here translated from the original Italian:

Undated [February 1813?]

To the most illustrious military commandante, the spirit of God has spoken by your mouth. You have been sent to Lagosta to re-establish the Temple at Jerusalem & to subdue the priests who ought to be subordinate to its head & superior. I am now the head of this clergy & stand in the place of the most illustrious right reverend archbishop. All the priests of whatever title owe canonical obedience to me, not to the Bishop of Malta nor to any other ordinary. This is your decision & you have guaranteed its being carried out. You have been constituted a mediator, you therefore will have the kindness to signify to the clergy of Lagosta these [are] my resolutions as their ecclesiastical & canonical superior.

In the first place they must accept my mandate of the date 30 July ultimo recognising me as archiepiscopal delegate in addition to the letter which I sent to them & which they must return to me sealed as it was, as it contains things which are cancelled by the following resolutions.

1. That the Reverend [Blank] shall be restored & incorporated into the congregation, annulling the minute of 12 August 1811 & all others put forth on this subject, because he had drawn his stipend in a case of necessity & proceeding which militates against no law or canon of our Holy Mother the church, for he has not abstracted any money from the chest as the books which I have examined testify.

2. That his share of the accustomed dues for masses shall be assigned to him as in other communities.

3. That the [Blank] of one part & another of the congregation shall deposit 100 piastres each in our diocesan exchequer with the consent of our illustrious & right reverend archbishop.

If the clergy of Lagosta do not subscribe to these my resolutions, I shall turn to you Signor commandante in order that you may second me & lend me 'hand & arm' that the said clergy may be forced to deliver to me the chest, keys, & books of the parish church, together with an exact inventory, that a schismatical conventicle which will not recognise as its head our archbishop, may be suppressed.

You signor commandante have seen that my claims in these circumstances are lawful, you with your kindness guarantees their being recognised, you will prevail against those who according to the principles of their religion have fallen under the church's censure for having wished to have recourse to another bishop or a secular tribunal. I subscribe myself in the most respectful manner, your most humble & devoted servant Antonio Quevich archbiepiscopal delegate. pro beasis fovauea [For your biased favour]

Now this was a most undesirable state of things; before I had time to turn round and make my arrangements and know who were my friends and with the perhaps, quick and arbitrary feelings of the day, on active service, I at once determined that I would have it settled without delay and accordingly summoned the rival priests to the 'Council', consisting of the 'President' and chief civil authorities, my proper advisers according to my instructions and support in whatever difficulties of a civil nature might arise. I laid the case before them and requested that they would relieve my difficulty and that they should take the necessary measures to have it settled and thus allay the *then* to me dangerous differences of the people.

My endeavours were vain; and after considerable delay, I dismissed the council and told the litigants to appear again, in the Council Room, the next day at the same hour, by which time I hoped their feelings would have become more conciliatory and that they would see that it *must* be settled without further delay. The next day they came again, but without any change of feeling or mind, each seemed quite convinced that he was the right man and that it was *his duty* to maintain his position &c &c, so that at last, as I felt it *my duty* to have the matter settled, I said I myself would hear what they had to say and decide at once as fairly as I could, who ought to be and should be installed in the chief office. It was indeed a trying and difficult position for one like me to be placed in; but I had no alternative' the affair *must* be *settled* and they were determined and obstinate in not agreeing. So, with all the patience and consideration I could command (and it is surprising how considerate and thoughtful I had become in the *very* few days of my responsibility)

I at last decided that 'Antonio Crucerrick, Pro Vicario Fovanco e delegato Archivescope' was the right man to whom the clergy of Lagosta owed and must pay obedience. The Parocho General (I do not, even now, know the distinction) i.e. the unsuccessful competitor, would not submit and was very violent I thought and recalcitrant, so I was obliged in this my first attempt at establishing my necessary authority, to act with decision and tell him at once that, ecclesiastic as he was, he must submit and that I would give him 24 hours to consider of it. And at the expiration of that time, I sent for him, when he was determined and defiant as ever, so without hesitation (what would the 'Times' or Mr Bright[1] say, or [what] would become of me these days?) I ordered a corporal with a file of men to conduct him and deposit him in prison until he came to his senses. He appealed to the *Bishop of Malta*, which was nonsense under the circumstances at such a distance, but before entering the prison door, he thought better of it, promised compliance and was released.

Thus ended my first difficulty, so little to have been expected or prepared for; but abstractly, trifling as it was, with regard to myself, it was a matter of no small importance as to how I might conduct it. But an *official* letter I next day received from the new Vicar General, i.e. the successful man, drawn up with as much pomp and importance as if it had come from the Pope himself, is really a curiosity in its kind and therefore I give the translation of it in extensor. It must be borne in mind that it was written to a *very* young officer and young man and a *Protestant*: certainly in this view, nothing could be more *liberal* (The original is now before me; *and those also of every document* quoted by me in this memoir and will be given in the Appendix).[2]

'Illmoce Signor Commandante Militare!
The Spirit of God has spoken by the mouth of V.S. V.S. has been sent to Lagosta to re-establish the Temple of Jerusalem and to subject to its head and superior, the clergy who ought to depend. I am,

---

[1] Mr John Bright, a radical Liberal M.P. who formed the Anti Corn Law League. He was a famous orator of his day.

[2] Note: Though here and elsewhere, Lieutenant Hildebrand mentions appendices to his recollections from 1809 to 1814, there are none in the MS, other than those relating to 1815.

therefore, the superior of the clergy and am in the place of my Illmo and Revmo Monsignor the Archbishop. All the clergy under whatever title, owe me canonical obedience, *not* to the *Bishop of Malta* or any other Ordinary. Such are your instructions and which you recognize with politeness'. (This style is always expressed in Italian in the 3rd person as a matter of extreme deference and respect and is not easily expressed in translation). 'V.S. has constituted himself a mediator: V.S. will therefore have the singular condescension to signify to the clergy of Lagosta my superior and canonical deliberations. They must in the 1st place accept my precept (precetto - official order) sent to them under the date 30th of last July, acknowledging me for delegate of the Archbishop, according to the letters I transmitted, which they should return to me signed, as they were, but containing things which are comfortable to the following resolutions'.

And here follow many particulars and admonitions which are not worth troubling my readers with, calling on me, as the commandant to aid and assist him with 'a strong hand' and all my power 'according to my instructions' that the said clergy should be *forced* to do so and so, and ending

'I am in the most respectful manner, most illustrious Signor V.S., your devoted servant Antonio Crucerrick, Pro-Vico and Delegate of the Archbishop Fovanco'.

Thus I was set at liberty to look after my more immediate duty, viz, preparations for defence as I was instructed, the possible and early attack from the enemy and according to my instructions, 'to make myself particularly acquainted with the nature of the country, viz positions, water, &c'.

I set out the next morning to reconnoitre. As this was quite consistent with and indeed connected with my double-barrelled fowling piece, it was a most agreeable recreation after such anxiety and I travelled far (nothing in the way of exercise or walking could tire me) in this kind of excursion, which I very frequently repeated, both as a matter of duty first and pleasure afterwards. The little island, about 6 miles in length by 3 miles in breadth, with four fine ports is of entirely volcanic formation, precipitous and high hills to the sea's edge and frequent narrow vallies [sic] which are very fertile and full of vines; nothing can exceed their tranquil beauty and the enjoyment they excite. Full of all kinds of game peculiar to that latitude, in their seasons quail, doves, &c in great variety and with abundance of never failing supplies of woodcocks of the first quality. But in summer, at first I was annoyed much by meeting so many snakes among the vines, especially which my dogs always pointed in a peculiar and terrified manner, which I immediately recognised. They stood as if terrified and fixed on an object which they were afraid of, but could not turn their back on and retreat from [them], with their hair on the back standing up.

On some occasions, when the dogs showed more than ordinary dread, I fired into the bush at hazard and almost invariably shot a snake, sometimes a long and rather substantial one, but seldom very venomous I believe[3]. On one of these excursions soon after I took command, I was much oppressed by the hot sun in the valley and ascended the precipitate and high rocky hill opposite me. The day was bright and clear and with such a cool exhilarating breeze as I never experienced but at Lagosta and the neighbourhood in the hot season and on arriving at the summit, a laborious and no small ascent, was delighted with the beautiful and tranquil sea in the obscure port beneath my feet and as if basking in the sunny heat, under the shade and shelter from every breeze, a most beautiful polacca[4] rigged, 3 masted vessel of about 300 to 350 tons, with every sail set and seeming the very image of security and enjoyment.

It was so beautiful that I could not resist stopping some time to dwell on it, but at length, turned and descended the hill, resuming my shooting and after making a slight divergence, following my game, re-ascended the same hill on the opposite side. On reaching the top of which, I naturally looked at once, for the vessel so much admired, but could not see it, or a vestige of it! I was so confounded and taken by surprise that I did not know what to think. There had been no wind and it was impossible it could have *sailed* away, so I knew not what to think, but earnestly and vigorously rubbed my

[3] There are no indigenous snakes that are venomous on the island.

[4] A polacca was a type of sailing vessel, similar to the xebec, frequently seen in the Mediterranean. It had two or three single-pole masts, the three-masted vessels often with a lateen hoisted on the foremast.

eyes in no small alarm, thinking I had suddenly lost my sight. But seeing *all other things* as they were, I could not long remain of that opinion and therefore with increased diligence in peering into and scrutinizing, the locks and little bays underneath me and which were at a considerable and precipitous depth, I at last discovered two boats creeping along the shore and as close as possible to where it was and something floating on the surface of the sea at a little distance, which appeared to me like masts or spars and sails; in which I found afterwards, my sight did not deceive me.

The circumstance was startling; and after a little reflection, I decided on returning immediately and summoning the Captain of the Port, to inform him of it and set him on his guard; for it was evident that something not quite right was designed and that I ought to be on my guard at the same time, I repaired thither, and sure enough found the two boats I had seen, approaching it and full of men, prepared to enter; the Captain of the Port keeping them at a distance with boarding and custom house spikes. It was evident that there was some foul play, as to the sudden disappearance of the ship. There was no doubt that some deception was intended. On enquiry I found that they wished me to believe that they had been shipwrecked. But they were deceived; I was on my guard and prevented their landing; but perceiving that they had no or very little possessions to all appearance, I sent them from my stores some pork and biscuit, delivered at long arm's length and ordered them to depart for Ragusa, whither they said they had been bound and expressed a wish to go.

I may at once say, that about 3 months after this, on our taking Ragusa, I there found the Capitano and men of these boats, who confessed their intended deceit; but pleaded necessity. The account they then gave was this, that they had really scuttled that fine ship, in consequence of their having *got the plague onboard at Malta*,[5] and knowing they would not be received into any port (the quarantine laws at that time [being] most stringent and severe) they took her therefore to a remote shore of the remote Island of Lagosta and scuttled her; hoping to recover 'a clean bill of health' from that island. I *then* believed this tale, but experience has since made me

---

[5] Malta did declare it had the plague at this time.

doubt it and attribute it to some roguery in Marine Insurance. No doubt that fine vessel was scuttled.

Day after day I went out with my gun and became quite familiar with every feature and part of the island, having with me in my walks, when they were not long, a very intelligent, well educated and talented priest of about 40 years of age, who was the maestro or schoolmaster of the island and Secretary to the Council, indeed the brains-carrier of the place and guide, in every step that was of importance. A man so superior to all the others, that it surprised me to find him in so remote a place, without the possibility of his meeting any one of his calibre as a companion.

I found afterwards that he was indeed considered a man of very superior qualifications, but had got into some scrape in his early youth, which brought him under the displeasure and censure of the Archbishop, who, with the undoubted discipline of the Romish Church, *banished* him from Ragusa for a certain time, not a very short one, to Lagosta. And I think, not without a view to the great advantage of sending such a man among so many ignorant priests; so utterly ignorant, beyond the mechanical use of their Missal and Breviary, that I was seriously requested by the Vicar General not to make any remarks on religious subjects to them, in my frequent evening conversazione (to which they were all glad to resort and enjoy conversations, and cigars &c) for he said he found that I had *unsettled* some of their minds on religious subjects!! Now, as I was then almost *totally ignorant* of even my own religious principles and knew only what I had picked up as a boy of 15 when I left home and on active Military Service since. And merely sported these remarks, as it were, which had been used too freely and thoughtlessly to these R[oman] C[atholic] divines in our conversations, and that these had *any* serious effect whatever, how great must have been their ignorance! How black their darkness! But, although I could not wonder at his anxiety, *I* of course *desisted* for the future and we got on as well as before. *They* had been lectured, and I hope better instructed privately, and were equally on their guard. I would avoid noticing such occurrences in my narrative if they had not impressed themselves deeply on my memory, as I started with the intention and determination to notice whatever I met with worth noticing, straight forwardly and without reserve, whether relative to *myself* or others and when this could be done without giving needless offence or, in any way, causing injury or pain. This is I find, a difficult line to take, for in the pursuit of my narrative, I shall be compelled to relate circumstances in simplicity and truth, which will oblige me to speak of *myself* on matters which might, if people choose and are sceptical, possibly cast some unfavourable impression on their minds, as to my freedom from self-partiality and egotism. But, when you bear in mind that this is written in the 73rd [year] of my age and in bad health, without a hope or prospect of a much longer continuance in a life that must and will probably, end in a short time, I can fearlessly appeal to your candour and humanity to *believe* that I have neither exaggerated or handed down to my children (especially for whom this is written) a single aspersion of which I feel, not only confident but can have any, the least doubt of being correct. The above lines were not premeditated but on the subject, I have given myself licence and relief by explaining at once and for all, my views, intentions, feelings and present situation and I shall say no more on the subject. I will henceforth narrate *without restraint* whatever befell me that I think worthy; without consideration of the bearing, for or against me personally, or the opinions that may in consequence be formed i.e. without looking to the right hand or left, the plain matter of fact and honest course.

But it is time I should give a brief sketch of my island, its town and fort &c. all humble (excepting the fort) and diminutive enough; but a beautifully secluded spot; hills and valleys in all directions, the granite formation of, I believe all the mountains of Dalmatia the neighbouring continent. The hills steep, rough and rocky, thick set with underwood, arbutus, myrtle and all kinds of odoriferous shrubs and herbs; (I know nothing of botany, geology or all the other ologies necessary to describe it as almost *any one* now, could do scientifically, but write from memory alone and an indelible impression of my delighted feelings at the time and therefore must pass it by as I can). The town a compact and substantially built little place, with some good sized stone houses and no very small and miserable hotels so prevalent in other places, altogether built on the slopes of the steep ascending hills surrounding it in the form of an *amphitheatre*, and having a very pretty, rural and prepossessing effect. The small valley at the foot, interspersed with gardens, vines, pomegranates and all the other fruit trees indigenous to that soil and climate. In short, a most desirable and but for its dull monotonous solitude, to one not averse to seclusion, delightful place to dwell in. But my most interesting object was the 'Fort'; perched on the pinnacle of the abrupt and highly elevated hill rising suddenly from this valley and as abruptly, when one attained its summit, looking down on the other side on the sea and port below.

A strong and formidable position, which with the four or five large guns, all but one of brass, two brass howitzers and two large mortars, with the garrison of 3 officers and 150 men and artillery men, ought to have made a stouter defence and given us a great deal of trouble and loss; but they were (excepting the gunners) *Italians* whose *hearts generally were not with Napoleon*, and, besides, the *rumours* of disaster from Russia, which had reached them long before us, made them wavering and faint hearted. And the knowledge that the people of the island had invited and took part with us, contributed further to the same effect; but still those officers should as a point of honour and duty have made a better and more effectual defence, it was a dastardly surrender, without the semblance of an earnest resistance. No doubt the people to the very lowest and youngest were our friends and utterly tired of, hating the French rule, which had destroyed their trade and forced them by proscriptions into their armies. Yet the French, although for good reason, they dealt as lightly as possible with the islanders along the coast, favoured *them*. And indeed it would be hard to find a finer, more independent, (naturally) brave people, handsome, open countenanced and open hearted. The female is most picturesque and becoming. And moreover it is to be recommended for its economy; the gala dress of all classes being handed down from generation to generation, as long as they retain a decent appearance and varying very little, excepting in the quality of the cloth or stuff. Its simplicity and neatness are indeed most attractive.

So much for the lively and still pleasing recollections of the early impressions of a now, very old man. Which afforded him so much pleasure when young! I passed some months of my happiest (and as it afforded me unusual *leisure* profitable for study and improvement which my contracted hasty and defective education so much needed) most valuable.

The barrack in the fort, which was sufficiently roomy and convenient for soldiers (but not on a grand scale) for the garrison and with very fair additional rooms and conveniences for the commanding and other officers, in which they almost entirely lived, excepting the commandant who had also a house or convenient lodging in the town. In a fort of such strength, close to the sea, a constant and vigilant look out and guard were essential to safety, therefore after due inspection and giving only necessary time to clean out my quarters and those of the men (a very necessary and often troublesome laborious operation after foreign troops, beyond what would be easily believed) I resolved on making myself secure there that very night and after going down to the town to see that my house there (that which my predecessor had occupied) was made comfortable and having dinner, I remounted the fort hill' a steep corkscrew path, not very smooth, which speaking from recollection, I think could not have been much less than ½ a mile and there took up my sleeping abode for the night.

This practice I continued invariably as long as I had the actual and personal command viz from 30th January to November 1813, when I left for Ragusa. And, indeed, the splendid view that met me every morning on turning out on the platform of that fort, was an ample compensation for the toil of mounting it the night before; besides when in it, I felt safe and slept soundly under the consciousness that I was *at my post* happen what might.

The only feeling a man can have who would rest fearlessly, with true independence and self-reliance, when placed in a position of risk and responsibility; having no fears for the present or for his honourable acquittal of all blame, whatever might occur in future.

3 or 4 days after the surrender of the island, Colonel Robertson's promised assistant officer arrived, a rather ambitious full lieutenant of grenadiers, Lieutenant B[utler][6], who, I found afterwards was one of 3 or 4 disappointed applicants for the command of the island on the day of its capture. He was by a few months, 2 or 3, my senior in the army and more in age, but still a young man and was I suppose unaware that he was sent there *only* at my earnest request, to *help* me in my duties for *one month*. He therefore began with a high hand, assuming the superiority in every way and I soon found that although my fears of the responsibility of the charge, so suddenly

---

[6] Lieutenant Richard Edward Butler was actually about eighteen months his senior as a lieutenant.

and unexpectedly thrust on me, had for the time, unnerved and led me to solicit so earnestly a *help*, that I had made a mistake and would have fared better if it had been rejected. He was not the kind of man or officer I would have selected and had been sent to me merely because he was *so little* my senior and the only one who could, according to the etiquette of the service, have been appointed to serve me as a junior, even for one month. And it so happened that that very day two country boats with French colours entered the harbour and anchored; seeing the French flag displayed by my new captain of the fort, as a *decoy* and having no knowledge that it was now our possession and they our lawful prizes.

They were not very rich in cargo, but had some thousand dollars on board, the fruit of their trading voyage, which we immediately took into our own custody and the next day sent off with the vessel to Malta to be examined under the court and declared there our lawful prizes and the proceeds transmitted to the Prize Agents in England, where it lay for some years and became not a little diminished, after the subject of dispute between myself and Lieutenant B[utler] on my finding that he had, assuming his army superiority, represented himself as the commandant at the capture and me as only serving as a volunteer under him[7].

This led me to write to the then promoted Lieutenant General Robertson, who at once, set me right because he there, incidentally gives the *reason* of his having selected me to the command of the island I had not the vanity to [expect], but which at the risk of being tiresome, I must give, in justice to myself. But 'tis so easy to relieve oneself of such a bore as these long uninteresting papers *by skipping a few pages* that at the risk of being tedious, I follow the natural course of my recollections in matters which were really both interesting and important to *me* at the time. We had no such lucky repetition of such prizes; and I turned myself earnestly, to the drilling and preparing the militia for whatever service might be required of them, which happily, by the sudden turn of events, on

---

[7] It is unknown how much John received in Prize Money, but Major John Slessor received 700 dollars for the capture of Lagosta and Korzula. But given that majors received eighty shares of the Prize Money pot and an ensign received only sixteen shares, his payment would amount to 160 dollars – but of course his would be diminished further because he did not participate in the taking of Korzula.

the utter rout and discomfiture of the French Army in Russia, never became a practical necessity, but which at this time we were both ignorant of and had not the slightest reason to expect.

Lieutenant B[utler] departed according to orders, at the expiration of the month and I remained quite alone, having only my sergeant and soldiers to talk to in my own language occasionally, on duty matters. The language of the natives was Slavonic as was that of all the neighbouring islands and continent; but a kind of lingua franca mixed half or less Italian was through their mercantile intercourse in their ships and boats, familiar to most, at least the sharpest and most intelligent, as was the case in all the neighbouring islands and the sea coast of the neighbouring main land Dalmatia. The few educated persons of the higher class of the priests were some of them good and most of them fair *Italian* scholars which rendered my intercourse with them both easy and pleasant. For otherwise how could I have carried on the *Civil* duties? (e.g. the examination of the priests and settling their dispute about the Vicar and Paroco General) and it may be proper here to state *how* it was that I became qualified, having left home at 15 and spent the last four years on active service. And this enables me to explain for the benefit of whoever, especially *young* officers, would wish to qualify himself under whatever disadvantages and that in a most pleasant and advantageous way; that it is within the power of any who desires and tries for it.

The fact is this. The very day immediately after my reaching Malta, where I was, the first time, (only 2 or 3 weeks, I believe), I engaged an Italian tutor, being determined to qualify myself by the acquisition of that language (I already knew a little French) to enjoy and take advantage of whatever chances I might happen on while in that country; and also that literature was my taste and ignorance and exposure of the common topics and affairs of the days and times in which I mixed, my dread and abhorrence. Therefore, I lost no time or opportunity and spared no labours of mind (and it was really labour, for neither my memory, owing I believe to early neglect nor capacity was of the first order) and spent late hours every night, however I passed the previous day or evening, when I could, at my books. I confess I had a natural aptitude to learn languages, but a very bad memory, which was much against its success and caused me much perplexing and vexation labour. After I left Malta I pursued the same plan immediately on arriving at Fort Salvatore in Sicily. I engaged a certain priest called Don Francisco in Syrestia (the Italian tutor general of the officers of the army who had the propensity for language learning) a very clever fellow and good tutor, but further I could not vouch for, or reverence him; [for] he had no great repute amongst his brother priests or countrymen. But I cannot but feel thankful for the foundation he laid in my Italian, which afterwards so much stood me in [such good] stead and benefited as well as amused and delighted me. This and the knowledge I had acquired, through the same laborious process, of the Slavonic language, when my lot took me into that region, made me equal to any duties of that kind that could present themselves to me at Lagosta; and I doubt not it was known to Colonel Robertson, *although I know not how*, when he appointed me to such a civil as well as military command; or he could not have done it. I would be wanting in my observations of Lagosta and its belongings and also in my hints for whoever in the same line should succeed at any future time in the service, not to mention every circumstance that might lead either to encouragement or as to preparation for like events, if they should arise. So I notice all that occurred that interested me and which in like circumstances would no doubt interest them, although perhaps appearing too trivial for remark as leading to no public useful deductions or instruction.

In 1813 the victorious Battle of Vitoria was fought in Spain[8] and the consequent triumphant entry of the English Army under Wellington into Madrid[9]. I of course, in my solitary and remote command, rejoiced and felt proud of my countrymen and speculated as others, on the results, but thought no more about it nor took any step beyond reading the despatch to my men, and giving three cheers on parade to celebrate it. But not so my ecclesiastical friends.

I was waited on by the whole body, the day after the news, to sanction the singing of the Te Deum[10] and all its accompanying

---

[8] This battle fought on 21 June 1813 sounded the death knell for the French occupation of Spain.
[9] He is in error here; Madrid had already been abandoned before the Battle of Vitoria.
[10] A Mass held to celebrate a great victory.

grandeur in the mother church and that I should as a matter of course be present in grand procession and display.

Now, although I had been present at several grand religious processions, High Mass &c in Malta, Sicily and Zante (in which sometimes no less than 1,500 soldiers of the British Army, with officers of all ranks and a general at our head, followed what was *said to be the body* of Saint Speridione[11]; all the officers with long wax candles in their hands) I was not prepared to undertake, *as chief* such an important and imposing ceremony on my small scale and having no zeal in the cause; and therefore I declined with as much respectful firmness as I could muster. But the authorities were determined and at last overcame all my objections with the observation that it had *always* been done by the *French* commandants on their announcements (often very lying ones) of victory and if I did not follow in the same line, it would have a bad effect on the loyalty of the islanders, which as we had been so short a time in possession and there were, of course many in whom much confidence could not be implicitly placed, was a serious consideration. In the face of my instructions to pay diligent attention to the laws and customs of the island, 'and especially the religious ones', and the approaching attack of the enemy which I was warned to expect.

So, I consented, leaving the arrangement of time, place &c to them. The next day was appointed and at the hour of service the priests with their Vicar General at their head came to my house, duly robed &c in solemn procession and conducted me (almost *bewildered* by the novelty and want of sympathy in the thing) to church, where I was received and fumigated and chanted in procession, through the aisle to the large state chair appropriated to the Archbishop on all grand occasions. Here I sat in full uniform for a considerable time while the service was being performed (I must say with solemnity and the impressive *dignity* peculiar to the R[oman] C[atholic]. services; besides the commanding and solemn effect of the deep toned fine Bocca Tomana musical chanting) and before releasing me from my chair to depart, they all in procession, passed before me

---

[11] Saint Spyridon died of natural causes in Cyprus but his body was twice moved to avoid being taken by the Turks when they invaded. His body eventually arrived at Corfu where it is held to this day in a church named after him.

with incense, with which I was again liberally fumigated by each as he passed, uttering at the same time a prayer which I could not understand, but could perceive it was always the same, a fixed form. This I had, in order to satisfy and keep up the loyalty of the islanders, to undergo two or three times afterwards on similar occasions and demands. Not to my taste; but really I believe it had a good effect and strengthened my position in the eyes and hearts of my people on whom my defence of necessity must so much depend.

There are a good many interesting peculiarities of this primitive people, whose habits and customs I have good reason to believe, have changed little or nothing for many hundred [of] years, which could not but interest me but which I dare not introduce, lengthening out of reasonable bounds, such an intended simple narrative as this; therefore, I abstain.

I am now come to a period on which depend very considerable results to myself and bearing much on the nature of our contest in the Adriatic in the year 1813. My intercourse with Lissa had been kept up without much or lengthened interruption from the time of my appointment, on the 30th January, and amid all the rumours which were from different sources coming thick upon me, those of the French disasters naturally were the most interesting and exciting; keeping us all alive and looking out.

Admiral Fremantle[12] in his flagship paid two visits to Lissa with a strong naval force in the early part of this year and of course, very active and important undertakings were expected. When he was gone from Lissa to the north of the Adriatic and all apprehension of *attacks* from the French had ceased, the thing was to attack and annoy them in every way we could; and I was no longer in fear of any attack of my island being made in my absence.

At this time, I heard that Colonel Robertson having gone from Lissa with the admiral, Major Slessor left in command at Lissa, had organised an expedition to seize Lessina, a large neighbouring island with a strong garrison[13]. I straightaway started in a scampavia gunboat, to beg to be allowed to go with him, but he as good and judicious as he was a gallant officer, at once refused and ordered me back without delay to Lagosta. I departed in a gunboat, slow and

---

[12] Rear Admiral Thomas Fremantle commanded in the Adriatic.

sluggish sailing, but being becalmed and wearied of the pace and seeing several lighter country trading boats which had joined us for convoy, I left my gunboat and got into one of them, which appeared to get on faster in the calm and ruffling weather of the season and latitude, unconsciously allowed ourselves to be drifted in close to the port of Lessina. In a few minutes we perceived two fully armed boats, with stout rowers dart from it, with all the energy and alacrity of making a certain capture. I was dismayed at the scrape I had got into and could not see a possibility of escape, which as I left my armed boat and was away from my island, would had I been taken, probably have ruined me professionally. But I always in those early days, from rash inexperience had an instinctive impulse to make the best of it and take the bull by the horns, trusting to chance and good luck. I instantly mustered my crew, consisting of 3 men and a boy, besides myself and, as to arms in the bow of the boat was a honeycombed 12lb old iron carronade, probably acquired because it was a useless cast off and stuck there to make a show of arms in their coasting trips; two old rusty muskets, one without a lock and an old cavalry pistol besides my own. Enough to make me despair and it did. I felt sure that a few minutes would transfer me to the enemy's boat a prisoner.

On enquiry, I found there was no shot to fit the old carronade, and only 2 or 3lbs of powder in a paper which the padrone had. But I was in despair and determined to try anything to escape capture. So putting a bold face on it, when I saw the approaching boat

[13] The regimental history incorrectly states that the expedition was sent from the garrison of Santa Maura, but John is correct in his claims that they came from the garrison of Lissa. The detachment sailed with Captain Hoste on HMS *Bacchante* and HMS *Mermaid* to capture the Island of Lessina on 8 November 1813. The following morning at 02.00 hours, the troops were landed. The 35th attacked the town, whilst Hoste and his marines attacked Fort Napoleon on the top of a nearby hill where the garrison slept each night. The attack on the town at dawn had succeeded beyond all hope. All but one of the French officers, who continued to sleep in the town every night, were captured still in their beds. But the Marines had found the climb to the fort harder than expected and the French garrison was fully aware of their approach. The attempt on the fort failed and the invasion was abandoned. Two days later, however, the French garrison threatened to murder their sole remaining officer, an engineer, and offered to capitulate unilaterally, to Major Slessor, who sent some troops from Lissa to take command of the island. Reference *The Backbone* by Alethea Hayter, p.255.

hesitate an instant, it was within less than ¼ of a mile and they were busy in plying their spy-glasses to scan our power and the possibility of perhaps, being too strong for them, I shouted out loudly to the captain of the boat, to pull its head round as quickly as possible, to face our foe and then, cramming into the cannon a large *handful* of powder in a paper and selecting as round and fitting a pebble stone, about the size of the bore, from the ballast with which it was provided, as I could find, I touched the primed gaping wide touch hole with a piece of burning rope, and let fly. I shall never forget the noise and din the discharge made. The stone flew into a thousand pieces and made a strange commotion on the calm sea which no doubt astonished them as it did myself. I forgot to mention that I had my light infantry uniform and cap on, with a pair of imposing epaulettes and as the boat was half-decked and low in depth, I before firing the shot, had purposely exposed my red coat and epaulettes, in *different parts* of the boat, creeping round and preventing the lower parts from being seen, so that they were evidently deceived and thought us full of soldiers and paused again, but not long. And perceiving this, I again repeated my stratagem, fired another wild shot at the risk of bursting the gun, which at once decided them to let us alone and return, as they did to port; and thus I escaped and got back to Lagosta that night. The next day the captain of a gun boat reported to me that the night before, Major Slessor had carried out his plan and in the dead of night, having previously arranged measures and secured by means of spies and the treachery of some soldiers the entrance into the Citadel of Lessina, by the sally port, and overpowering the guard, went quietly from one quarter to another and took twenty two or twenty three officers out of their beds, transmitted them at once to his gun boat and carried them all back to Lissa with himself (among the rest, the 3 officers we had captured at Lagosta only a few weeks before and who had been liberated by the terms of the surrender) and some to Lessina.

This is among the most daring and well planned surprises that I ever heard of. Major, afterwards Lieutenant General Slessor, was one of those which such times brought out, or rather gave scope to put in practice his own natural talents and previous experience of service. Cool and *quiet* habitually, but capable of remarkable dash and decision whenever called on to exert those valuable qualities.

Left: A portrait of Lieutenant John Hildebrand.

Below: Greek Light Infantry, 1813, by Denis Dighton.

Above: Lissa today. At the Battle of Lissa in March 1811, the French commander was killed and the French routed.

Below: Forte del Santissimo, Salvatore, Messsina, is still a military property.

Above: A painting depicting the Battle of Lissa, by Thomas Whitcombe. The French defeat at Lissa in 1811 led to a rapid collapse in their strength across the Adriatic. British and Greek forces where then able to capture French-held islands throughout the region.

Right: A Captain of the 35th Foot, circa 1811.

Above: A recent view of Lastovo Town.

Below: Ragusa was besieged by Allied troops between 19 and 27 January 1814.

Above: General the Hon. Sir Charles Colville. (Anne S.K. Brown Military Collection, Brown University Library)

Right: Captain Hoste by Henry Edridge. Hoste fought at the Battle of Cape St Vincent and the Nile, but his greatest successes were in The Adriatic.

Chas Stadden 1800
ROYAL SUSSEX

Above: In 1805 the Republic of Venice (seen here in a painting by Turner) was incorporated into the Kingdom of Italy. This lasted until Napoleon's defeat and abdication in 1814.

Opposite page: Right:Private, Grenadier Company, 35th Foot (Anne S.K. Brown Military Collection, Brown University Library)

Below: British troops bivouacked in the Bois de Bologne, 1815. (Anne S.K. Brown Military Collection, Brown University Library).

Left: Kibworth Church.

Below: The Hildebrand's grave stone, obverse.

Bottom: The Hildebrand's grave stone, reverse.

This expedition of Admiral Fremantle's quite altered and permanently deranged, the previous arrangements on that coast.

Colonel Robertson with all the troops he could spare, accompanied him to all the important ports on the eastern coast as far as Venice; and as the expedition was unpremeditated to that extent, as far as we knew, *left us* in rather an uncertain position.

The colonel had in his hurry left Lissa, with an old German captain in command of the German Legion by army seniority, [a] command with 20 other foreign officers and a few men, whatever forces he left, expecting I suppose to return in a short time from a naval dashing expedition and therefore making no permanent arrangements: and without the intention of leaving Captain Barbier[14] in permanent authority of any importance. But the colonel did not return[15]. The expedition led him to Zara, Fiume, and Trieste; out of all of which they drove the French and took military possession of the forts and fortifications and as a matter of course in those days, of the full civil and military power. Thence they passed over to Italy, took possession of Verona and every other place to (Reggio?) up to the headquarters of the combined British and Austrian Army under Count Nugent at Parma and thence to Genoa, &c, its conclusion and that of the war.

But I must go back to Lagosta and my own particular interests and proceedings. The summer of 1813 i.e. from 30th January to the middle of November, passed there notwithstanding its solitariness, by means of shooting, studying the languages and the incidental matters of duty, rousing me to a kind of energy now and then, without any disagreeable tedium, for I was always thus although quite alone fully employed. But I was roused one evening, by receiving an unexpected despatch by gun boat, from Captain

---

[14] Captain Barbier, a Swiss, actually commanded two companies of de Roll's Regiment and was made Chief of Police on the island.

[15] The Austrian General Count Nugent was offered the support a portion of the British garrisons in the Ionian islands and two companies of the 35th and some foreign troops commanded by Colonel Robertson were landed near Trieste by Admiral Fremantle on 12 October 1813. Although they did not participate in the siege of this fortress, the French garrison amounting to 800 troops and 53 cannon surrendered on 23 October. General Nugent then proceeded across the Apennines and Robertson's force accompanied them, seeing action at Ferrara, Reggio and Parma, before capturing Genoa in April 1814.

Lowen[16], the commandante of the larger island and garrison of Curzola, a few miles from me nearer the main land. Captain Lowen was an Englishman but an officer of the *Corsican Rangers*, an old and experienced soldier. I believe he had seen much service at one time in the French Army, I know not in what rank or *how*, but he had then been some years in our service and was a valuable and good officer. He had been placed in command of Curzola on its capture, a day or two after that of Lagosta, with 150 men for its defence. He was then about 40 years of age and with much experience. Hence his opinions on military and other matters demanded my attention and respect. I am thus particular, to account for my having engaged in what might appear to some in an expedition which carried me further and led me to run greater risks than I thought of, or, had I been left to my own judgement, would have considered quite prudent to undertake. But I was precipitate and sanguine then in any military enterprise. To make the matter short, he wrote a note to me saying that he had from good information, been assured that the people at and around Ragusa were ripe for revolt against the French and well organised to resist it, strong as the force of the latter was and the strength of the garrison. That they were quite prepared to establish a blockade and in a short time, starve them into a surrender, if they could get a very moderate support and countenance from the British army; merely enough to give them countenance and an appearance of our determination to support them in their undertaking if necessary. Captain Lowen asked me if I would *join* him in affording them this help; that he could spare only 50 rank and file himself and asked how many could I join to them?

The temptation of success in such an undertaking was great, with a prospect of gaining distinction in the service, if successful, and all its concomitant advantages and glory, which, with the natural impetuosity and military ambition of youth, at once decided me on

[16] Captain Pearce Lowen, Royal Corsican Rangers. He was an Englishman (born Dover 1773) and he initially served in Villette's Regiment in the British Army, hence probably John's mistaken belief that he had served in the French Army. Lieutenant General William Villette had attempted to form a regiment from Albanian troops at Corfu in 1799, but although a number of officers were appointed, including Lowen, the Albanians proved 'difficult' and the attempt was abandoned by 1801 at the latest.

seizing the opportunity. I replied that I could only, with prudence take 15 men with me, but thought that these with his 50 would suffice for any undertaking we were likely to encounter in a mere blockade or surprise; of which I then had but a very imperfect conception and indeed of the whole undertaking. But I ended by saying that if he would inform me of the time and place where we were to meet I would not fail to be there with my 15 men.

Two days after by his appointment we met at Curzola and there it was decided that on a certain day we should rendezvous at *Ragusa Vecchia*[17] which is on the shore within two miles of the fortress of Ragusa where was a large garrison, under the command of a distinguished French general. But we had command of the sea-board and had been too much accustomed to all kinds of risks and adventures to be easily deterred by any such disadvantages.

---

[17] Now known today as Kavtat, which was actually about four miles from Ragusa itself to the south-east.

Chapter 10

Ragusa Vecchia 1813

John and Pearce Lowen had agreed with the leader of the local Ragusan insurgents, Count Caboga, to land a small contingent of the 35th and Corsican Rangers at Ragusa Vecchia, to aid the insurgents if possible in blockading the garrison of Ragusa by land in October 1813. It is certain that the Navy was required to transport them there. The British flag was raised over the town church, Caboga was proclaimed commandant of the town and it was announced that the laws of Ragusa were now in force.

Around this time, although he does not mention it, John would have received news of his promotion to the rank of lieutenant, dated 23 September 1813.

Captain William Hoste in HMS *Bacchante* sailed into the bay of Ragusa Vecchia on 15 November 1813 and he ordered the Union Jack to be removed and the Ragusan flag of St Blaise raised in its place. With a twenty-one-gun salute, Hoste proclaimed the independence of Ragusa, with no thought given to the reaction this would get from his Austrian allies. Hoste however had little time for the Croatian insurgents, his role in his own eyes, being merely to clear the French out. Indeed, he wrote to Admiral Fremantle that 'I can give you no hopes of Ragusa soon falling ... I do not possess the means of reducing it.' He spoke disparagingly of the insurgents and the blockade, 'like all undisciplined troops ... sometimes there are two thousand before the place and the next day probably 100.' Hoste then promptly sailed away again, more interested in the capture of Cattaro.

Having deposited the troops at Ragusa Vecchia, it became incumbent upon them to establish what they could do to support the Ragusan insurgents in their blockade of Ragusa itself. It was a walled city, strongly garrisoned with about 600 men under the command of the experienced French General Joseph Montrichard.

Therefore, John and Lieutenant Archibald Macdonald made their way to view the defences of Ragusa and to meet with the insurgents, in an attempt to agree a way forward. But John again showed his youthful naivety by removing his uniform and donning the garb of a local. By doing so, he forfeited all rights to be taken as a prisoner of war, rather he was now liable to be shot as a spy, and to make matters even worse, he only missed being captured by a hair's breadth!

A second visit by all three officers on mules also came close to being captured, and after the shock of meeting such a ragtag group, but finding them well armed and determined in their cause, the decision to support them was made.

> Ragusa Vecchia is an old and small town at one time [of] more importance, but then poor and almost deserted by the gentry of the modern Ragusian territory. But good old roomy houses, built substantially of stone, afforded excellent quarters which the inhabitants readily and cheerfully opened to our use and the enjoyment of their hospitality. Here we were joined, by Lowen's arrangement, by Lieutenant Archibald Macdonald, senior lieutenant with a kind of roving commission to annoy the enemy anywhere (almost immediately after captain of the 35th Regiment[1]) with whom we settled the mode and plan of our proceeding, first as to what was expected from us, then how we were to act. For up to this time it seemed Lowen had acted solely on what information he had gleaned (although a rather indolent man he was a consummate linguist and well understood the nature and habits of foreigners, especially of Italians and others on the Mediterranean and Adriatic) *from the natives*, and in truth, as far as I could learn at this first interview, the opinion I could form was anything but clear and encouraging. But we had embarked, in a degree compromised ourselves and in a great degree by taking up quarters and having meetings with the inhabitants had implicated both them and ourselves in the necessity of at least endeavouring to meet their wishes and expectations. There met us here a certain

---

[1] He became a captain on 7 October 1813.

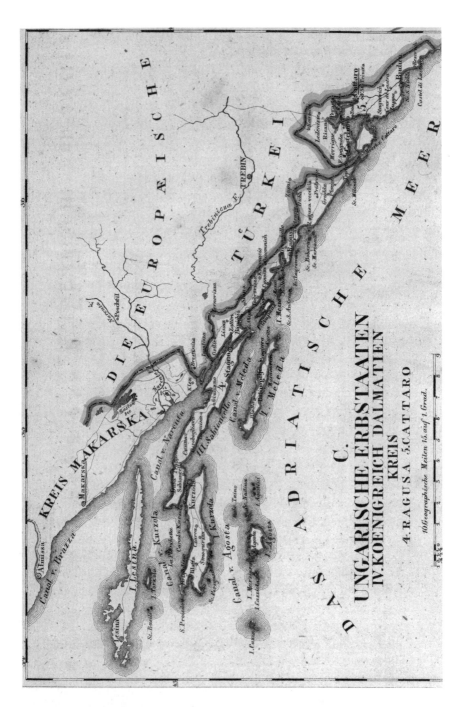

Above: An Austrian map of Ragusa and the islands.

Count Caboga[2] and one or two other Ragusian noblemen who, I found were at the head of the movement.

But before forming any plan for our own movements, it was necessary we should visit and inspect the country around Ragusa and see where and how we could fix our posts and act to advantage in the proposed *blockade*, which against such an enemy and garrison, the more we looked into it, appeared more formidable and perhaps unpromising.

But Macdonald and I, both very young men, undertook to start *the next morning* (we were healthy and strong and accustomed to long and trying marches) but I had been suffering and much weakened from dysentery at that particular time and was altogether out of order and would have gladly deferred the expedition if possible for a day or two. However, we had made a beginning and a day or such delay would inevitably have brought a visit from the French garrison, therefore I resolved to go, *if equal to it* in the morning. But then I found [myself] so much below the mark that I started with a feeling of certainty that I could not sustain any lengthened fatigue. Still, time pressed and I did as best [as] I could and in the best spirits I could muster to meet the occasion.

We two (Lowen did not go with us) advanced (each clad in a *shooting jacket* and its accompaniments) and a doubled barrelled gun, *loaded with ball*, to the very foot of the ramparts, a walk of 5 or 6 miles by mountain path and even advanced (foolishly enough), went up with a considerable concourse of country people, men and women going to the market on a market day, to the very gates of the public entrance to the city. I observed that we were by our complexions and appearance I suppose, the marked objects of their observations, but with a kind of reckless fatuity, we still proceeded in our reconnaissance quite leisurely, as if there was no danger or cause for caution, quite under the fortifications of Fort Napoleon[3] (their stronghold) and within pistol shot of it. When, on a sudden,

---

[2] Biagio Bernardo di Caboga. The Caboga's (or Kaboga) were a very senior and ancient family, based in Ragusa.

[3] From his description, this would appear to be Fort Imperial, which stands on a high hill overlooking the town. Its construction was begun in 1806 and it was completed on 15 August (Napoleon's Birthday) 1812. Hence the name, which it appears was later changed by the Austrians.

Macdonald called out to me 'Hildebrand, we are observed and waylaid; look around, there are several parties out to catch us'.

I was of course startled and did look around me, when I saw several parties of armed soldiers, scattered so as to force us into one point like in the bag of a net!! There were so many parties all round that there seemed no possible chance of escape, except by running the gauntlet and trusting to speed, taking chance of the shots which would certainly come thick on us.

This was no pleasant discovery, and it left us not a moment to deliberate. My friend Macdonald, always cool and collected under any circumstances, said cheerily 'Come Hildebrand, we must give them leg bail and try to beat them' so we started on the instant and he, as active and vigorous as always, but after running 50 or 60, or it may be 100 yards, my weakness and dysentery told and I could not go on. Macdonald urged me to exertion and said if I did not we should certainly be taken prisoners, but I could [only] reply 'My dear Macdonald, I *cannot* but *you* must not be taken to save me; even if you could, but that is impossible: so good bye; get on as you can without thinking of me'. He looked back on me with evident sorrow and regret and then did as I advised, starting on with all his speed and vigour. I threw myself, quite exhausted and helpless, down, without selection into a myrtle bush on the edge of a goat's path (the brush wood of the country) *unable to move a yard further*, or to take any steps to conceal or cover myself and *this* within 100 or 150 yards of Fort Napoleon and within view of the whole ramparts. There I lay, only able to grasp my gun, which, so raw and inexperienced was I, I held ready to resist whatever attempts would certainly be made to take me when I was discovered. I felt ashamed to yield to *any* force, with well-loaded arms in my hand, without resistance and kept debating in my own mind what I should do; but never came to a determined decision what that should be. However, it never occurred to my mind, for an instant, but that the *worst* that could happen was my [being] taken prisoner and detained possibly only a short time. Little did I contemplate the dreadful fate that awaited me had I been taken! Which I will leave to be related in its proper place. Here I lay for a considerable time, to my astonishment almost openly exposed, without being seized; and while lying there quite uncovered excepting by a few leaves, a peasant (Dalmatian) passed *close to me* on his way to Ragusa, saw me plainly, but continued his path, without in the least turning his head or regarding me (he knew who I was, but we had come he knew to help them shake off the French yoke; but his self-possession as well as his generosity has been a subject of my admiration and gratitude ever since). I tried to look around me for some time but could only perceive that the pursuing parties had decreased and almost ceased in number and I could only suppose that they had caught sight of Macdonald and pursued *him*, supposing I was with him. At any rate, by God's providence there I lay, undiscovered until dusk when having recovered my strength a little and inspired by unexpected and therefore natural *hope* I was able to crawl out of my bush and eventually to grope my way (the night was peculiarly light and bright) to Ragusa Vecchia which I was nearly never seeing again.

But one soon forgets dangers escaped. A sound sleep and mitigation of my complaint soon told on me and the next morning I arose both better in health and spirits and more than ever excited by my situation and enterprise. Soon after a hearty breakfast, Lowen, Macdonald and myself entered into close and cool consideration as to what we should do. It was clear that the undertaking was much above what we, at least I, had anticipated, and that we had attacked the position of a strong fortress and with a more than sufficient vigilant and powerful garrison and that therefore we were committed to a serious and dangerous measure. But there we were at Ragusa Vecchia within 2 miles of that fortress and garrison, who were not likely to leave us long undisturbed, if we did not take the initiative and move ourselves.

So what was to be done? With Lowen's 50 and my own 15 soldiers in such a position, it was clear that they would in resentment for our insolence and conscious power, pounce upon and try to overwhelm us and thus nip the blockade and seditious movement of the natives in the bud. These as yet we had not seen; nor did we know further than that they considered themselves powerful enough and had risen against the French and were waiting for and expecting our support and *assistance*; that they had in a manner, commenced a blockade of the city and hoped and expected that by cutting off their supplies on the land side, the sea being always under the control of our cruisers and gun boats, we would and as they fondly supposed, very soon, reduce and take the place by famine. *They* had no idea of how long experienced, courageous and determined men could resist under such circumstances; nor had *we* at least I can answer for myself. But to go at once to the point, we decided on starting the next morning on another expedition of reconnaissance, in order to find our real position and thereby settle our plan of proceeding. Therefore Captain Lowen, Lieutenant Macdonald and I arranged that we should start *on mules*; Lowen was a fine tall and large man, but not active and equal to long walks as *we* were and it was necessary to pass by the fortress 2 miles on our side, to the modern town (if it be so called) of Ragusa, to inspect Gravosa⁴, really a fashionable suburb and place of recreation on the water side from the city, about a mile on the other side and all the road over [the] mountainous and rocky rough and uncultivated country and incapable of it, making a considerable detour necessary to avoid the forts and guards and more especially 'Fort Napoleon', into which I had been unconsciously but too nearly roughly introduced the day before, we prepared for a long and exciting ride. Having no horse or conveyance of any kind of our own, we had recourse to our usual resort in such necessities, and which as the people in all those regions had been long accustomed to it under the French and other military nations, but which was immediately responded to. We sent for the Mayor or Podesta, of Ragusa Vecchia, told him our need and intentions (in which his heart and inclination went with us) and desired him to send out a requisition for and supply us with good and safe mules for the occasion to be at our door at 6 o'clock in the morning.

Sure enough at 6 o'clock, three mules likely looking enough were there; one especially, a fine looking powerful animal intended no doubt for Lowen, both as senior officer and with a view besides, to his long legs size and weight. And so we started, in high spirits and quite prepared for and expecting and disregarding attacks from pickets and all kinds of things on our way. We proceeded a couple of miles quietly enough (giving a wide berth to Ragusa) under the guidance of 3 stout peasants each with a substantial stick, for the purpose of attending to and urging on the mules in the rough and usual way of the country and in our direction at last were obliged in following the only practicable goat path which led us nearer to Fort

⁴ Now known as Gruz.

Napoleon than was agreeable or desirable in any way; from the rampart of which we were saluted with a warm welcome of musket balls, but without our suffering any more serious inconvenience than the annoyance and whizzing of a few musket balls. This we soon passed and went on swimmingly again, when all at once the mule on which I rode, a likely looking animal enough, took sulk, I believe from having been urged beyond his pace and could not be got on either by stick or coaxing, the nature of the animal. And just at this moment (we were not above ½ a mile past Fort Napoleon) Macdonald who was in advance of the 3 and better mounted, called out 'Look behind, we are closely pursued' and in truth, there was a strong party of infantry soldiers in close pursuit and very little in our rear.

Of course we were in no little bustle. Our guides urged [us] to drive on the mules as fast as possible, which in Lowen's and Macdonald's case was effectual; but *my* brute could not be made to mend its pace and as the pursuing party was numerous, well-armed and gaining on us (we had only our pistols and swords), it became really a serious matter, when Lowen in an impatient tone shouted out to me to make haste or we would be taken. What could I do?

I bullied the guide &c, but got on none the faster. My man had thrashed the brute till he was exhausted and broken two good sticks to pieces on his hide, but to no purpose. I had also broken my own stick to pieces, all but about a foot remaining in my hand. Lowen became excited and out of patience, and turning around said, with great wrath, 'Why don't you jump off the brute? And jump up behind me?' But I had brought with me the only saddle and bridle I had, almost a new one and was loath to leave it a prey to the French, yet at last in despair (for I was now a considerable distance behind the other two) with all the venom and bad temper, of which I was at the time full, struck my mule, intended as a last farewell and in dire spite, with violence at the *root of the ear*, by mere chance, when in an instant he started forward and by keeping up the game of this application, kept him to it, at a fair gallop until I got the lead and continued it until we fairly outdistanced our pursuers and got off. But I should here explain why we were pursued only on foot. The fact was that the roads, it may be said *no* roads of that mountain district made it impossible to employ cavalry, and only two or 3 dragoons were stationed at Ragusa, to carry occasional despatches on the only practicable road (but a good and broad one) along the coast, to keep the communication between Venice and all the fortified towns as far down as the Morea, a noble military road. We had to descend a precipitate mountainous narrow and rough path, from the high table land we had just traversed, down to Gravosa, really the port, and a most noble one, of Ragusa about ½ a mile off, in which large fleets could ride in safety and with the (universal in the Mediterranean) deepest water even to the shore. Gravosa itself was a mere offset, a place of resort for recreation and pleasure from Ragusa, about a short mile distant and the delightful residence of a small population chiefly consisting of captains of mercantile craft and their usual accompaniments, and country houses of the gentry. It is at the extreme end of a long and noble basin, with some few fine old, but now unfashionable and neglected houses of the formerly wealthy and aristocratic Ragusians. The rest are of humbler pretensions, more modern and with a peculiarly neat and tidy appearance; those on the sea side especially and occupied by the best sort of capitanos and their families, altogether almost completely landlocked.

Here we found the force we had been invited to come and assist in blockading the strong and strongly fortified Ragusa, commanded by a distinguished French general[5] and in importance the seat of an Archbishop. And indeed it would not be easy to describe the allies we were introduced to, nor my sensations at first sight. It was all so perfectly new to me and therefore unexpected, that I felt quite bewildered, and could make no probable conjecture what was really expected from our small force, or how we were to set about it, so different all appeared from what I had expected and [had] been accustomed to see in preparation for active warfare with regular troops. But, not to dwell on this, we found I should suppose, but 'tis mere guess from recollection, about 600 to 7 or 800 perhaps many more fine looking men, [armed] to the teeth, determined looking athletic (generally) men assembled to meet us, who appeared at the time excited and enthusiastic beyond measure; without, to all appearance, much order or discipline (but in this afterwards I found I was wrong, for there was much of both in their own way) and at their head, two noble hearted, courageous noblemen, with them as

---

[5] General Joseph Montrichard commanded at Ragusa.

their retainers, called Sluga, but perhaps not correctly, more properly their retainers a very humble and dependant class of servants, although either by necessity or choice always remaining fixed and attached to the soil; Count Caboga of a family for many centuries famous and powerful in the small Republic of Ragusa, and Marchese Pietro de Bona, and perhaps some others of noble families. But Count Caboga, a gentleman of about 40 years of age, was evidently the moving and ambitious commanding power, the Marchese a fine young high spirited nobleman, about 25 or 26 years old. These two were distinguished by their proud and commanding look, and the rich and broad silk sashes, and showy plumes of white feathers in their caps. The common men were dressed in all ways like mountain peasants, but armed with long Dalmatian guns, and pistols and daggers in their belts, a most formidable if not a very regularly military array, certainly most formidable and defiant. I found afterwards that there were some hundreds more like them, under my command, determined, active, sharp fellows and all good and certain marksmen; few of them unaccustomed to arms and hardy mountaineers, the guerrilla soldiers only completely undisciplined, and ready at all times when wanted.

We three officers, with the count and the Marchese de Bona immediately retired to the house of which they had been some days in possession and fixed on as the headquarters, to consult what was to be decided on and done without delay. For the outbreak was so sudden and the combination of English forces, the numbers of which they must have been ignorant of, with the insurgents apparently so formidable, that the French must at first have been completely at a loss how to meet it. Although it was evident they would not allow it to go on long without disturbance and that *our* parts must be at once decided on and commenced.

After due consideration it was decided that Captain Lowen should remain with our very modest force of rank and file, at Ragusa Vecchia, as a *reserved* post to retire on if necessary, that I should take command of the natives and reside with them in the house we were then in, as headquarters and that Macdonald, who was like myself, quite a volunteer and independent, should consider himself as one of us and help us with head, and hand, and watch over us in his fine gunboat, a large boat (mounting a 9lb brass gun and pulling 20 oars of fine young fellows, his own training in daring and activity) to remain with me or go as he liked and saw necessity, taking the command of and regulating the movements of the four gunboats I had brought from Lagosta. On him was my chief dependence and certain trust, in case of need. Of the courage, and zeal of the count and Marchese there could be no doubt; but with all so new and strange, I could not but feel some hesitation and, to speak out, apprehensions as to what might be the result. It seemed impossible to anticipate a happy one with such disparity of forces and positions to begin with; nor could I see excepting from some gross and cowardly (not at all to be expected from the French officers) error how we could succeed. But nevertheless, I found myself committed and for a hundred reasons bound to begin with every energy and [to] do my best. Besides that, but for the position in which I had placed myself, with regard to my having acted without orders and instructions (which always lay like a log on me) and my enhanced responsibility thereby; my anxiety for the chance I had of success in some degree, and the excited hope of finding some way, of getting out of it *creditably,* at last urged me on without allowing me to look too far to the right hand or left; in fact, to fix my eye and exertions on the *one* object.

Chapter 11

Blockade of Ragusa 1813–14

John's relation of events during the actual blockade of the fortress of Ragusa is impossible to verify as there do not appear to be any records covering the actions of the insurgents. However, what little we do know regarding the personages of the Ragusan nobility who led it and the actions of their partisans do match his description of them and indeed his story does generally ring true.

The Royal Navy had effectively stopped the French coastal trade, hence Ragusa was forced to rely on deliveries of supplies overland, this is what the partisans strove to prevent.

His decision to work closely, if not actually lead this determined bunch, was certainly at odds with his orders to command on Lagosta; and his decision to stay with the Ragusans actually in their headquarters under the guns of the fortress, was rash and perhaps shows his naivety.

The carelessness of the partisans to danger was particularly highlighted in their haphazard and indeed downright dangerous way they prepared new cartridges each night, loose gunpowder everywhere and smoking cigars as they worked. But his efforts to help lead them with the assistance of the boats brought by Macdonald certainly seem to have bolstered their efforts, and on one occasion undoubtedly saved all of their lives.

He therefore chose to ignore all 'orders' from Captain Barbier to return to face a court martial, assuming that Colonel Robertson's orders still stood. He clearly felt that if he was at the sharp end, in the thick of things, then he could not be wrong.

> I felt sure, at once, that we should be attacked most earnestly by the enemy so near and so much interested in the hope of *soon* nipping it

in the bud. Yet so far, from what I had already seen of our house, as a post for defence, I had much confidence in its capability. It was a large roomy house, but still compact and the armed natives were already settled in it, the house of their own choice, and we were all together under the same roof. By the way I must give some idea of a place which was destined with its brave and dauntless garrison to make so stout and triumphant a defence ere long. It had been I suppose, the roomy summer house of some wealthy, perhaps noble Ragusian with Venetian taste and [an] ample fortune, as a retreat from the cramped up garrison city and as such, situated on the water's edge of the beautiful Port of Gravosa, not a mile away, most delightfully large, roomy and aristocratic as it was fitted up within as to stair cases, hall &c so in the most substantial style. There was one large room on the first floor, besides many other smaller, but still above the common dimensions and a fine roomy entrance hall and larger hall on the ground floor, but the mansion at the time I mention, had become by neglect and deterioration not what it had been in former days and fallen off in dignity and consequence. Yet still a useful, substantial and *for our purpose*, an accommodating abode.

The entrance from the water's edge was arched over, as we see in great houses in this country for a public thoroughfare and as a carriage road at the grand entrance door; and over this arch was a flat roof, with a parapet around it of about 2 feet high or less, leading partly over the water, used I believe as a kind of balcony, and place of recreation in the open air in summer, by a communication from the large room above which I have described, for the family and visitors; about 20 or 30 feet in length and 15 in breadth. (I speak from guess [work], after an interval of very many years). I am thus particular in describing the rooms &c because it soon became the scene of a serious and sanguinary encounter, *in defence*, against a most formidable attack, intended by the French from the garrison as they openly boasted, to be our utter destruction and annihilation; in fact to put us all to the sword.

This was fixed as our advanced outpost and headquarters, of which I then and there planted myself in full command. Our garrison consisted of a very few soldiers, ten or a dozen, I forget exactly how many. Count Caboga who as the originator of the movement and chief over the natives assumed a kind of command, but, although I hardly knew my own position in such a force, with perfect deference and friendly intercourse with me, the Marchese Pietro de Bona, a young man of about 27 or 28 years of age and about 60 armed and warlike Dalmatian followers of the count were within, all ready and armed for service. But I am at a loss [how] to describe in order and clearly and succinctly, this to me then motley group, as I was just introduced myself among them and hardly at all acquainted with their language and could only understand or make myself understood by them through the Italian language to their chiefs, and therefore could comprehend little of their military arrangements, although it appeared I was to be the head of all.

Yet, through the discipline of its kind, which the count and his friends had established, all seemed to go on well and above all, plenty of determined fellows were at hand whenever and for whatever purpose they were wanted. Wild mountain and irregular warfare was familiar to most, if not all the men generally above 30 years of age or perhaps much under it. I was led to understand that my force, in that way, extended over at least 1,500 or 2,000 of these fine fellows. Still it was not encouraging for I could only act second hand through their chiefs and could not see how they were to be handled and made use of against regularly disciplined soldiers if I should, which seemed too likely, be brought into open contest with them. And *very soon*, I had an opportunity of testing and forming an opinion of what might happen.

I found a considerable number, say 2 or 300 men, around the door of my post before I had time and opportunity to examine into my position and set things straight; all full of enthusiasm, burning to commence battle and show their defiance of the enemy who had cowed and kept them down so long with a rod of iron and now, having me a British officer at their head, they would *at once advance*. The thing was so strange, [it] took me so much by surprise and was so unexpected and disorderly to my mind, that my first impulse was to recommend more consideration and caution; but soon found that any hanging back on my part, or hesitation to do as they wished, would be a bad beginning of my enterprise, indeed stopped it altogether, or set me in a wrong position with those who had placed their hopes and expectations on our aid; certainly with hardly any consideration in their own wild impetuous way. So I at once consented to join them, but in mere impetuosity and without the least idea of what was to be done and excepting taking a prominent place in the advance (because they wished to display their acquisition of a British officer in uniform with 2 light infantry epaulettes at their head) I really had nothing to do with the first movement nor took any interest in it; which was merely, as I thought, a senseless bravado without an object and without much order or accuracy, in open file, in line, up to the walls of Fort Napoleon, our wild men firing and showing all signs of defiance and provoking contempt. All the time, firing random, or perhaps directed shots (for they were good marksmen) and that in no stint, at the soldiers on the ramparts, drawn out as much by curiosity as anything else to see this unusual and irregular wild commencement of hostilities.

They of course responded from the fort and a well sustained but not very effective musketry fire was kept up on both sides. I confess I felt both humiliated and annoyed by the, to my mind, utter absurdity of such a movement, but went on with them without showing my feelings or in any way discouraging them. It occurred to me that I was 'in for it' and must not damp my best chance of ultimate success by losing their confidence in my courage and zeal. The result of this first day was humble enough. We had one or two peasants killed or wounded in this senseless way, but, beyond seeing one of them carried from front to rear, at a most deliberate dogged and defiant pace, on some sticks or poles picked up on the ground, and that very many walked beside him, like men at a funeral, and quite as leisurely, I had no opportunity, from not knowing their language, of learning anything particular about it.

We returned to our quarters before dark, and then I had the first opportunity of examining my new, and as I thought, temporary mode of life and expectations in it for the duration of the blockade, which I then looked forward to, and unless our hopes of success and confidence in our strength failed us, of considerable duration; such as I had little contemplated when I joined in the enterprise. Of course all the rooms and especially the staircase were anything but neat and tidy with the open and unrestrained intercourse of so many men and under such circumstances, there was no appearance of carpets, or furniture of any kind. At best it was but such a military post as could be seized on by any guard or picket in the severest service.

In the upstairs largest room were two or three rough deal tables, or rather boards placed on trestles, on the largest of which in the centre we all together took our meals, served in abundance of the finest ox beef and vegetables twice a day and the same cold at any hour we chose. In fact it was an advanced guard or pickets space (but not, as generally, for a certain specified number of hours) for every and all days, till the affair should end by success or defeat; each finding the best place he could to rest or repose on, night and day. It was in truth hard service and rough fare. Although winter, i.e. from late in November to the beginning of March, the weather was mild and on that score we had not much to complain [of]. But complaint of any kind never entered our minds; had such a lengthened affair been foreseen or contemplated, it might have been otherwise and perhaps I would at once, early in it, have *returned* to Lagosta, but we were in constant *excitement* and delighting in daily enterprise and that went on from day to day, in hope, and with the intention of seeing the *end* and acquiring the glory of taking so important a place as Ragusa. And were thus allured on, the daily and constant skirmishing and never ceasing musketry, dropping fire of the outposts, for most vigilantly and effectively did they shut up the garrison of Ragusa from all outward communication and being good marksmen and never ceasing the watch, precluding the possibility of any one or thing gaining ingress or egress from the garrison or town. Indeed, so closely did these irregulars attend to this that, on the pathway which led from Fort Napoleon to the town, by which they all relieved their guards and pickets and supplied provisions, I saw, for several weeks, the corpses of two soldiers, who had been shot when endeavouring to run from one place to the other lying across the pathway in their clothes and more than half decomposed, no one from either fortress or fort daring to venture out to remove them. Thus all aid or assistance from either to either was completely cut off, so well and courageously did these men fulfil the duty they had undertaken. And every now and then the whole body chose to vary the thing by indulging in an occasional defiance and provoking walk in distended line to menace the garrisons of both places, in the manner I have before described; to accompany which I was generally earnestly invited and sometimes did merely to keep up my prestige among them, for it was an unmilitary manoeuvre.

But I should have explained how it was that our headquarters was safe and could be occupied so near the French forts and garrison. Thus Fort Napoleon was on the ridge of a high and precipitate hill or little mountain just above us, so elevated that they could not depress their guns to batter the house immediately below further than, now and then, sending a chance shot through our roof. At first they tried all they could to attain greater depression of their guns, but after a few days found it was wasting ammunition in vain and so gave it up. And between us and the town, there was a considerably rising ground which prevented the delivery of cannon shot and somehow or other (I never could quite understand it) they hardly ever did us any damage by the shells, with which they occasionally favoured us. But popping with muskets was *always* going on especially on our side and daily with some fatal effect. And this constant consumption of cartridges was every evening repaired by all, or most of our hands turning to, to make cartridges, at which they were expert, but which they certainly did in their own wild way and in the most reckless and dangerous manner on the large table in the dining room, which, when the expenditure had been greater than usual and therefore they were more wanted in haste, for next day, I several times saw them making from a heap of gunpowder *emptied from* a keg, I always supplied from my gunboat store on the centre, the makers sitting round, chatting, with candles, and some smoking with the utmost composure and thoughtlessness.

This always made me wince, but, shut up as we were and expecting *every night* a fierce attack; every precaution [was] set aside for the great absorbing one, and preparation for it, I dared not express, or show any, the slightest fear *of any kind* to these habitually rough mountaineer warriors who would have only understood it as timidity, and so matters went on from week to week, when I had *commenced* the affair without a thought of undertaking anything which would last, or detain me, from my island more than a week or two. And what made my position more tantalizing and anxious, was a despatch I received, on the 2nd week, from Captain Barbier, the German Legion Captain who had been left (as fit for no active duty) at Lissa in command of the few troops left there; who took it into his head that he had succeeded to all the authority of Colonel Robertson of every kind and that as I had, as he argued left my command without *his* leave, it was his duty to check my career and order me back to it forthwith or that he would bring me to a court martial.

It was perplexing because I felt I had [acted] precipitately and without authority in embarking in this undertaking; but, having undertaken and identified myself with it, as I would have done had

Colonel R[obertson] been at Lissa, I resolved on remaining and seeing it out, whatever risk of censure or even worse I ran. And I replied that I could not now leave the poor people already under arms to the vengeance of the French, which they would certainly be visited with, if I were to withdraw. And moreover that I was appointed by Colonel Robertson to the *independent* command of Lagosta to correspond on it only 'to him' which, when he left Lissa with Admiral Fremantle, he had not rescinded or altered, I would therefore take the risk of being able to satisfy him on the subject. In a fortnight Captain B[arbier] sent over a gunboat with another angry and threatening repetition of the former letter, but with no effect. I would not leave Ragusa and I told him so, with due respect. And thus, not only day after day, but week after week and even months passed away; and I found that it required no short time to starve out such a garrison as Ragusa.

We daily *heard*, through our spies, how straitened they were in provisions and in how few days they *must* give in, but the desired event came not. And still the French did not attack *us*. I had reckoned, with certainty, that they *must* have done so long before, that it was impossible to understand how such a strong garrison as Ragusa, under such a distinguished general and officers, could have abstained so long from, at least endeavouring to dislodge and drive us away and open out his previous freedom of intercourse and supply with the country round him; but I never doubted for a moment that when they saw a proper opportunity and necessity, they would pounce on us if only for very shame, in a death struggle; and that they were only biding their time.

I never doubted it for one moment night or day, nor ceased expecting it; but the long delay, when I thought that both their honour and interest ought to have urged them to do it without a day's unnecessary delay, quite puzzled, and brought me almost to, at least, suppose that after all, they did not intend coming and the constant watchfulness wore me, and I know Macdonald and perhaps almost all our garrison down to lassitude and indifference. We had been harassed and kept on the utmost watchfulness and activity and consequently [were] utterly [in] want of natural rest or sleep, for at least 2 weeks.

But we had almost hourly reports from our spies, that the time was *really come* in which our long expected and wished for struggle would occur and on the night of the 8th February[1], 1814, we were so persuaded of it that Macdonald and I sat up, as usual in the long public room the whole night, the men making cartridges till about 10 o'clock, when my friend Mc said, 'Well, H, I can bear this no longer, they won't come tonight I am sure, so I shall go off to get a few hours' sleep and I would recommend you to do the same'; and off he went forthwith, I knew not whither, to his billet. And seeing this, my model of a man and incomparable soldier act so, I went also having previously got a billet from Count C[aboga] *for the night*, on a house within 30 or 40 yards, which I had never before seen; but was guided to it then; but found on my going to it in the dark that between it and my quarter, the water, a small salt water inlet, intervened and I had to go around a short tongue of this inlet, to reach it.

The distance was so short and I so utterly wearied out and 'beat' [that] I did not take much notice of this, nor, if I had, could I in my worn out state have objected or suggested a change. So in less than 5 minutes, we reached the house and were received in the most cordial manner (notwithstanding the late hour, the dreaded supposed attack and my warlike equipment) by a neat, tidy looking middle aged woman (I found afterwards she was the widow or wife of a capitano of a small Spanish trading vessel, living, in her husband's absence, at Gravosa) and her daughter, a young handsome girl of 17, but their appearance &c could not at that wearied moment attract from me hardly one glance and I begged them to show me to a room, where I could lie down for an hour or two. [Being] unobservant or hardly noticing at the time the kind civilities and interest they seemed to take to accommodate me in the best possible way; but after all was over, I remembered and often since have remembered with pleasure and gratitude that reception. I was shown up to a small but clean and tidy bed room and instantly, before they left me or even hearing all the civil welcomes they were offering, I stripped off my uniform, sash and sword, which I placed close by my bed side on a small table, with my drawn sword and a pair of loaded pistols on them; and then, without taking off my boots or anything else, so tired was I, jumped on the bed and in far less than 2 minutes was as fast asleep as a man could be.

---

[1] Ragusa surrendered in late January 1814. Therefore, if correct, the date of this suspected attack must have been around 8 January rather than February.

Chapter 12

A Near Run Thing,
8-9 January 1814

As the garrison became more and more straitened and hence desperate, the inevitability of a sortie in an attempt to break the blockade became increasingly likely. Despite his own trepidations, having feared such an attack, John had eventually gone to bed, only to be awoken abruptly to the sound of gunfire. It would seem that some 300 of the garrison, half of the total available, had launched a determined attack to destroy this rebel post and to break the blockade.

Emerging from his house, John instantly found himself the main target for the French infantry and the wall behind him was soon peppered with the marks of the numerous musket balls which had mercifully just missed him. The situation was one of great confusion and looked quite desperate, but his gunboats saved the day. Plying their packed assailants with shot at very close range, this devastating fire soon changed the situation and the French retired again within the fortress, having suffered significant losses.

The blockade had held.

And thus I slept for, I believe, four hours and would have slept on for 20; but, at about 5 o'clock (bear in mind this was in a very dark morning of February) I was startled and awoke by the mother and daughter rushing into my room with a lighted candle, in the utmost terror and at the same moment, the sound of [a] heavy fire of musketry close to me, which I instantly understood as being a fierce attack on our quarters come at last; and it was indeed a terrific fire, and I was so bewildered at the alarming and sudden *surprise*, having sprung that instant from such [a] sound sleep in a strange room and the heavy and increasing firing, with the frequent discharge of the cannon from my gun boats close under my window, that I had some difficulty in getting on my coat and arms and was indeed so agitated (I am not ashamed to confess it; for it was not from fear, of which at the time I was utterly devoid, but an instant consciousness of the responsibility I had incurred) that I quite nervously shook all over in trying to put on my coat. The poor terrified landlady was clinging to one of my knees, the daughter to the other and when I made a move towards the door without thinking of anything but to get out as a matter of course, they clung to me and begged so hard that I should remain indoors, for I must be shot in an instant if I ventured out, that (I should be ashamed to confess such want of feeling on any other occasion) I not only tried to shake them off, but finding that of no avail, [I] actually in my anxiety and agitation kicked them both off on to the floor before I could escape their grasp and get out of the door.

Now this little house was situated directly opposite to our post, only about 20 or 30 yards from it, but on the other side of the inlet which I have described; and therefore the moment I opened the door in the blaze of the discharge of 2 or 300 muskets and my two gun boats, kept up as fast as it was possible, all pointed at me exposed as I was in full uniform, the whole fire was concentrated on me and a rush from the other side to get around and seize me. I never heard of or could imagine such a clatter of musket balls as saluted me. But the one and only anxiety I then had was my *position* and *responsibility*. *In an instant,* it flashed through my mind that my fortune and everything depended on the result of this attack, if we should be overcome I would be ruined in the army, and therefore I thought of *nothing else* than to struggle through it if possible to victory. The sense of personal danger never for one instant occurred to me and the perfect storm of musketry poured on me from the moment I showed myself was at the time, not even heard or noticed by me; [only] *afterwards* I recollected it, with a kind of horror and astonishment. I first tried to run round the point and get into our post, but that was impossible and luckily so, as it turned out.

The soldiers headed [towards me] and fired vollies [sic] on me at once, and with a quick and apparently overwhelming fire and had almost had their hands on me. But my gun boat captain, whom I had hailed just before and [who] was anchored just between me and the house a few yards off, after some delay in the confusion sent his little boat to take me aboard.

All this time there was a perfect storm of firing about our quarters and all the neighbouring houses and on the gun boats, and when I got on board I saw in a moment that my capitano had in his plucky courage (for he was as these capitanos were generally more than usually plucky) to get nearer to the enemy and have more effectual, as he thought and more terrific effect of his great gun, had moored her the moment the house was attacked, *close to it*, leaving no room for the action of grape and canister shot, the only thing that could in such a position act effectively to tell to its best and proper effect; but no doubt the effect of this gun decided the contest and gave us the turn of the victory. They were taken in flank with it [whilst] crowded; [by] a raking fire which they could not withstand.

The door of our quarter was beset with, I understand afterwards, at least 300 [hand] picked and many other volunteer soldiers with hand grenades and everything destructive and likely to forward them in forcing the doors and breaking into the house, and putting (as they exultingly and loudly expressed their determination) everyone in it to the sword. And indeed they appeared at that moment very likely to effect their purpose of forcing an entrance, but I cannot even now believe that any such number of French soldiers, or any others, could even when in have overcome such a valiant and determined garrison of the stoutest of hearts and brawniest of arms who had already kept them off after 2 or 3 hours fighting.

But, by good fortune, black as things looked, one of the gunboats prevented it coming to that extremity. I placed her a little further off, only about 30 or 40 yards and poured on this crowded [mass] in a narrow open passage such a constant succession of grape and canister that it [was]immediately startled, and [it] soon thinned the assailants. This was immediately followed by hesitation and they soon after moved away in swift retreat; which a few grape shots converted into a hasty and confused rout and the defeat became complete; we had won the battle!! Which, if it did nothing more important, at once and instantaneously removed a load of responsibility and anxiety which had oppressed me ever since I had commenced the enterprise and [which] was almost unendurable during this contest, but which, in a moment, elevated me to absolute ecstasy. I, of course, immediately set about seeing [to] the killed and wounded, scattered around our post and found it, in proportion to the numbers engaged on both sides, awful. I could not get near the house without difficulty; so many crowded [in] from all quarters, the moment they perceived from the ceasing of the firing and the sound of the retreating foe, that the fight had concluded, and in our favour. These were all crowded and mingled with our own faithful and brave companions. When I forced my way through and entered the hall of the house, [which was] of considerable extent, I cannot forget the awful sight. The extensive floor was closely packed with dead and dying all lying on their backs; and (as if they had sprung up from the earth thus immediately) two or three monks or friars perhaps more (for I was so confounded and confused that I could not take minute observation or recollect) kneeling, and with noiseless lips confessing the sufferers, with crucifixes held over their faces, or pressed to their lips; I never saw, and trust that I never shall see such another sight, God forbid it!

And, rushing out I found propped up on two ladders brought for their support close to the door two fine men, one a chef de bataillon[1], the other a lieutenant of grenadiers, both vomiting blood from their internal wounds and evidently dying. And upstairs on the balcony, my young friend the Marchese de Bona, prostrate with a shot through his chest and four poor gun boat boys, all under 16 years of age of Macdonald's barge lying dead. And many, many others wounded, to be yet seen to.

Now it must be plain that any one in command, especially of one side of this sad loss, cannot but, even at this distant time, feel sorrow and regret. But at the same time it should be remembered that I was on *the defensive,* and the party sent against us [was] so powerful as to *ensure,* as they thought, a certain victory and had expressed their determination to put us all, without exception, *especially myself,* to the sword, so great as the slaughter was, I can only regret, but not repent the result of the defence, grievous as it was. It was my *duty* and I had no choice but to resist to the death or be killed with all those around me. And I could not but exult in the result. But I must now narrate its extent.

No doubt the attack was of the most formidable kind, a sortie organised under a great French general with all the appliances and

---

[1] Equating to a major in the British Army.

resources of a great fortress and garrison such as *Ragusa* which had supplied the title, to one of Napoleon's choicest generals, [and] of a dukedom[2], and therefore calling for every effort to sustain its importance. Even in the matter of a sortie on a blockading post which had been established for some time under a subaltern close under their guns, and as it were bearding them in defiance and who they knew well had resolved to resist and with God's help repulse[d] the attack they expected would certainly be made on them; In short that they were *determined* not [to] give way, or shrink in the slightest degree before *any* force brought forward to dislodge them whose object was thus to terminate the strict blockade, under which the French garrison had so long writhed; and had moreover long expected and who had, daily fortified themselves against the determined and formidable attack they *expected* without shrinking, or even for a moment thinking of giving way as long as they had life; and who never from strong courage doubted the success of their resistance.

This was certainly no ordinary affair against a common outpost or picket. And, as far as I could ascertain (for I had so much to excite and occupy me to attend to, as to what had just passed and in preparation for what might be coming, that I could not pay attention to or look up minute particulars, or even expect regular reports under such circumstances; and so far in such confusion not only from the gunboats &c but from the native warriors, who had fought so irresistibly and suffered in killed and wounded so severely; that obliged as I was to attend to other things, I really never learned nor could I had I had leisure, easily have obtained a report of our loss. Nor of that of the enemy could we form any reliable estimate). The only thing palpable was that they left in killed and wounded on the hall floor and outside the door above 40 dead (2 officers and 38 men) and, as the distance from the spot from which they started on their rout, in pell mell[3] (without thinking of delay to look behind them). To the gate of Ragusa, was hardly ¾ of a mile and a good road, we cannot but feel certain that they must have carried as we heard they

---

[2] Marshal Marmont was sent to Dalmatia in 1805. He defeated the Russians stationed there and was made Duke of Ragusa. The modern name of Ragusa is Dubrovnik.

[3] In disorderly retreat.

did in the crowd, *very many* of both dead and dying with them; so it is not easy even to *conjecture* what the loss of the French [actually] was. Our own melancholy task was not so difficult, first and foremost my young gallant and ardent friend Pietro Marchese de Bona fell early in the fight from a musket shot (which took him in his right breast, and went out just under the shoulder blade in his back) of course, it was thought when he dropped as is usual, that he was killed; but not so, my experience in other wounds of this kind and from which I have heard from others, leads to the conclusion that at least 1 out of every 3 such wounds recover. I found also several French soldiers severely wounded (the two officers before mentioned did not survive many minutes) and I had *no doctor*. In our irregular and wide spread warfare around and from Lissa, to be carried on by small detachments depending principally on what medical aid they happened on, through the Navy surgeons, it is no wonder. As Colonel Robertson had only one surgeon and an assistant attached to his force, that when he appointed me to Lagosta he had not the means of leaving any medical staff.

And afterwards going to Ragusa in the hasty way I did I had no such resources nor, if I had should I have thought that in that *short* expedition (as I supposed it then would be) anything could occur which might render it necessary. But now, with the Marchese de Bona so badly wounded and so many men requiring surgical aid, it occurred painfully to me what was I to do? I am not naturally of a desponding temperament and had run many kinds of risks and got out of them hitherto; but this really was a difficulty which I could not see my way out of; so I consulted Count Caboga and our *chief* civilian supporters and warriors, and consulted with them what was to be done. Count Caboga was no ordinary man, but one of tact, deep reflection and resource, besides his indomitable fearless courage as so lately experienced. I think he suggested that we should seek aid from the French general in this difficulty, as we had some of his own soldiers in hand. I therefore sent in, or rather went with a flag of truce to the barrier and soon met with a friendly and courteous reception and answer. Our plea was that we had a young Marchese of Ragusa, whom the general knew well, and several French soldiers wounded, for whom there was no medical resource and if left so, probably most of them would die. Would the general generously lend us the assistance of a surgeon?

After some parley, still under the flag of truce and with only two attendants at the barrier, it was agreed between the French officer and myself (I do not recollect whether Macdonald was with me, for they would not treat with any one of the *rebels* as they termed my irregular supporters) that a French surgeon should attend to our wants, in this way. I was to meet him at the barrier every evening and having blindfolded him, conduct him to our post where the wounded all lay, and after he had seen to and directed all they required, he was immediately to return to the barrier again under my guidance and subject to the same blindfolding. And this we continued for 2 or 3 weeks, perhaps more, but I cannot recollect how long. The French doctor was a most skilful surgeon, an accomplished gentleman and most humane and considerate man; so that during the whole of this trying intercourse, and such unfavourable precautions, we got on admirably together, until his attendance was no longer necessary. After the flag of truce had been so favourably received and acted on, the first thing I saw on going up to the bed chamber of the Marchese, were his mother and sister until then perfect strangers to me, on either side of his pillow tenderly attending to his wants. They had been sent out of Ragusa for this purpose, by the humane consideration of the general and I may as well at once terminate my account of this intercourse by stating that through the skill and daily, sometimes twice a day's attention of the doctor and this soothing and affectionate nursing, the Marchese recovered so fast, and so far, as to become convalescent in about 6 or 7 weeks; and the poor French soldiers, most of them also recovered, some few did not.

But what became of my poor wounded gunboat men I hardly know further than that, among themselves they had a kind of surgery which made them very careless of and indeed more than that, *our* medical staff. And here I cannot but intrude a circumstance bearing on this point which really astonished and interested me, even in those careless days and ever since, in a great degree. When I was on the deck of the gunboat which acted so efficiently and effectually in repulsing the sortie, three or four men were standing around me under a tremendous fire of musketry directed to the boat, asking for orders of different kinds and receiving my directions, when one in the very act of speaking to me at once dropped his under jaw, and with *open mouth* endeavoured to speak, but could not. I saw he was badly wounded through the throat and almost immediately he sank down and could not rise again. We were so warmly engaged and I so anxiously employed, that it passed as a matter of course and [I] really thought no more about it and neither enquired nor heard what had become of him.

But, some 6 or 7 weeks afterwards, when again under fire in the same boat, this man with great vivacity started up at my elbow to excite my recognition. I was startled and questioned him, but to be as brief as I can, on my asking him *what means* had been used for his cure? (the ball had entered near his wind pipe, far on the right side and as is not unusual in gunshot wounds, had made an eccentric circuit around it, coming out very much in front of the left side not far from where it entered) He replied with the utmost simplicity, 'Commandante, they poured oil and wine into the wounds and it cured me!!' I cannot describe my astonishment at this reply from a man who I am persuaded, knew nothing of scripture and had never heard of the parable of the Good Samaritan (which means of cure no doubt had and has always puzzled very many to understand it). But on cross questioning I could get no other reply or explanation, which he gave me to understand was an ancient well understood and indisputable cure of such wounds in Dalmatia!! I relate *the fact* and leave others on a more appropriate occasion to comment on it.

But to return to my post, having ascertained that all had been seen to and made as 'comfortable' as could be, so far with the wounded; it was a matter of considerable consideration what was next to be done; for I could not for a moment doubt that the French would take the *earliest* possible moment, smarting under the exasperation and shame of their defeat, to renew the attack with superior power and determination.

Chapter 13

Seeking Reinforcements

Knowing that it was more than likely that the garrison would launch another sortie, a council of war agreed that efforts should be made to persuade Lowen at Ragusa Vecchia to release up to half of his small contingent to bolster the partisans at their headquarters. John was deputed to make a very difficult and dangerous journey through the mountains to circumvent the French area of control. It was achieved after some adventures, but John simply received a blunt refusal from Lowen to release a single man, not even the fifteen that John had brought over from Lagosta.

Having failed in his mission, he sailed across the bay and thus returning much more quickly and with less personal danger, although a storm on route nearly sank his boat.

Given this refusal, Count Caboga suggested enlisting the support of other partisan leaders and John duly set off again to gain an audience with Count Natali, a very influential leader at his island castle. With time to reflect, John had realised that his actions may be deemed inappropriate and he was worried by Captain Barbier's constant threats of a court martial. He therefore requested Macdonald to write a full report of their actions and success at arms to Colonel Robertson.

The relief is still palpable when you read his memoir, when he finally received a reply from the Colonel, which not only approved of his actions but commended him for his audacity and judgement. But more than that, Robertson also sent an offer of a captaincy in his newly raised regiment, the Piedmontese Cacciatore and ordered him to join him in Italy at the earliest opportunity.

Unable to believe his luck, and doubtful that the colonel could actually make such an offer, he delayed sailing for the Italian coast for a bit longer, because after three months of blockading Ragusa he was determined to see it finished.

After as much reflection as I could spare time for, I consulted with Macdonald (who was as anxious as I was, as to how we had better proceed; although we were not in the same situation as regards responsibility, for *he* had a kind of roving commission on which he always acted as pleased him, hence his being at the Ragusa blockade without any order and could go with his armed boat where and do as he liked, but *I* was without as yet, even an intimation that my expedition was tolerated and with Captain Barbier's two repeated threats of a court martial hanging over me as my reward) and with him, held a council with Count Caboga to discuss the matter in our present threatening circumstances. The more threatening in consequence of our victory and the sore and exasperated feeling sure to result from it.

We all agreed that Lowen ought, at once, to come up from Ragusa Vecchia with at least my 15 men and 10 of his own and strengthen my post to repel the expected attack when made, in [as much] as we could not but expect what the enemy would consider and prepare for, an overwhelming force. But, from the previous manner in which Lowen had hitherto resisted our requests to bring his men nearer to Ragusa, fearing his responsibility, we could hardly hope [for it] prevailing now, having failed so often before. I wanted Macdonald to go; but he declined, resting on his complete freedom from any other demand on his duty than was consistent with his armed boat service, although he would remain and help us to resist as long as we might require his aid. At last it was agreed that I should go and try what could be done by making a night march as the most expeditious although somewhat dangerous (that very night) to Ragusa Vecchia and to return the next day. For it was not deemed safe for me to be absent two nights; and as the excitement of the morning contest had somewhat subsided, I naturally wished to look over the scene of battle and make my observations; and begged Macdonald to go with me.

I was indeed astonished at our success and could not but admire and honour the valour of our civilian friends in having resisted so long, such superior power and their repeated and strenuous endeavours to break into the house, and the (what I would have called at any other time, and under different circumstances) *ostentatious* courage and defiant carriage of Count Caboga and the Marchese, noticed so strongly [and] marked on their countenance and uplifted foreheads, surmounted with their conspicuous large white plumes, as they moved to and fro amidst the combatants in the hottest of the fire in defence of the post; which could not but have given confidence and excited the courage of those they had brought there. I am unwilling to doubt that these valiant men *could* not and would not have gained the victory by their own arms alone; but when I saw the effect of the gun boat's fire on the whole force assembled round the door and at that time busily and vigorously employed in forcing it; and the quick effect two or three discharges of grape and canister had in dispersing and driving the enemy so soon to flight, it is evident to what to impute the final or at least unexpectedly quick result; so much so that had we had another such contest of equal severity without the easy command and necessary room and choice of position to make use of it, I would have greatly dreaded the result.

As we were looking over these things and examining our various stations and movements in the fight, the small gable end (I believe of a butler's pantry or such other diminutive structure) close to the house in which I had been so roughly disturbed and left so abruptly in the dark of the morning. The tremendous musketry firing to which I was exposed; in fact regularly platooned for several minutes, while I was hailing and giving directions to the gun boats, I standing in front of it on the water's edge, too anxious in directing and contemplating the possible result to even notice or think of, exposed object as I was, from the blaze of the discharges all around; the balls striking thick like a storm of heavy hail, each one giving its sharp 'ping, ping' against the wall behind me and at my side; and I said to Macdonald 'let us go over (it was over the narrow inlet I have before mentioned) and see, for I am sure we shall find the marks of very many shots'. We went and it was indeed a riddled target; and when I thought of all those shots having been directed at me, at a distance of about 30 or 40 yards and that I stood there alive, it was astonishing. And this proves how many near shots a man may escape in action; for we counted on the white washed wall of about 8 or ten feet in length, no less than 42 shots that had struck close to me and under my height. I can in no way account for it but by supposing that, being nervously anxious about the observance of the directions I was shouting out to the gun boats and constantly moving it may be a yard to the right and another to the left, never standing on one identical spot during the whole time I was there, I must have been to the right, when the shots struck to the left and vice versa so that I came off with only three tears, one in the collar and 2 [in the] body of my uniform jacket and 3 buttons all [with] the evident effect of musket shot; myself untouched! We now went again to the chamber of our wounded friend the Marchese and as having no time to lose and finding him much in the same uncertain state, then and there discussed how I was to get over to Ragusa Vecchia that night and return before the next evening.

At last it was decided that I should start on the poor Marchese's horse with an escort of 5 mountaineers over the mountain by the nearest route, which it was hoped would bring me there before daylight. The weather was tempestuous and pitch dark when we started, so much so that before we had advanced 2 or 3 hundred yards, my guide the chief of my escort, said it was not safe to proceed on horseback and that I must dismount to ascend the mountain before us and be very cautious indeed over the dangerous goat paths until we had better light and weather. A subsidence of the storm; and as a proof of the difficulty and danger of our path, he made me dismount and take hold of the end of the *tail* of *the horse*, which he said could see and manage better than I could and I was to follow close and creep on cautiously for the present; that the storm of thunder and lightning and hail which was terrific, would soon be over and then we could get on very well, but the storm continued and increased as we ascended, until at last my guide said it was *impossible* to *advance*; but that there was a 'Campanella (or small mountain) chapel' not far off which they thought we could reach and shelter in until the violence of the storm subsided. It was certainly a refuge to get in anywhere; for never before, or since, was [I] in such a storm as on the top of that bleak mountain.

I had not seen anything for the last hour and had only known that I was accompanied, by the hold [the] four men kept of me to keep me from losing my foot and being precipitated from the goat path we followed over the precipice of that Dalmatian mountain which I could not discern from the darkness. We reached the 'Campanella' (a little chapel 14 feet square with the smallest and humblest of altars in a corner and all else, in like dimensions and humble pretensions) led by my guides, themselves carefully *groping* their way and not seeming quite sure they were right, in the most complete and profound darkness; excepting from the incessant and terrific lightning for a few moments now and then; and, without having any suspicion of the kind of place I was in, was at last led or rather dragged forward by my mountain escort, to a blazing fire they had just, i.e. in a minute or two, kindled from some dry leaves and sticks (which, from their readiness of finding, I supposed were left in a corner for the accommodation of any such chance visitors). I must confess that, having travelled on as it were completely in the dark so long and only sensible that I was under the guidance and protection and in the complete power of any one, by and only by the clinging grip of my guides, I was astonished and startled at the sight of my escort for the first time as they were sitting grouped around the bright blaze, to which they invited me and which I was so glad to avail myself of, wet as I was, drenched to the skin and cold enough.

Here we were detained by the storm at least 2 or 3 hours; during the whole time my escort (5 Dalmatian mountaineers armed to the teeth) were sitting huddled up in a corner, by the fire and talking all the time with the greatest excitement and animation, not one word of which I could understand; at last from their fierce looks and the depressing influence I suppose, of fatigue and the storm, I began to feel fidgety and a caution I had had before we started, just after I had been warmly assured by Count C[aboga] of the valour and fidelity of these men who had fought most valiantly with us the morning before, viz 'that these fine fellows would cut my throat for my fine buttons if they should find it a temptation or to their interest'.

Accordingly, I asked them in the best way I could make myself understood, why we stopped so long and said that I thought it was time to start as the storm had somewhat abated. But I had to repeat my remarks many times before I could get any other reply than that it was impossible yet. So I was obliged to suppress my impatience but could not so easily reassure myself in confidence that my friends were so trustworthy as they had represented and I began to try about what suggestions I could offer by which to test or tempt them. I knew their need of and the consequent value, of *gunpowder* in their estimation and it occurred to me, on urging as speedy a departure as possible, to remark as if inadvertently in a quiet way, that I was *very* sorry at the delay; and by way of explanation, to add I had hopes of reaching Ragusa Vecchia before morning, for I had ordered a gun boat lying there to sail for Gravosa early in the morning, from which I had intended supplying them with a barrel of powder. It was quite true, the boat was to start at the time, but the present suggested itself to me on the instant, as a kind of stimulant and bribe to expedition; for I began to wish myself rid of my fierce looking companions; although *now*, with some shame I feel convinced that, on that duty and for the furtherance of the cause in which we were all engaged and for which we had so recently fought and striven, they *deserved* every confidence I could place in them. But, be that as it may, they did very soon start and we reached the boat, in time to fulfil my promise to their great delight and satisfaction; they got the barrel of gunpowder.

On consulting with Lowen, who was in snug and pleasant quarters at Ragusa Vecchia very different from those I had so many weeks occupied, how far he would help me with soldiers to strengthen my post, I found that he remained apprehensive of the step he had taken in *coming* there, and of its consequences in case we should meet with mishap and lose our men or any of them. So there was no hope of bringing him with me. At last I decided on taking my own 15 and running the *risk* of a more formidable attack, which Lowen thought inevitable, and starting on my return to Gravosa early next morning by sea, the shortest way (although exposed to the guns of Ragusa about mid way) but both to gain time and avoid such another mountain journey as the night before, I decided on it, and sent for the 'Intendente' the mayor or chief official, from whom we had got the mules before, and I made a requisition (this was the short and easy way to have our wants of *all* kinds supplied in those service days and would become so again under like circumstances of active warfare). With no Mr Bright, (having power to hamper officers in their duties) for a good serviceable country boat and crew to convey me the next morning early to Gravosa. He of course made all the usual official difficulties in finding and supplying a boat and crew fit to convey the commandante; but it was to be done without let or difficulty and without further objections.

The Intendente had long been accustomed under the French and other military rule to this peremptory way of managing such matters and he departed to set about it at once. In the morning he came to announce that he had pressed a boat and crew such as would perform the service admirably and I started to the shore to depart. But here I met with two discouraging circumstances, first the evident, indeed strongly expressed *reluctance* of the master and his crew of four men to comply under any circumstances and secondly, from the Bora or Tramontane wind (most tempestuous and fierce violent wind, not unusual in the Adriatic in winter) not only threatening but as they all assured me most energetically was not only imminent but could certainly come on us in an hour or two and deprecatingly urged my desistance from a risk of all their lives. In my anxiety to return and the natural impetuosity and thoughtlessness of youth and from military custom in those days, I listened to none of their arguments or entreaties (thinking the real cause of their reluctance was the necessity of our passing so near the batteries of Ragusa) but insisted with all the determination of military authority that we should start *immediately*.

The weather, to me looked favourable and sufficiently settled to promise to continue fine, long enough for our object. And with much difficulty, I got them on board and seated myself at the rudder. In that climate the seafaring men are seldom mistaken in their prognostications of weather; and in this case they were unfortunately, too correct. We had not proceeded above 2 or 3 miles when the wind suddenly veered about and began to blow a fresh breeze from the N.N.E. threatening a Bora squall and my crew instantly became alarmed and began to reproach me severely for having forced them out under such circumstances. But although from the rapidity and violence with which it came, I was myself under no little apprehension, I took care not to show it and did all I could to reassure and encourage them to hope it would not be so bad.

Yet in a very short time there was no possibility of ignoring the increasing danger. For so small a boat, the sea became fearful and at last the men, one and all, *threw up their oars* exclaiming that they should all be inevitably drowned and that *I* was the cause of their deaths. One said in agony 'I have 5 children who will be left orphans', another the same with four children; in short all had families and all blamed me in the most desponding and bitterest terms for being the cause of their deaths which they made sure of and the bereavement of their widows and children; and all threw themselves down on their knees on the sides and bottom of the boat and frantically prayed to God for mercy. This was indeed a fearful scene and to myself more than a severe affliction and alarm; in fact, although I did not for a moment let my fears be seen or relax from my earnest endeavours to encourage and rouse the men to some exertion, I was myself all the time in terrible alarm and sitting there in the midst of this fearful tempest with every certainty that a very few minutes if not the next wave, would swallow all up. For the first and only time of my life I gave myself up to inevitable and instant death, while by the cessation of the rowers, the boat broached her broad side to the waves, which came pouring on us in rapid succession and the boat began to fill.

Yet the men would not move from their prayers of despair, nor could I by persuasion or threats get them to do their best to get our head to the wind, our only chance of being saved from swamping.

At last I, in despair, began almost unavailingly to try to throw back the overflowing waters of each successive wave with the only vessel I had within reach, viz my cocked hat, the military headdress of that day. With which I with all my might, at every slight lull, did my best to bail out and on a moment's respite, I succeeded in once more getting the crew to their oars and got the head of the boat to wind; and by a most wonderful intervention of providence, when there did not seem to be a possible chance of shelter we were driven by the wind and water close to a small pietra [or] rock not more than twice or three times larger than the boat itself, but (being elevated) which lulled the water under its lee so that an active and frightened fellow *sprang* upon it with a rope and wound it round a projecting point holding us fast; but almost without a hope of being able to hold on till the wind abated. At this very moment we saw a frigate scudding before the squall without a stitch of sail set (the *Bacchante* with Captain Hoste[1] going to Bocca de Cattaro[2] which he had been besieging, with the most energetic and extraordinary perseverance and exertions for several weeks and frequently passed us at Ragusa

---

[1] Captain Sir William Hoste R.N. commanded HMS *Bacchante* and was instrumental in the seizure of French vessels in the Adriatic and capturing the Greek islands. He finally captured Cattaro, a major success, on 8 January 1814.

[2] Also known as Boka Kotorska.

on his visits of inspection and encouragement of the operations there). The frigate passed so close to us that we all thought as they must see us and observe our danger and signal of distress, we should have been succoured by her, but she passed on before the violent storm and perhaps *could* not, in any way, aid us, at any rate we received no help nor recognition of our appeal for succour.

But by a temporary lull we were enabled to hold on under the lee of rock for above two hours, when the gale began to mitigate and finally after 3 or 4 hours, it passed away to a moderate and manageable breeze, and we not only escaped, but with most determined exertions and threats I prevailed on my cowardly crew to turn their boat's head once more towards Gravosa and seat themselves at their oars. Now, although it may appear that from its short duration, there could have been no such great danger as I have described, it was not so. I for several minutes, perhaps ½ an hour, completely abandoned all hope of escaping a watery grave and as I have said gave myself, the only time of my life, quite hopelessly up. Sitting at the rudder and all the men shouting and reproaching in despair on their knees, all the affections and reproachful transactions of my past life came into my mind as it were in a moment and I had a fearful vision of the judgement which appeared instantly threatening and staring me in the face. It was certainly an awful half hour, as vividly now on my recollection as at the moment and I cannot but hope it has had some beneficial influence on my life ever since.

We managed to escape the shots fired at us on passing the citadel and fort and by God's mercy escaped the dangers of this perilous day and reached my post at Gravosa, late in the evening.

The next day was devoted to seeing how all matters with regard to my charge and post stood. The French doctor had regularly visited his patients and had great *hopes* of many of ours, the Marchese was certainly in a most precarious state, indeed I had no idea that he would recover. He was still little more than alive to all appearance his mother the dowager and his sister sitting as I left them, one on each side of his pillow, but when he could breathe out a word or two it was cheery and spirited. Thus he continued with little variation for several days in a most uncertain and anxious state. In the mean time our good and skilful French surgeon continued to meet our flag of truce at the barrier and submit to be blindfolded, with evident earnest anxiety that he should render his visits efficacious, every evening and at other times previously arranged by himself, according as the necessities of his patients required his advice or aid. Nothing could exceed the humane and devoted attention of this good and skilful man to our wounded as well as to his own. I have ever since thought of him with gratitude and admiration, and only regret that the lapse of years has obliterated his name from my recollection.

Thus, matters went on for a few days as before the sortie, but with if possible, increased anxiety and watchfulness on our parts; in fact, the blockade was kept up with a strictness and closeness that nothing and no one could possibly get into or out of Ragusa, or communication be kept up between Fort Napoleon and Ragusa and from the constant *reports* we had from our spies, they were reduced to great straits. So much so that it was said and delivered by all I met with, that the French general had killed and disposed of publicly his chargers for food.

But I was called on for another and to me puzzling duty within a few days. There was a certain Count Natali, of very considerable influence in that immediate district, a Ragusan noble of great repute for his property and above all his talents, sagacity and influence, who had not yet joined the movement and who had hitherto kept himself aloof from it. Count Caboga and the leading persons unitedly and earnestly asked me to try what I could do with him, to bring him over to take an active part on our side. I felt more than unwilling to make the attempt to persuade one whose repute was so influential; besides that I had always hanging over me the want of *official* authority in the whole affair; but my ardent temperament and sincerity in the cause overcame these feelings and scruples and I promised to visit him at his house, situated I was informed at the mouth of the long harbour about 6 or 7 miles off on a very small island called Scolio[3] and literally so, being only large enough to accommodate the house itself and a small garden with scanty offices. But when I had *considered* things more, I was reluctant to engage in a matter which must be of no small importance to him, as to which side he might take. That of the French, who were in full command

---

[3] I have been unable to identify this island with any certainty.

and power of all he possessed, or his Ragusan brethren in this as yet, venturesome and uncertain and hazardous attempt, to wrest the power from the French general and resume the ancient Ragusan rights themselves.

In my absence of any authority from my superiors in my own service, I felt at a loss to imagine what arguments I should use to persuade him or what inducements from British authority I could hold out. But I was committed and with my habitual confidence to do the best I could and risk the consequences, I started in my gun boat, taking another gunboat to accompany me, with a gentleman of noble family to guide and direct me as to how I was to gain access to Count Natali[4], whose house I found perched on the pinnacle of an abrupt rising little spot of an island, ancient, small and fortified after the manner of some past centuries and with two towers and turrets at the extremities, connected by the dwelling house in the centre; altogether a most romantic picturesque and warlike abode; which in old times, must have afforded safety and security against such attacks as in those times were much needed, especially on that coast. I was surprised at finding it thus formidable and took precautions accordingly before committing myself to his power; anchoring the gun boats in advantageous positions and when I landed, as a precaution against a nobleman who had most perseveringly kept back from declaring himself and whom it occurred to me might be delivering me up to the French, [to] make an advantageous understanding for himself. I have often, since, when thinking of those days, felt ashamed of myself for having entertained even for a moment any such suspicions, or rather possibilities, since I have known the honour, value and worth of that nobleman. But I had so much responsibility resting on my young and inexperienced head and had already taken so much on myself and run so many risks of being taken prisoner, that I could not but feel that I could not be too cautious with those of whom I knew so little and they foreigners; and when I perceived the fortified house and its strength it instinctively made me suspicious or at least cautious.

So, when I landed and was met, which I found that had been arranged by the count and found him there to receive me, I

---

[4] Count Giovanni de Natali.

cautioned the captain of the gunboat to keep a watchful look out on the house and as I understood I was to remain there for the night, to allow more time for our conference, to watch well in the early morning for any signal from me and [to] act accordingly. And if I should be detained against my will and made a signal, both gun boats were to open fire upon the house, without regard to my being in it and rescue me.

But of these precautions I did not however give the slightest cause to suspect; but entered the house with the count, who received me in the most courteous and cordial manner; yet I could not before our dinner nor indeed till the next morning, extort from him a single word which could implicate him or give us authority to reckon him as one of our active partisans, so cautious was he and so seriously did he look on the attempt, which I had embraced almost without hesitation, although without his possessions, I had *everything* of importance to myself at stake on the result.

We had a capital dinner and first rate wines, and at 9 o'clock, seeing he was not inclined to become more communicative I hinted that being fatigued I would like to retire. His quaint old butler, of the old style even of that day, in a very stately manner brought candles in, in two large massive candlesticks and preceded me to my bed chamber. I followed him, in some surprise through some narrow passages to the foot of an equally narrow stone spiral staircase and having ascended two flights without a word, we came to a small narrow *draw-bridge*, which was let down by someone in attendance and having passed it, entered on another flight of stairs of the same kind, which led us to a considerable sized room surrounded with gloomy looking, but I dare say, rich hanging tapestry, very thick and very gloomy. The bed which was in the centre hung with heavy dark green stuff, (or some such thing) curtains and large enough to hold a ½ dozen persons and with all the appearance of its being a state prison or room not often, certainly not recently occupied and with no fire. The attendant having ushered me in, made a most obsequious and formal bow, wished me good night and disappeared and immediately after I heard the clanking of the chains of the descending draw bridge by which I knew that I was at the top of the tower and if they had any reason, or chose it, their well and securely confined *prisoner*. I speak now only from my impressions *at the time*, but from after experience, found that I had no further ground of apprehension than the strange depressing impression of my novel position.

As there was much to arouse a kind of suspicion and apprehension of the consequences of my having placed myself in time of war in such a position, in the house of a gentleman of whom I knew nothing but by his repute and evidently from his conduct to myself, very reserved and uncertain as to what part he would embrace and having me so completely in his power, in case he should decide against me. I felt anything but easy and satisfied with myself; again the quaint old fashioned room and heavy arras[5] (of which I had read so much in olden times) the immense cold, even chilling to look at bed which I was to occupy apart from every living creature as far as I believed and no bell or means of alarm, all this depressed and made me very unfit for rest; and I resolved to sit up all night, really to *watch*, as on guard. But I was fatigued and drowsy and after a while began to find that sleep was mastering me and at last, having gone carefully round the room and examining the arras on both sides where I could, threw myself *on* my bed, not in it ('twas too uninviting) and, with my pistols and drawn sword at my head fell into a doze; but I was altogether so unnerved and restless that I got but little sleep and when I heard the sound of the morning gun from the gun boat, it was indeed reassuring and refreshing and I arose almost surprised that I had got over the night in safety. This was I doubt not, altogether the nervousness of over fatigue and constant excitement and anxiety and an older man, with more manly self-confidence and perhaps less superstition (for I confess the draw bridge and green curtains and the dark arras had not a little to do with the uneasiness of that night, which I have never forgotten) would have slept it out, but certainly not comfortably in that bed. I was visited early by the old butler and descended to a substantial breakfast which then never came amiss to me, the count doing the honours of his house in the best style of a well-bred man, but did not give the slightest indication from his countenance what had been the result of his night's reflection on the anxious subject I had come about, until breakfast was over, when to my great satisfaction, he

---

[5] A wall hanging made of tapestry in medieval times usually used to conceal an alcove.

expressed his resolution to embrace our cause and reinforce us with his dependants, who were I believe, like all the rest, a kind of serfs, of the old Venetian custom in those provinces, but really, as far as I could see a *contented* and well used and taken care of people.

I immediately gave the signal and we departed on our return fully assured of the value and sincerity of our new adherent. The capitano told me they had become uneasy at my long absence and the appearance of the place and had consulted more than once with the other capitano whether they ought not to demand my restitution; for we had been in nothing but unusual difficulties and warlike movements for so many weeks that such suspicions and watchfulness were not only natural but proper precautions. On our return to Gravosa we found all much in the same state, the *blockade* carried on even more anxiously and vigorously than before the sortie; and I was again assured that, as nothing could enter or leave the garrison and [that] they were in the greatest straits, the place must *surrender* in a *very short time*; but as I had had many such assurances before, I had [set] but little reliance on this.

Macdonald was still there, and as I had written no report of our late encounter and victory, I begged he would write an account. This I begged, as I really had no *leave* to be there, but on the contrary was under repeated threats of a court martial for the step; so I knew not on what terms to write and address to Colonel Robertson; who was then with General Nugent's (Austrian) Army in Italy[6]. Macdonald readily (as he had a kind of roving commission to be at Ragusa or where else he liked and saw his way to do some service) had no hesitation and wrote the despatch, which I was too busy to care much about, or even see and all was tranquil with me until Colonel Robertson's opinion and approval or non-approval should arrive. It was about 3 weeks before this occurred; and when it did I can say with the most thankful and joyful sincerity, it almost elevated me to ecstasy.

The colonel not only highly approved of my conduct, but in the face of the representations of Captain B[arbier] and evidently intended reference to his reports, published in *public orders* and had

---

[6] General Laval Nugent von Westmeath (1777–1862) was an Irishman by birth who served in the Austrian Army.

read by the Adjutant on parade, his 'high approval of Lieutenant Hildebrand's undertaking and conduct at Ragusa' and that although from the reports he had received from Captain B[arbier] there was no doubt, a somewhat of *irregularity* in the proceeding he could not bring himself to *censure* an active, enterprising and successful young officer and that therefore he expressed his 'high approbation of his zeal!!' and this he repeated when the order was read out to the regiment. Here was by very far, more than my reward. But it did not end there, [for] two days after, I received a despatch from the adjutant of a newly raised regiment, the Piedmontese Cacciatore, which was then at Parma in the Austrian Army under Count Nugent and of which Colonel R[obertson] was colonel, who had raised it, that Colonel R[obertson] has 'as he was authorised to appoint three captains to the said regiment, lately raised' he had appointed *me 3rd Captain* of it, and ordered me to join it under his command in Italy, immediately I was released from my duties at Ragusa! The adjutant wrote that he was to command and pay my company in the mean time. When I read this no one could imagine my astonishment and ecstasy; to be thus advanced, from the very junior subaltern of Colonel R[obertson]'s force, to be 3rd Captain of his regiment, with the *established* rank of that of all the other foreign corps, then so numerous and quite ranking with the British Army.

But, although I could not bring myself to believe this sudden and unexpected elevation, two or three days after I received letters of congratulation from Macdonald and two or three other officers of my regiment in the army under General Nugent. The thing appeared certain, beyond the slightest doubt. But so great was my astonishment and indeed inability to realise in my mind its certainty, that I wrote to Major Slessor, Lieutenant Colonel of the newly raised corps and who had acted with it in Italy and was then with Lord W[illiam] Bentinck, commander in chief at Malta, to ask his lordship whether I should be confirmed in the rank of 3rd Captain of the Corps. Soon after I received a letter from Lieutenant Colonel S[lessor] saying that he had, that morning, breakfasted with Lord W[illiam] B[entinck][7] and had put my question, the reply was 'Colonel R[obertson] had the appointment; and therefore there can

---

[7] Lieutenant General Lord William Bentinck was in command of the forces on Sicily.

be no doubt of its being confirmed. In fact tell Mr Hildebrand 'tis as certain as anything can be which has not actually taken place; the next Gazette will bring it out, so Mr Hildebrand can have no possible cause for doubt'. So, for the time being it ended and I only longed for the capture of Ragusa that I might join my regiment with the Austrian army of Italy, under such promising and flattering circumstances. But day after day and week after week [it] still tantalized me. Yet I could not leave Ragusa till all was over, of which we seemed as far off as ever.

Chapter 14

Ragusa Surrenders

The garrison of Ragusa were now desperate for relief. Even General Montrichard had publicly handed over his horses and watched them being slaughtered for their meat, but he was aware that things were only going to get worse.

Much to the evident chagrin of John, around the 13 January, the Austrian General Milutinovich[1] arrived with a force of two Austrian infantry regiments, to blockade the fortress, but strangely they brought no siege artillery with them. Milutinovich immediately took command of the situation and largely ignored the partisans who had maintained the blockade for the last few months. John was clearly appalled, as was Count Caboga and his men, but Milutinovich was playing a political game, ensuring that there would no opportunity for the Ragusans to take the fortress themselves and perhaps attempt to proclaim an independent state. This inevitably led to constant squabbles and bickering between these two forces, who both actually really wanted the same outcome.

Yet this was not all. Towards the end of the month, the braggart, Captain Hoste, seeing another opportunity to again see his name in lights, arrived off Ragusa with HMS *Bacchante* and *Saracen*[2] determined to take the fortress, just as he had done so successfully at Cattaro.

John remains completely silent as to the Royal Navy's contribution to the eventual surrender of Ragusa and he claims that Hoste merely sailed

---

[1] General Theodore Milutinovich (1766-1836) had been appointed commandant of Cattaro and Ragusa and sent with two regiments of Croats to capture them in the name of the Austrian Emperor.

[2] A brig of eighteen guns.

in to the bay to sign the terms of surrender at the very last moment. This would appear to be very unfair. However, sited on the opposite side of the fortress, it is quite possible that John genuinely had no idea what Hoste was actually doing on the other side of the fortress to bring the siege to an end.

Hoste made a full reconnaissance of Ragusa and its defences and then agreed at a meeting with Milutinovich, that the key to taking Ragusa was to take control of the hills on which Fort Napoleon stood and which dominated the city. The difficulties of moving artillery to the crest of these hills should not be underestimated, however Hoste found a novel way of achieving it without too much difficulty. He landed one of his main deck 18-pounders and two mortars brought from Cattaro and then moved them to where the aqueduct, which served water to the city from the hills above, ran. This channel of water running along a low-built aqueduct was actually covered with a roof of flat stone slabs, and Hoste had decided to trundle the guns up the steady incline of the aqueduct roof to the top of the hills. Using this novel trackway of only ten feet wide with a mercifully small drop on each side, they did however push the guns onto the hills above and to set them up in an area of dead ground out of the view of the guns of Fort Napoleon. The naval gunners continually manned this battery in the wet and cold of a Croatian January without any form of cover out of the elements.

At this point, Hoste records that Captain Macdonald arrived with about fifty men of the 35th Regiment. This can only mean that Macdonald had brought up the majority of Lowen's contingent to join Hoste on the eastern edge of Ragusa, whilst John Hildebrand remained with the partisans on the western side, hence John would have also been oblivious to these movements. It is also interesting to note that Hoste records that Macdonald had mentioned that the garrison had launched two sorties, in which Montrichard had taken the opportunity to bolster the garrison of Fort Napoleon. But it is also notable that Hoste claimed that Macdonald had also stated that the partisans had simply fled before the French; this is in direct contradiction to the evidence of John's eyewitness account and I suspect that Hoste's statement may well have been made to make his own contribution appear even more important to the eventual outcome. The two mortars began firing at Ragusa, all be it rather ineffectually, on 22 January, and only on the 26th did the far heavier

18-pounder finally make it to the gun position. Hoste was well aware that his cannon could now fire on the entire town with great accuracy, whilst the guns of the defenders could not elevate sufficiently to fire back.

On that day, Montrichard called a council of war to discuss surrendering, but his senior officers pointed out that no breach had yet been made and he was overruled. On the 27th, Hoste ordered some ranging shots which struck the area of the main square, serving as a warning to the city of just what exactly was about to descend upon them. The populace rioted and whether orchestrated by Montrichard or not, it certainly gave him the excuse to open negotiations and at 16.00 hours under a white flag he asked for a ceasefire whilst terms were agreed, which was accepted by the Austrian general.

In talks with Milutinovich and Hoste, Montrichard agreed to surrender, without the full honours of war, at midday on the 28th, with the French troops being immediately transported to Ancona. But Milutinovich had no intention of handing Ragusa over to the partisans, he was going to ensure that it was kept for the Emperor.

Warned that the Ragusans under Caboga planned to claim the city fortress as an independent state and concerned that the partisans might wreak terrible vengeance on the French garrison, a secret agreement was made with General Montrichard. The Austrian troops were actually allowed to enter the fortress surreptitiously during the night and only Hoste's party of Marines were formally admitted at noon the following day as a diversion. This trick prevented Caboga and his partisans from entering via the Porta Ploce until noon as arranged and when they did enter, they found the Austrian troops already firmly in possession and Caboga and his men were forced to retire again. It was over.

Hoste had also been worried during the negotiations, when his senior officer, Captain Edward Levenson-Gower arrived in HMS *Elizabeth*. Sent by Admiral Fremantle, specifically to prevent Hoste claiming such another victory to his name. But Leveson-Gower saw how the land lay and remained at anchor far away from Hoste, specifically so as not to supersede him and therby steal his thunder.

Hoste wrote to his father about the capture of Ragusa; 'After some fag and trouble we have succeeded in taking Ragusa … the fatigue and labour we have had has almost knocked me up, we have arrived here with a large sick list.'

John took his leave of Ragusa and the partisan bands only a few days later at most.[3] He was clearly upset, because he felt that his own contribution and that of the rebels had been completely ignored by the Austrians. His anger and sense of frustration and betrayal is still palpable even as he wrote about it all some seventy years later.

> We heard almost daily reports that an Austrian force was actually advancing from Venice under General Milutinovich, to take possession (by treaty with the Allied forces, on the final disruption of the Napoleon power) of all the fortresses on the eastern coast of the Adriatic and of course Ragusa amongst the rest. Therefore, we pushed on our blockade to try to anticipate this with renewed earnestness and nothing of the kind could be more effective. But no sign of surrender and at last, an advanced guard of Croats made its appearance before Ragusa, followed in a day or two by a large force of 2 or 3,000 men under General Milutinovich who summoned it to surrender, without regarding our so long established and effectual blockade and our hard-fighting force, as having anything to do with it; but the French general did not surrender, on the contrary, he appeared more determined than ever waiting for instructions from his Emperor; therefore the Austrians sat down regularly before the place, supplanting our pickets and in fact shoving us aside; to the great mortification and disappointment of myself, Count Caboga and all the other brave fellows who had attacked, and so long carried on the blockade, and which had these troops not come up no doubt *must* have very shortly ended in our success. Being more than usually mortified, and put out by this unexpected interruption of my own individual expected glory and success, it occurred to me to endeavour to take Fort Napoleon by assault and that I would undertake it if General Milutinovich who was now really chief in command would encourage and aid my attempt.
>
> I did not *then* perceive, nor had I an idea that this was exactly what he would have desired should not take place. Long afterwards

---

[3] Although John himself states that he remained there until early March, he was already receiving mail from Ragusa in late February which clearly indicates that he had already written to them previously on 4 February. This shows that he must have left before this earlier date; it is, therefore, my belief that he left almost immediately after Ragusa fell at the end of January.

I could see how raw and crude my ideas and speculations were; that it was the general's interest and evident desire not to terminate the siege by allowing a surrender to the undisciplined Ragusians, nor to risk a single life to expedite matters, which *he* knew, but of which I had no idea at the time, must be *shortly* settled in consequence of the treaty of the Allies by a quiet surrender of the place to himself.

At the time I had no suspicion of this, and only wanted to acquire some credit and repute by taking Fort Napoleon as soon as possible.

So I went to General Milutinovich and earnestly urged on him the probability of my succeeding in seizing this stronghold, if he would only give me a moderate support and aid from his troops.

He treated me in the kindest and most considerate manner no doubt in consideration of the active part I had so long taken in the blockade (great and proud, as I afterwards learned, as was his repute and position in the Austrian Army) and after much argument and urgent persuasion we separated, as I thought, perfectly and satisfactorily; he was to give me the support I required, and would send a captain of engineers to arrange the proceedings, of time and manner of attack.

The captain met me and we arranged that I should take 15 soldiers with me and assault with earnestness, a determined and *real* attack, the front of Fort Napoleon, facing the fortress and that he should *send round* (for my post was nearest at hand) two other pickets to points I pointed out, of resolute men, whom I urged he should accompany, make false or real assaults as circumstances might decide in support. And it was fixed that we were all to start for our several posts at the foot of Fort Napoleon that evening, each according to the then fixed time and that there all should await in the utmost stillness the firing of a rocket as a signal when the attack was to be made, which signal he was to see to and make provision for. Macdonald, as was his wont when anything enterprising was intended, was with us that night in the great room which was full of our irregulars, all anxious to aid in, as far as they were allowed and could, the attempt. Among the rest there was the captain and a lieutenant of Austrian engineers, who were to direct the proceedings, but evidently (I now have no doubt, seeing how *unnecessary* the risk was for their ultimate object) with no heart in the matter; so much so that Macdonald, always penetrating and plain spoken and whose courage was not to be questioned, said to me 'Hildebrand, I see plainly these fellows do not intend fighting tonight, I will go back, so good night'.

However, I was not quite ready to give up my expected success, and its consequent honours, of our taking Fort N[apoleon] by assault that night and therefore I remained awaiting patiently the hour of the departure of the Croats, as arranged to their respective points of attack and at the appointed time I moved off with my small band of rank and file, two sergeants and 1 corporal, with a bugler, and as the distance was short, soon found myself at the door of the sally port which had been the means of [getting] in and egress, till the blockade had put an entire end of it; by the side of which, by the help of ladders and climbing, we hoped to surprise and overpower the garrison. But I *now* think it was a very *doubtful* enterprise and had we failed, must have ended disastrously. But as there were two other points of assault, where not having had a hint of any change of arrangement, I then felt no doubt the attack would be made simultaneously with ourselves, I felt no great apprehension and we ensconced ourselves as closely as we could under the foot of the wall, in the extreme darkness.

There we remained, for the distance around the base was too great and the path too intricate and rough, to allow of any intercourse with the others without great risk of discovery, for some time listening for and momentarily expecting the signal of attack from the other side. But half hour passed after half hour without anything of the kind and not a sound was heard of a movement in any direction, until the day began to dawn, when we were soon discerned by the enemy who were drawn up under the rampart walls and an immediate pop, pop firing commenced at us. My sergeant then came to me to know what they were to do, which I could, on seeing how we were situated, only answer by directing an immediate retreat, by *running* down the hill in single file as hard as we could, in which being all young and active fellows we completely succeeded [doing] in safety and within a few minutes were at the door of our post in no little rage and disappointment at the shabby and we could not but think treacherous way our allies (who had, if they even started, which I doubt, returned almost immediately and had been all night ensconced in the house, in safety and sleep, leaving us to our fate, without a hint or warning of their abandonment of the enterprise). I could not describe the indignation and contempt I felt at such cowardly treatment and with the impetuosity too natural to me, hastened forthwith to the Austrian general's quarters and had an immediate interview with him, when forgetting my subordinate rank and but little impressed with respect for what I had hitherto seen of the Croat troops, I gave vent to my irritated feelings at such conduct, in no very measured terms.

The fine old General Milutinovich instead of calling me to order as he might, made more than due allowance for my disappointed and irritated feelings and no doubt, also seeing the justice and reasonableness of the cause and attributing it to some mistake, spoke kindly and soothingly to me, and standing opposite to me, advised me to be pacified and, with the action usual with foreign nations, placing his hands at the top buttons of the two rows of my uniform light infantry jacket, stroked each side down to the bottom as if marking each as a step, saying at the same time, I 'should be covered with orders' for my conduct. I confess that, having seen the profuseness with which his Croat troops had been be-plastered, compared with what I saw and could imagine from them, I would not at the time, have cared a farthing for a bushel of such orders and therefore did not answer very gratefully. It must be remembered that up to that time and for years after it, *no medal* was worn by a British soldier who, with pardonable vanity and pride, we thought both in courage and exploits infinitely their superiors, and although entertaining the highest admiration and respect for the distinguished general himself, I left him rather abruptly and not at all reconciled to the treatment I had received and could never afterwards bring myself to look on his troops more favourably or with common patience.

But it could not be helped and my hope of glory and success by taking Fort Napoleon fell to the ground. I would gladly have left Gravosa then and there, but for the persuasion of Count C[aboga] and his party. Indeed, as the blockade had not yet been *raised*, although we were shoved aside from the higher place, I did not see how I *could* leave until Ragusa surrendered to the Austrians, which it appeared evident must now be the result. Therefore, I waited to see the end, which soon came. The French general in command would not of course, now that their power was superseded, capitulate to the Ragusian *rebels*, as he called them (strictly and correctly enough) but chose Captain Hoste the distinguished commodore of the station and who had been exerting all his energies during the whole time we had been occupied in the blockade (and astonished all at the things he had achieved at Bocca de Catarro) to whom to surrender and who accordingly accepted it, perhaps previously arranged and settled the arrangements of the evacuation. This was all Captain H[oste] had to do with the capture of *Ragusa*; he never landed there during the whole course of the blockade, nor fired a gun against it. No doubt *he* had good and weighty reasons for not interfering with the attempt and could see as *I* could not even suspect the course events were taking to render all such enterprises both useless and perhaps embroiling, with a view to a final European settlement. I knew nothing of such matters and therefore was groping my way uselessly in darkness.

In the mean time General Milutinovich proceeded onward to Catarro and the south and General Miloradovich[4], also a distinguished chief, succeeded him with us. In fact, all was now in a way of immediate surrender and settlement between Austria and the allies with regard to Ragusa. A treaty of surrender was signed, I do not know whether Captain Hoste was a party to it excepting as a representative, as the British government consenting as an ally, but it was communicated to me by General Miloradovich that the town and fortress of Ragusa were to be delivered up to him the next morning and offering *me* the honour, as I had had so much to do with it, in preference to his own troops to command the party which was to take possession of Fort Napoleon the next morning; and accompanying the communication with, courteously inviting me to dine with him that day and to meet the French general to whom I had been so long a thorn and a nuisance.

At dinner all went on amicably and kindly, as far as in a party so composed could have been expected; but I perceived the French general fixed his face steadfastly on me during the whole time of dinner, with a peculiar and I thought malignant meaning; so much as to a certain degree to disconcert and annoy me; but I of course, took no notice of it, yet after dinner the stare was resumed and at length the French general (I cannot bring to my recollection his name

---

[4] It has proven impossible to identify this Austrian officer with any certainty.

although he was an old and distinguished officer) with a remarkable significance addressed me 'Are you, Sir, the young gentleman I was so nearly catching when you were so diligently inspecting my works lately? How you escaped I cannot for my life imagine, nor can anyone else. You had an *escape*, Sir, indeed *from being hanged*'. I was so nettled at the expression that I answered warmly 'General, what do you mean? My escape was indeed wonderful from being taken prisoner, but what do you mean by my being hanged?' I shall never forget the determined and emphatic malignity of his countenance when he replied 'Sir, if I had taken you, you would not have been alive five minutes: my provost marshal would have had you dangling by the neck over that fort', pointing to Fort Napoleon, 'in less than that time'. I was still more irritated and replied 'hang me! A British officer! You dare not'.

To cut the matter short he replied 'You were a *spy* within my lines in disguise and (with double emphasis) if I had caught you I would hanged you as a spy, in five minutes, nothing could have saved you'. I confess that in a moment I was struck dumb and confounded. I had *unconsciously* placed myself in the position and acted as he said, I being within his lines in a shooting jacket instead of my uniform i.e. in disguise, making inspection and observations of his fort and in one moment, the story of Major Andre's execution under similar circumstances in the American War[5], occurred to me with overwhelming conviction to my mind. The general perceived it and repeated over and over again the certainty of my fate had I not, he knew not how *escaped*, at a moment when all considered me as inevitably in their hands. Even at this distance of time the sudden impression this discovery and its unavoidable consequences, makes such an impression and strikes such horror at my heart, that I never will allow myself to think of it but for a moment; and *never* if I can get rid of the thought.

There is not the slightest doubt that, but for a wonderful interposition of providence, I must have at once come to an ignominious and dreadful end. Had that peasant who saw me in the bush but who turned his head purposely aside to avoid the

---

[5] Major John André was a British officer who had been hanged by the Americans as a spy during the War of Independence.

observation of those on the ramparts acted as 10,000 would have done under like circumstances, my fate was then and there sealed, although, at the time, I had no idea that anything worse than a French prison for a while would have been my fate. I cannot dwell on the circumstances without intense pain and a feeling of sinking of my heart *even now*. So certain and so dreadful and disgraceful must have been my lot, but for God's Mercy!! Had I had the slightest suspicion of it, when I was lying under the myrtle bush, I should not have hesitated a moment as I did, as to whether or not when my expected captors would have come up to seize me, I should have discharged my two barrels at them immediately. My fate then would have been infinitely preferable to what would have occurred had I been taken alive.

The next morning (I lost the exact date with many others; and *letters* which would now be of great service to me if I had them in France on a subsequent active and bustling campaign 1815, which places me now in no little difficulty to recollect and mention what I would relate). The next morning, I, as had been arranged by the two generals, took my little band to join and *lead* the force destined to receive over Fort Napoleon from the French to the Austrian forces and into which fort I marched, at the *head*, as the post of honour, I must confess with a disappointed and mortified heart, after all I had risked and done with the confident hope of a very different result and with anything but a feeling of exultation or gratified ambition.

But I must not dwell on this any longer in pity on the patience of any one, if there be ever anyone having had [the] patience to read my narrative thus far, lengthened out as it has been in spite of myself to so great an extent and so much about myself. I shall merely say, in *conclusion* of this blockade of Ragusa, that as I had been requested and had promised, I immediately the fact was accomplished and the men dismissed, waited on General Milutinovich to take respectful leave, but to my *relief*, did not find him at his quarters and in no little dudgeon at the necessity of quitting the scene of so many labours and risks in such a way, left my card &c to be delivered to the general on his return and hastened down to the port, thus having in boyish pet [petulance] lost my chance of the (Austrian) medal, with all speed [I] embarked in one of my gunboats and in less than an hour, was well out of port and at sea, with Gravosa behind me. Now, it may seem very strange that I have not retained the exact date at least of my landing at Ragusa Vecchia in November 1813 and my leaving Gravosa in February 1814, but for the reason given above, they were lost to me in France in 1815.

But from some letters I *still have* from the Marchese Pietro di Bona, Count Natali and the Presidente Questiche of Lagosta, I can gather that the former must have been towards the very end of November and the latter about the 5th or 6th March[6]. I have a letter from Presidente Questiche addressed to me, as Commandante of Lagosta *at Lissa*, dated 14th February, giving me a report of the proceedings at Lagosta to that date. But I would not think any such things worth the time to write or anyone to read them[7], only that in a somewhat extraordinary narrative of so many exciting transactions crowded so quickly in succession together, I think the greatest accuracy as to dates in my power, is due to my own credit in recording them. And such things as the blockade, the sortie and repulse from and capture of Ragusa can be easily tested, if thought worth the trouble, and *verified*. Such things even in the absence of official notice of them can *never* be lost to the mind and recollection of the inhabitants of Ragusa who may, as no doubt some do, survive at present, especially in the families of Count Caboga and Marchese de Bona who was wounded so severely and Count Natali, who struggled nobly for the recovery of their independence.

---

[6] As explained previously, John must have only remained in Ragusa until late January as it is clear he was writing to Ragusa on 6 February.

[7] He is wrong; they are important in establishing his memoirs as a faithful record and they are reproduced in the following chapter.

Chapter 15

Italy 1814

John sailed past Lagosta directly for Lissa, where he met Captain Barbier in a more amenable frame of mind, having received commendatory replies from Colonel Robertson. Here John received mail including orders repeating those for him to sail on to Italy to join Colonel Robertson and his troops who were then cooperating with General Nugent's Austrian army as it advanced across Northern Italy. Although some of his correspondents seem to indicate that they believed that it was more of a jaunt, to see the sights of Venice. Perhaps both were true.

John sailed up the coast towards Venice via Zara and Trieste. He was apparently keen to join Robertson to claim his captaincy in the Piedmontese Cacciatori but news eventually arrived that the unit would pass into the army of the King of Sardinia and his position was therefore null and void unless he also switched his allegiance, this he declined to do.

Robertson, with the two companies of the 35th, with detachments of De Roll's Regiment and his fledgling regiment of Cacciatori continued to serve with General Nugent's army after Trieste fell and they marched with them through Ferrara, Reggio and Parma, eventually meeting with Lord William Bentinck's force to take Genoa on 22 April 1814.

A general peace was looking ever more likely in early April but was not certain yet and John moved on to Padua in chase of Nugent's army. But John whilst there received further orders via Captain Barbier, to return to his regiment which was then ordered to aid in the capture of Corfu before peace was officially declared. He eventually decided to obey his orders and to return, thereby retaining his commission in the 35th, his position in the Piedmontese Cacciatori never having been formally ratified.

Corfu held out, but with Napoleon's abdication signed on 13 April, the new French government ordered the French General Donzelot who commanded at Corfu, to hand the island over to the British, which he did on 24 June 1814.

The war was finally over.

John and the rest of the battalion could now look forward to a period of rest and recuperation, whilst forming the garrison of the beautiful Island of Corfu.

> I passed Lagosta in my gun boat much, as I was interested in it and longed to land there once more and made in my anxiety to go straight for Lissa, where my instructions, to repair to Colonel Robertson in Italy were lying for me and not to lose a day more.
>
> Here I *found* my order to repair to Colonel R[obertson] with the Allied army under General Count Nugent, then at Parma, but, if I found it had removed, to follow and join him wherever he was with the utmost despatch. I therefore took leave of my friend Captain Barbier whose dignity I found had softened down and whose demeanour was something more than respectful, and without disembarking, continued on my passage up the Adriatic in my gun boat.

It would seem that John's stop at Lissa may have been of a few day's duration rather than hours, as witnessed by letters then sent to him.

> Lagosta, 8 February 1814
> Sir,
> The bearer of this will bring to you the four [collonati?] For the purposes named by you in your dispatch. He is the captain of the vessel sent for the transport of your baggage. Receive signor commandant the assurances of my esteem. Your obedient servant, Questiche president of the council.

> Lagosta, 8 February 1814
> Most Noble Commandant,
> I expected your letters from Ragusa & I see they come from Lagosta, you cannot imagine with what grief I hear of your proposed cruise with the Italian fleet, not that I wish to oppose myself to you, but that it removes from me many most valued

occasions of embracing you. My dear commandant, believe as much as I express in these letters which I wish could sufficiently convey to you my feelings of deep gratitude for your goodness & friendship to me. I was convinced that your mediation on behalf of my brother has not had the desired effect. I beg you most warmly to write in his favour as you propose doing in your letter. I am not of the opinion that he would have shown himself attached to the infamous French government. I know & can assure everyone quite the contrary, but necessity forced him to take some steps which may have roused the suspicions of government. I beg you to mention this statement, which is reliable, in your letters to your friends. I have already sent you another letter to Ragusa & one to my brother who has returned from Zara, as I had no means of ascertaining the determinations of your superiors as regards yourself. Dear commandant, take care of yourself & write to me from Italy that I may know your movements, in the meantime I shall not omit to remember you in my poor prayers for your most worthy & to me beloved person. With these sentiments united to the highest respect & esteem, I have the honour to subscribe myself unalterably your obedient servant & affectionate friend Nicolo Perichi.

Guippana[1] February 1814[2]
My friend,

If you think the conduct of some of those at Ragusa strange, what can I say when I am a Ragusan! My nation armed itself for its independence. The Ragusans made war so to speak on their brethren in order to escape the French yoke. Our brave paesani as you yourself testify have supplied the want of cannon with courage; & their constancy has kept them to the siege of Ragusa without rations, & without pay. Besides we have suffered all the inconveniences that attend an undisciplined movement. The aim of the whole nation was one; war on the French government, for its own liberty, they desired no more. Our citizens of Ragusa united

---

[1] The Island of Sipan in Croatia was also known in Latin as Gypana, meaning 'Island of the eagles'.

[2] Undated except 'February', but clearly sent early that month before his excursion into Italy was known to have happened.

themselves to the besiegers, imprisoned the French garrison, unfurled the national flag & placed at their head some of the old aristocracy. To avert the excess of vengeance & the disorder that would ensue, they did not wish to admit any armed paesani within the walls. The principal persons in Ragusa hastened to communicate these events to the Austrian general, rightly trusting to receive protection & help in restoring our ancient & legitimate government. There was no need to fear those armies which are so glorious, because they make war against a system of oppression & usurpation. This was our common hope, this the resolve of the whole nation. My dear Hildebrand, with dismay we have seen ourselves deluded. Others have reaped the fruit of our labour & in the treaty we see again reigning the abhorred French system. General Milutinovich has changed the officials in the different posts. He shows himself the friend of the nobility, but the weight of the civil law still exists. Do not think however that I have ceased to hope, our cause will be decided for peace, hundreds of events may occur which may be favourable to it, besides it is in itself too just & the state of Ragusa too small. Now that I have spoken to you of the Ragusians in general, let me tell you of my particular interests. For doing my duty as Governor of Ragusa, in maintaining the independence of the island against various attacks direct & indirect, I think the authorities bear me little goodwill. If my position as governor be restored, I am indifferent to it, but if not, it might do me harm in the future. In either case I have the satisfaction of having preferred duty to interest & I trust to merit the approbation of the governor I have the honour of serving under, whoever he may be. If you are still at Lissa you will perhaps know that I have made my report to the governor there & asked for instructions from here. The reports however are trifling. The English are not precise in these matters, so I have suppressed a detailed account of the general's speech & the conduct of the Commissary General! My situation is at present not a little curious. I have written to Captain Hall[3] & to Captain Harper[4] at Lissa & have not yet received a reply. I do not

---

[3] I have not been able to identify this officer as either an army or naval captain with any certainty.

[4] Captain John Harper RN commanded HMS *Saracen* of eighteen guns.

know to whom to apply directly, nor where to turn. I thought that my former position, together with your recommendation would have procured for me, in preference to others, an honourable & lucrative position in Ragusa, the latter of which conditions, my dear friend I much need as my fortune has been much diminished since the arrival of the French at Ragusa. As to the probable continuance of my position I have spoken to you above. You wished me to write to you. Here is a long letter 'en reverges' I shall expect an answer. Write to me when you leave for Italy & I shall hope to see you again at Ragusa. If you had delayed to set out, you would have found some amusement at Ragusa Vecchia, but if you are already in Italy, the carnival will have afforded you some gaiety, my family desire to be remembered to you. Believe me, sincerely your friend,

Girolamo Comte di Natale.

I have heard from Ragusa that the civil law has been abolished & the national code put in force, this gives me much pleasure & I look upon it as the beginning of a happy future.

Anything more delightful than that passage (barring the confined and close accommodation, for the weather had become rather warm) I cannot imagine. To turn out at gun fire in the morning with the splendid sun rising in that clear atmosphere and with the feeling of having just escaped from such [a] long and most anxious service to perfect liberty and with the near prospect of joining my regiment and that on active service too, on a large scale was delightful.

We got on slowly in that heavy boat, but at last came to Zara[5], having passed innumerable beautiful islands and there, on landing, a perfect stranger, not knowing whither to go, for hotels such as are now to be found there and everywhere on that coast and elsewhere, were unknown in those days (long before steam packets &c) I was fortunate enough to be addressed by a nobleman then walking with his wife on the pier, who seeing I was at a loss, offered me most politely to be of what [ever] service he could in directing me. And he was indeed of great assistance and hospitality to me, for the 2 days I remained there and I have mentioned this circumstance chiefly to

[5] The City of Zara was in Dalmatia and is now known as Zadar.

exemplify what I had before observed, that such acts of kindness often meet with a very early and unexpected return when there seemed no chance of it.

We took leave of each other the next morning, on my re-embarking and I proceeded to Fiume[6] and Trieste and here, on landing, I had a letter from the nobleman from whom I had so recently parted, sent there by despatch, no such posts then as we now have long had, informing me that he had just heard of the death of a near relative in Sicily, by which a large and scattered property descended to him, which required his immediate and personal presence and begging me to get him a passage if possible, in some ship of war to that station. I have said [that] there were no packets, nor regular communication between countries so situated. And it happened that at that very time there was a brig of war at Trieste, whose captain I was acquainted with and by whose kindness my friend got the passage he wished, for which I long after, received his thanks.

At Zara I met with Major Slessor, our second in command from the first, at Lissa and who had accompanied Admiral Fremantle's and Colonel Robertson's expedition from Lissa taking Zara, Fiume, Pola[7], Trieste &c all along the eastern coast of the Adriatic up to Venice and as 2nd in command of the British contingent to the Austrian Army, then carrying on very active service under General Count Nugent, gaining fame which kept increasing and continuing to promise to do so for some time to come, and to join which I was then on my way. When all at once I received another gunboat despatch from my old torment Captain Barbier, informing me that I was not to proceed further towards Italy, but turn about at once and make the best of my way back to Lissa and thence to Corfu to join our forces there to take hasty possession of it, as peace had been agreed on between France and the Allies; that the war was at an end!!

This unexpected and to me *disastrous*, news, as cutting short my career then at its height of promise in the army, astounded and grieved me beyond measure. But being now with the leave of and in fact in company with Major S[lessor] who encouraged me to accompany him up the Gulf of Venice whither he was bound on his

---

[6] Fiume is in Croatia, it is now known as Rijeka.
[7] Pola is a province of Croatia.

way, then just opened out over land[8] to England and, worse than all, my promotion to the 3rd Captaincy in the Piedmontese Cacciatori, destroyed by the handing over, with all its arms &c &c the regiment by treaty to the King of Sardinia, to whose service I was determined not to accompany it. So I decided on seizing the first opportunity which offered, to return to England to look after my promotion, or make such arrangements as I best could for leaving the service with advantage; all my military prospects seemed utterly gone and no possibility of seeing more active service to prop up my claim; in this however strange and unexpected circumstances ordered it otherwise. The Battle of Waterloo, with all its glories, the storming of Cambrai, taking of Peronne &c &c and the capture of Paris, were still before me and that at a very short distance; plenty of service for one more year.

I will not enter on anything not referring to my own narrative, but leaving Fiume and Pola &c, [I] proceeded at once to Venice, then being rapidly filled with Austrian troops and reporting myself to the brigade major, who received me with great distinction, as Commandante of Lagosta and having served so actively in the capture of Ragusa, and with the attention paid then to all British officers, was supplied by billet with an order on the Palazzo of a Principessa in Piazza St Mark at which, on my presenting myself billet in hand, (to which all persons on the continent or at that time at war were well accustomed and never thought of resisting or objecting to) was received by a very smart footman, or I believe major domo, who informed me that the Principessa could not admit me to the part of the palazzo she occupied, but had given him orders to separate off a sufficiently convenient wing of it and that he would see that all my wants, meals &c should be met satisfactorily. This I did not consider very civil, but I heard afterwards that the lady, whom I never saw, was in deep grief and indignation at the

---

[8] If John's recollections are correct regarding meeting Major Slessor at Zara whilst on his way to England, this clearly had to happen at a later date as we know that Major Slessor was at Zara between 6 and 10 April, Fiume 12-14 April and Trieste 14-21 April 1814 at the beginning of his journey to England across Central Europe. Reference *The Backbone* by Alethea Hayter, pp. 270. We also know that John was at Chioggia that same day. It therefore seems more likely that if they did meet, that they met at Trieste or Venice where they crossed as John returned from Italy to Corfu.

evacuation of the French (a superior officer of which service she was much attached to) and the succession of the *hated* Austrians, for such they were at that period at Venice and at all its former Provinzia and at many other ceded places; I remained in the house however, with every accommodation and attention from the servants for ten days until I left Venice; but must confess the lady had so far relented that she invited me more than once to wait on her; which I took no advantage of; for all my thoughts and affections were then fixed uninterruptedly on war and warlike movements and I was anxious, having satisfied my curiosity at such an eventful and stirring time at Venice, anxious to be off to Italy.

I must mention a characteristic anecdote before I conclude with Venice. I was lying one morning very early, in the splendid bed room allotted to me, thinking about rising and my day's work, or rather the pleasures of the day, when my door was suddenly *burst* open rather than opened, by two [rotund?] looking men in scholastic or collegiate long gowns, wigs and cocked hats with a long folded up scroll of paper in the hand of the foremost, who began abruptly after some unintelligible and hasty apology for their early visit, to read it at my bed side, with all due form emphasis and respect. It consisted of many pages of fulsome flattery to the Officiali Englese, which before he got to the end drove me out of patience. I drove them in quick time out of the room. I had until a few years ago by some accidental mixture with other papers, more fortunate in their fate than others of greater interest, this very poem in my possession, an unintentional memento of former days and too contemptible to be preserved carefully.

There is no doubt that John continued to receive letters in Italy from his recent friends in Ragusa, keeping him up to date with events there, as well as from Lagosta, which he still retained the command of. But what is very clear from these letters, is the esteem with which he was held by all.

Ragusa, 27 February 1814
Dear Friend,
Scarcely an opportunity has presented itself for me to reply to yours of the 4th instant which I received six days ago. My dear Hildebrand I am very grateful to you for the remembrance you have of the

esteem & affection I have always professed for you. My family who respected you when they had the honour of knowing, have through unavoidable circumstances not been able to show their attachment to you, but when you return to Ragusa, as I hope you will, I beg that you will use my house as your own, being assured that all of us are greatly desirous to see you there. As to politics, on looking around my country I am still in a state of uncertainty, but from the accounts which we receive I trust our hopes of our old governor being restored to us are not without foundation. My dear friend, who then will be happier, than I & my family? Caboga has been made head of the Commissary department, all the others in our company have been appointed except Giovanni & some of my family. Although we have sought for one, they have not been offered any appointment. In order to merit the laurel crown it was necessary to act from unworthy motives; to deceive everyone & only to consider one's own interest.

If Europe has been freed from the French, it does not follow that the rule of honourable men will return. The vice of self-interest naturally reigns in the heart of man & the wretches who have become rich by the operations of the good will continue to triumph & be distinguished. The man of honour can only hope to receive the reward of his actions in heaven. I am now quite well, some days ago I felt a pain in my chest, but now I am quite as I was. I hope soon to have news of you & ask you to tell me of Macdonald, to whom I send most sincere regards. Adieu my dear friend, believe me, your most affectionate friend,
Marchese Pietro di Bona.

Ragusa 23 March 1814
My dear Hildebrand,
You cannot believe with what pleasure I received your letter of the 12th current from Lissa. I wish to send you a reply by the first opportunity that presents itself. Macdonald is then no longer with you! I hope that you will go to rejoin him as you wished. At the same time I am very sorry that you are going still farther from me. I have heard of your fame, but I recommend you dear friend, nevermore to take part in such operations, which only tend to deceive an innocent nation. You yourself wished me to speak to you with my usual sincerity. I have read your letter to Pietro, to which he says he has already replied, but not being on this occasion dated from Lissa, he

sent it to Ladestanos[9]. It may perhaps therefore be lost. He does not write now to you, as the continual discussions have again wearied him & he is not well. Do you wish to hear what has happened at Ragusa since your departure? Caboga has been appointed head of the commissariat. The administration is pro tem under the French system, the civil law of Ragusa has been put in force for the time being. The original code continues to be that of France, we hope only for a time. Some of those in office have been superseded. Those commissioned & the clergy, have taken the oath of fealty & obedience to the Emperor of Austria, King of Dalmatia & of Cattaro. A few days ago General Milutinovich passed here with our troops to take possession of Cattaro[10], but was compelled to retreat to the frontier by a Russian colonel who met him[11]. This colonel is for the present governor of that province.

We believe that steps are being taken for the reestablishment of our republic. A month ago a Russian courier brought letters from the Duke of Montenegro & from some members of our old council resident at Constantinople addressed to the President & Council of the Republic of Ragusa. Not finding these authorities however, he took back the letters & we are ignorant of their contents.

My father has presented a memorial to the Emperor of Austria, in which he has represented the burden of the nation, our taxes, the promises made by the allied powers & has not scrupled to censure the conduct of the Austrian & British commanders at the siege of Ragusa. The minister has entered into correspondence with him. Why does England not take up our cause? I become more confused daily concerning our prospects. My mother, my sister, all my brothers, the Count & Countess of Carmagna thank you for your kind remembrances, they ask you to let them hear frequently of you & I beg you to write continually to your devoted friend,
Franco Marchese di Bona.

---

[9] Greek for Lagosta.

[10] Cattaro had surrendered to Captain Hoste in January, who had handed it over to local partisans as there were no elements of the Austrian Army in the vicinity. Milutinovich was now moving to reclaim it for Austria.

[11] The city of Cattaro lies in Monetenegro and the Russians were unhappy for Multinovich to cross the border to retake it for Austria. However, it was given back to Austria at the Congress of Vienna.

Island of Mezzo,[12] 27 March 1814

My dear friend,

I am very grateful for the esteem which you profess for me. Friendship has incited you to do more for me than I could have ventured to ask. You should receive a long letter, had I not much to write concerning your councils & the time is short. I have already made my report to the admiral, but it was addressed to the Cavaliere [Grigomane?], I now make a copy of it, which I beg you to translate into English, for which reason I leave it open. May I ask you to send the other to the admiral? I ought again to repeat my thanks & ask you to excuse this request, but you are a generous & sincere Englishman & you know that I would do all in my power for you when occasion offered, therefore I desist. The news you have sent grieves me much, if you have better, write to me of your charity! I hope my dear Hildebrand, that you will remain our governor & I flatter myself that I shall be able to show Perichi how useful your recommendation will be to him, my brother also will do all in his power. Enjoy yourself in Italy & remember your friend.

Comte de Natali

Ragusa 30 March 1814

My friend,

I hope that you will read this token of my affection at Lissa. Write to me I beg of you before you leave, telling me exactly when you set out & for what place.

I thank you for the pains you have taken to procure me the handkerchiefs. Until now I did not know their value, had I done so assure yourself, that notwithstanding all our friendship, I should not have ventured so far to inconvenience you. They remain an abundant proof of the affection existing between us. My family charge me with a thousand messages & thank you for your kind remembrances of them. The news which you give me is almost the same as that which we received from General Milutinovich. Every day fresh regiments of Croats arrive from the siege of Catarro, but it is said that two Russian officers will soon come from headquarters, to settle the affair between Vladimir & the Austrian general. My dear

[12] Known today as Lopud.

Hildebrand nothing remains for me but to beg you to write &
continue your friendship to me, your friend from the heart,
Pietro di Bona Marchese

I then bethought myself of being really, off to the army in Italy,
without delay and engaged a boat to transfer me from Venice up the
Trenta[13] to Chioggia[14], the nearest landing place to Padua, where
(about 7 or 8 miles' journey) as soon as I could after reaching it, I
reported myself at the fort major's office as a British officer on his
march to join General Nugent's Army and left my card for His Royal
Highness as a mark of respect. Within ½ an hour I had an invitation
to dine that day with the Viceroy the Prince Hesse Homburg[15] and I
believe a brother of the then Emperor of Austria in these words and
written on a scrap of paper not much better than cartridge paper,
the consequence I suppose of the freedom from ceremony in
wartimes, the original of which I have now before me:

Padua 6 April 1814
His Highness Prince Hesse leaves his invite to his dinner table.
Lieutenant Hildebrand Captain of the English troops.
De Rivolance, Captain Adjutant of the palace[16]

I went dressed in the best I then had; a tolerably decent light infantry
jacket, with the advantage of a pair of the then usual epaulettes, at
the hour appointed and was not long left in the neglect I expected at
so grand a dinner of high personages. On the contrary, the prince
immediately I made my appearance, approached and took my arm
with the princely condescension and frankness and the
condescending freedom of a soldier, so that I was at once at ease.
The prince walked up and down the long anteroom for I should

---

[13] He actually means across the Veneta Lagoon.
[14] Hildebrand consistently spells it Pioggio, but from his description of its location,
it is definitely Chioggia.
[15] I believe that Hildebrand has confused two people here. He actually means
Friedrich Joseph Ludwig Carl August of Hessen Homburg (1769-1829), who was
an Austrian general and became Landgrave of Hesse Homburg in 1820. But the
Viceroy of Lombardy-Venetia was actually Prince Heinrich XV of Reuss-Plauen.
[16] The original of this is not in the archival records.

think at least an hour before dinner was announced, having me still on his arm and of course talking of the eventful military transactions and speculations of the day, the then absorbing subject of every conversation and anxiety and the more so when one mixed however accidentally in the interested and higher circles; even I, a boy almost and a mere subaltern in the British Army, was worthy of the notice and friendly conference with the prince viceroy, who to my utter surprise (unaccountable but for the uniform I wore and the excitement of the period) placed me in the seat on his right hand, at the dinner table, with the only lady present on his left; and such an elegant, accomplished lady I have seldom before or since met, who was perfect master of several languages and to my astonishment, after her having said she had never been in England, I found spoke English not only fluently, but elegantly in pronunciation and every way.

There were at that table several noblemen and gentlemen of high rank in diplomatic positions (I think 14 from various and many of them distant countries, congregated) at that court under the pressure and anxieties of that eventful time and the conversation was carried on in no less than so many different languages. Behind each chair was an attendant dressed like a field officer in all appearance. Altogether, an imposing and grand introduction to one of my age and grade. The prince was most attentive and condescending to me, said very many civil things in an encouraging way and amongst others, he remarked my familiarity with foreign languages, in some of which I was sufficiently conversant to carry on conversation tolerably well; and at last he asked me 'can you speak German?' and on my reply that I could not, he said with some emphasis, 'then learn it directly, it is the language of a soldier'.

On such an occasion, I was too much flattered and pleased not to take in and cherish the advice and accordingly, at the earliest opportunity that offered itself I did not fail to profit by it; until stirring events in another quarter diverted my duties, studies and endeavours to other pursuits; and therefore, although I eagerly *began* and vigorously, it brought forth no available fruit and I never did learn German, so as to be useful and as I had made up my mind and intended. The next morning just as starting for Parma, I was (most disagreeably, at that particular time) stopped by the diligent perseverance of the capitano of one of my gunboats, for which I must say, in my temper, I neither admired nor was grateful for as I ought, which capitano had traced me up the Adriatic to Chioggia and thence on to Padua, where he pounced on me with an exulting look at his success with a despatch from my far too worrying (to me) senior officer, Captain Barbier, to the effect that I must, if overtaken by the messenger, arrest my advance to the Army of Italy which was broken up and retrace my steps to Lissa, with all celerity where I would find orders, directing me to embark in a frigate, hourly expected with all the men and non-commissioned officers I could collect on the station and proceed forthwith, with my Lagosta garrison and all the men I could collect, to *Corfu*, of which General Maitland[17] intended to possess himself as soon as it could be accomplished and evidently with the intention of anticipating any obstacle that might intervene to retard it.

---

[17] Lieutenant General Sir Thomas Maitland became Governor of Malta in July 1813. As the war was finishing in 1814 he rapidly sent troops to gain control of the island of Corfu. During the subsequent negotiations it became a British protectorate.

Chapter 16

Corfu 1814

Corfu was handed over by its French garrison and the island became
a very important post by which Britain maintained her influence in
the Adriatic for many years. It is a large island formed in a sickle shape
measuring some forty miles in length by a maximum of twenty in
breadth. Ceded to Britain by the Congress of Vienna, it was unified with
Greece by the Treaty of London in 1864.

John found himself involved in some very unsavoury work at Corfu,
the soldier's quarters being infested with fleas to an unbelievable
degree. Garrison life was not much to his taste either and he requested
'sick leave' as he was apparently suffering from a liver complaint, but
little expecting it to granted. But it was and he proceeded home by ship,
arriving in England in late 1814.

He was fortunate to be at home when news of Napoleon's escape
arrived in March 1815.

> The fact was that it [Corfu] was to be *secured* and made such
> advantage of, as the British and Allies should afterwards decide on;
> but in the mean time it was without any delay to be seized and
> possessed by the British, for which purpose every exertion was made
> to collect a large and imposing force from all quarters, to rendezvous
> there. Now I am aware that, in a not very courteous remark elicited
> by a letter I (from very strong feeling of its impolicy and deep regret
> to see all the conquests we had so slowly and gallantly made of the
> Ionian Isles, &c surrendered without a struggle) had written to the
> 'Times' paper, I was contradicted by a gallant colonel, who assumed
> no little authority and official knowledge of this capture and
> unequivocally denied that it was a *Military* conquest.

156

I had no doubt on the subject and was gratified to read the speeches of both Lord Derby[1] and Mr Disraeli[2] in parliament, both confirmative of my opinion and statement that it was a real military conquest; but being at the time I wrote no longer a soldier but of a profession which made me unwilling to enter into a public military controversy upon a matter in which I might be thought to have had no longer any right to interfere, [and] as I did not covet *notoriety* but very much the contrary, I let it pass; yet as I might now without going out of my way in the course of my narrative enter more fully into it, I will do so, having been witness of it from the beginning to the end and having landed in the first of the frigates boats to take possession as we supposed at once by a previous surrender by the French general[3] on summons and really expecting to have no more trouble than to walk into it.

But it was not so; the French did not generally and readily surrender any place until forced to it and although an agreement had been entered into between the French general and our commander (General Campbell[4]), yet, as the French general commanding at Corfu had not received military instruction to deliver up the place and for which he was waiting before he would allow us to take possession of even the outworks, and that reply came very slowly; we did not really get possession I think before, I believe 2 or perhaps 3 weeks. It certainly appeared a long time and our duties of pickets &c were as diligently and carefully carried on for that time as if the event might still be thought doubtful. And, as the *British* were the only assailants, with all these precautions and urged on the obtaining immediate possession as a matter of much importance to accomplish it, independently of any allies (to be dealt with afterwards by treaty *with us in possession*) nothing astonished me more than to find a British colonel, assuming the certain knowledge of all that took place,

---

[1] Edward George Geoffrey Smith-Stanley, 14th Earl of Derby (1799–1869) was Prime Minister three times and a renowned orator.

[2] Benjamin Disraeli, 1st Earl of Beaconsfield (1804 –1881), twice Prime Minister.

[3] General Baron Francois Xavier Donzelot. He later commanded a division at Waterloo.

[4] Lieutenant General Sir James Campbell was governor and commander in chief of the Ionian Isles until 1816.

deny that it was a military conquest. However, it is over and that bright gem of the British crown has been since surrendered, to be in some future day [be] reconquered as it *must* with sad loss of blood and treasure to please and truckle to a miserable clique of Quaker traders without any feeling of national honour and renown. I trust I shall be pardoned this [out]burst but I could not easily restrain my feelings on this sad humiliation and I am persuaded, great national sacrifice.

Even at Corfu, he continued to receive letters from both Lagosta and Ragusa, informing him of events and asking for his advice and his influence to be used in their favour, including another from his favourite cleric!

Lagosta 15 May 1814

Most esteemed commandant,

I have just learnt that you have returned from your pleasure tour & have enjoyed yourself at Trieste & Venice, where however still some traces remain of the invasion of the modern Goths and vandals. I rejoice still further that you have returned safe & sound & also because you are now the only person who can restore my fortune. A month ago I received from Ragusa a species of permission to leave the diocese, consequently I wrote to you on the subject, but as you had already started, my letter was returned to me with my complaint. I wrote at the same time to the Justice of Peace at Comiza[5], I now write to you again on the same object & also to the said Justice of Peace. I constantly receive new tokens of allegiance on the part of the inhabitants of Comiza & nothing further is needed but the approval by the governor of the votes of the people, but this I fear will not be given as the governor strongly upholds the parish priest of Comiza. Last Easter the congregation received an order from the governor not to nominate their priest by ballot according to their custom. I mention this in order that you may know how to act in this matter. I have already suggested to the Justice of Peace that a memorial should be presented in my favour, but not without first submitting it to your approval. Dear

---

[5] Comiza is a small town on the western coast of the Island of Lissa or Vis.

commandant, endeavour to obtain for me a necessary income & to liberate me from a place in which I have undergone more discomfort in a short time than in the whole course of my life. The archiepiscopal court assigns to me a parish to which I am unable to go on account of my bad health & the scarcity of provisions there. At Comiza I should have two assistants or coadjutors & enjoy a stipend which would procure for me a comfortable existence in my old age, to provide for which now seems hopeless & without resources. There are not wanting most effectual means for procuring me this. I hope much & almost take for granted the success of your intercession for me. In conclusion I beg you to be assured of my most lively gratitude united & most sincere affection & esteem. Your most devoted servant & affectionate servant Niccolo Perichi

My mother presents her compliments to you.

Ragusa 18 May 1814

My dear Friend,

You cannot imagine our joy on hearing of your safe return from your delightful journey. We are all gratified by the remembrance you cherish of us & assure yourself that it is responded to by us most warmly. My brother Francia has been at Stagna[6] for a few days on family business & in his absence; knowing you so well; I took the liberty of opening the letter addressed to him. Before replying to the questions you have asked him, I wish to remind you of a promise which you made to us, that on returning from Italy you would come to Ragusa. An Englishman must never break his word, so we await you with an inexpressible anxiety, solely proceeding from a sincere friendship, on account of which we desire that you should join us.

The news which you heard of my sister is quite false & it is much more probable that there has not as yet been any communication between Caboga & my family, but all this depends on the wishes of my father, who always expresses himself in a most metaphorical manner. Regarding my unhappy country we know nothing, in the mean time our hearts follow the same footsteps. My Hildebrand if

---

[6] Eighteenth century maps show that Stagna was the old name for Donta Doli in Croatia.

you know anything, communicate it to me. We continue to hope. God grant our desires may be fulfilled.

Napoleon has ended his triumphs to the destruction of these miserable ones, but who knows if we shall see the pride of our traitors abased? Caboga has been decorated with the Cross of Leopold[7], a decoration which makes all the country murmur. He who merits the rewards of foreigners no longer deserves the gratitude of his own country. Let us say no more on the subject. General Milutinovich has up to this time made three voyages by the canal with his brave battalions of Croats but Cattaro has not surrendered. I will write to you another time, but in the mean time I beg you to accept the sentiments of esteem & friendship of all my family & particularly of myself. Your sincere friend,

Pietro Marchese di Bona.

About an hour ago I received a communication respecting the subject above names (my sister & Caboga) just now I have not time to particularise on it, but I will take the first opportunity of enlightening you. I will send it to you with the two books of the history of Ragusa. In the mean time I send you these, take care of yourself!

Mezzo 28 May 1814
My Friend,
Your letters to me arrived late, but they are always welcome. Although I do not know if you are still at Lissa I wish to write to you. It is true that I have received a most satisfactory reply from the Lord Admiral. My reports have shown him the situation of the islands I govern, which before he knew nothing of. He has forwarded them to His Majesty's minister at the court of Vienna. I am very glad to have met with the approbation of my superiors & to have obtained the esteem of all the English whom I have known. They are a nation, which as you know I honour & love. It also gives me pleasure my dear Hildebrand to believe that I have perhaps been useful to my country without ever having failed in the duties of my

---

[7] The Imperial Austrian Order of Leopold was founded on 8 January 1808 for bravery in the face of the enemy.

position. The admiral has casually been informed of the affairs of Ragusa, through my reports, & consequently the minister also to whom they have been forwarded. It is always best that the truth should be known. The tonic which you made was short but pleasant. Italian hospitality amazed you? Were you then my dear English friend led to expect the contrary? You have seen the beautiful city of Venice. The papers announce that the republic is to be restored. As a republican & a Ragusan it interests me. But if it be true what will the allied powers say to it? Austria will perhaps not be satisfied with recovering only her own states? But of politics we must talk not write. We are all at present watching for the new organisation which is to prevail in Europe. I myself am curious to see the return of the French prisoners to their own homes. They will number about 300 men from different garrisons. Their number is insufficient for the present state of government & politics. The result remains to be seen. At Trieste you may have heard that public report wedded you to a Montenegrina. My wife tells me to say we made fun of it but with great discretion. I endeavoured to take part in the discussion by saying that judging from my knowledge of your genius for geography, you would have had to consult a map to discover where Montenegro was situated; but come to us & we can laugh over it together. In the mean time write to your affectionate friend,

Girolamo Conte di Natali.

Lagosta, 30 May 1814
Most esteemed commandant,
The memorial signed by various individuals has reached us here from Lissa. In the mean time awaiting the result of the position I have the honour & am also obliged out of sheer necessity to entreat you again on my behalf. You will have received my letter sent from here on the 19th current but of an earlier date. You will excuse my having sent it by an unknown messenger. In it I begged you warmly to interest yourself for me in the affair of the parish of Comiza together with the Justice of Peace of that province to whom I wrote at the same time. I beg now to remind you again of this matter, you promised to second me to the utmost, you have unbounded influence & Captain Barbier is quite at one with you. You are my most intimate friend & the only one I have in my present circumstances. I trust to you alone & feel sure of obtaining what I

desire with your help. For some things I should be more than content & remain at Lagosta, you may believe me, for you know me to be sincere & loyal, but on the other hand my bishop is not friendly to me, you guessed as much & I would not believe you, but thus it is, I am now assured of it. If I did not trust to your friendship I should be most miserable in the ecclesiastical province in which I now am. I hope for no help but yours, after God & I trust to receive what will be to me a happy appointment obtained for me by my true friend, Signor Hildebrand. Assure yourself of my most sincere esteem & gratitude joined to the most lively affection. Your devoted servant & affectionate friend,

Niccolo Perichi.

Lagosta, 8 June 1814

Most Esteemed Commandant,

I have received two most welcome letters from you, one of April 7th, the other May 15th at the same time. In the first was an enclosure for Captain Barbier, favoured by me & this I sent to a Lagostan who will immediately forward to him. I do not know by what means the second arrived. I being in expectation of a reply to my two previous letters think & fear they must have been lost. They were of great importance to me. I am now at liberty to accept the proposals made to me by the Comizans & the Governor of Lissa agrees to recognise the liberty of suffrage of the people. It requires much patience to submit myself to the continual reverses which come upon me & this is wanting to me.

The archbishop is very badly disposed towards me, this you warned me of, however I am assured of the justice of the cause which I have maintained, but up to the present time everything has been against me. I fear very much that the Governor of Lissa may have taken the part of upholding the priest of Comiza against the votes of the parishioners. I have not yet received their decision. At Lagosta I am constantly meeting with disagreeables which almost make me weary of life. I do not know on which party to depend & I have no one who can render me any assistance. In such a condition, I can assure you that I used much, very much patience in order not to succumb. You alone by your active friendship after God, comfort me. I expect no consolation from anyone else. I trust that the Comizans may have learnt that you have returned to Lissa, but if you have not received any of my letters, where am I to address this to?

I beg of you to assist me in liberating myself from a place which of all others has been rendered insufferable to me & to procure for me a position absolutely necessary to my condition. You will find great help in the friendship of Captain Barbier. I therefore write to him a private letter, which I send open, subject to your approval. If you think proper, forward it to him, if not give him yourself a clear statement of the circumstances, but I assure I am in need of prompt assistance I remain in expectation of the result, which I trust will render less unhappy an existence, which for a hundred reasons is wretched. Assure yourself that however my affairs end, I shall always be most grateful for your friendship, with which sentiment united to the greatest esteem. I subscribe myself unalterably, your devoted servant & friend,

Niccolo Perichi.

When we got possession of the formidable fortress which had set us at defiance, in spite of our successes almost everywhere else, during the whole course of the war, we were astonished at its strength and the gigantic artificial and scientific means that had, as it were, been exhausted by our powerful and ambitious enemy, but the immediate duties on which we were called immediately, left us little time for leisure and admiration. Everything excepting the fortifications themselves and their armament was in an apparently neglected and certainly a state of dirty confusion. One instance of this was so striking and remarkable that I have perfect recollection of it to this day. I was one of several officers having fatigue parties, altogether of about 200 men, sent to clear and clean out the barracks of the citadel and the first thing suggested by the quarter master, most used to such duties, was to take out all the ticking beds which appeared to have nothing but a little chaff left in them and that little settled in the corners; we carried them down to the sea beach to empty them there, as there was evidently a large admixture of fleas of the largest size and in high condition.

We reached the beach the first time but not without considerable grumbling and annoyance and stoppages in consequence of the dreadful torments of the fleas, amounting to an impossibility to proceed, the men gradually stripping off their linen fatigue jackets and shirts to get rid of their tormentors, but after a while we got all to fall in again and march back to the citadel and repeat the same task; but we had not got many paces before every soldier of the party was stark naked, saying that they could not endure the torment and thus returned again down the hill to the sea in which alone they could shake them off. I remember that when the corners of some of these beds (as they were called, which probably had lain unused for years, while these creatures were feeding on the remains of the chaff) were shook out, large *lumps* of fleas, in balls formed by their tenacious clinging to each other and one would fancy almost devouring each other, were shook out, a truly wonderful and disgusting sight! So strange as hardly to be believed excepting by those who beheld it.

The garrison duties were heavy, and although the weather was beautiful in November the men began to sicken; many were seized with low fever and not a few of our finest and healthiest looking young light bobs died. I have since heard that such is not unusually the case with the troops of that garrison.

For my part, having had enough for the present of rough campaigning for so long a time and being dispirited at the prospect before me of half-pay, or mere tedious garrison duties (and slow promotion) to which I had not been accustomed and had no taste. For I at once made up my mind for leave of absence to go home to look after the confirmation of my new appointment as captain and for anything that might turn up for me for a profession or livelihood, but without [real] hope of succeeding.

To my astonishment, recommendation for my leave was immediately conceded and the result was my termination of my career in those countries and an immediate passage home, [which] in those days [was] not an easy, or even calculable expense, as now in steam times.

Chapter 17

Belgium 1815

Having arrived back home with his family in Berwick on sick leave, John did not neglect to begin to consider how likely it would be for him to gain promotion within a reduced army after the peace; or whether he might need to look for a new profession. But whilst he contemplated these matters, the news that Napoleon had landed in France and that he had become Emperor of France again without a fight, led to certainty of renewed war and John sought opportunities to be involved.

His experiences in the Adriatic had certainly not quenched his desire for excitement and adventure. Yet he still belonged to the 1st Battalion, and by rights he should re-join it at Corfu. But he was officially on sick leave with a liver complaint and he had only recently informed Horse Guards that he was still not fit for service, enclosing medical certificates to prove it. How on earth therefore could he officially request permission to join the battalion in Belgium? However, it was obvious that all of the excitement was now to be had in Belgium and John made a typically impetuous decision in making his way to join the 2nd Battalion in Belgium as a simple volunteer. He risked a severe reprimand, if not a court martial, but on arrival at Courtrai, where the 2nd Battalion was based, he was fortunate enough to find a warm welcome and a 'blind eye' being turned by his superiors to his actions.

He was lucky enough to be placed in Captain Robert Cameron's company; Cameron was in Belgium but ill and was not present at Waterloo. But it would appear that John is incorrect in stating that he commanded the company, as Lieutenant Samuel Scarfe was also in the company and his senior by some eight years[1]. John also states that he was temporarily adjutant as Lieutenant Christopher Breary who was Adjutant, was ill. If he was sick, then he returned to duty before the battle, as he was certainly present and received a Waterloo Medal.

The 2nd Battalion had been sent to Holland in December of 1813 as part of a force sent to help free the Low Countries from French control. But the ensuing storming of the fortress of Bergen op Zoom on 8 March 1814, although nearly a stunning success, actually ended as an inglorious failure with thousands taken prisoner. The battalion was perhaps lucky this day not to suffer any casualties as it was held in reserve and was not committed to the attack. With peace coming the 2nd Battalion was placed at Ostend as the garrison of this vital port.

With the news of Napoleon's return, the battalion was ordered to march to Courtrai[2] where it became part of Major General Johnstone's 6th Brigade along with the 54th, 2/59th and 2/91st in Lieutenant General the Honourable Sir Charles Colville's Fourth Division.

The battalion was stationed with pickets on the banks of the river directly opposite the French and it became very obvious on 15 June that the French sentinels had changed. Up until then they had been line troops, now they were only National Guard, it was the first sign that things were on the move.

John admits that the troops were taken by surprise when the order to march finally arrived at 09.00 hours the following day. Unfortunately, the troops had been out on a long march just after dawn and had only recently returned to base for breakfast when the hurried order to march was delivered, but they still were ready to leave by 11.00 hours. They marched on interminably, but John admits that the combination of two months of garrison life and having already made a long march that morning, the battalion was scarcely up to a long, strenuous march in the hottest part of the day, to join the army and many had to fall out.

Finally, they arrived at their destination, at Enghien and sought to get some rest. On the 17th they moved a little closer to the main army, to Tubize, where they guarded a road that Napoleon may have attempted to use to outflank Wellington's army. Strangely, John does

---

[1] Lieutenant Samuel Scarfe's seniority was dated 28 November 1805, whereas John Hildebrand's was 23 September 1813.

[2] It's route, according to Major Slessor, took it via Bruges, Ghent and Oudenarde to Courtrai.

not mention the extremely heavy rain of that evening, which so many others suffered from. Perhaps being divorced from the main army where the opportunities to obtain a dry billet for the night were much better, meant that it was not such a problem for them.

When I ended the narrative of my Adriatic and Ragusa Campaign (1814) it was under the firm impression that all was over as to war and that I should never again have to draw my sword in our service; and although so bitterly disappointed as to the confirmation of my captaincy, in consequence of the mal a propos peace and the consequent re-arrangement of private, as well as national rival claims, made on the Duke of Wellington on so sudden and unexpected a termination of his exalted command, leaving him no choice of listening to the claims of those who had been employed in any quarter distant from his own immediate army and command, there was no choice left me, but either to accompany the new regiment to the service of the King of Sardinia, or fall back upon my former position in the British army which was still open to me from my not having been gazetted before the peace. Being determined against the former, I hardly knew what to do or what to think of my changed position. I could see that I had *no* chance with the Duke, hampered as he was with all kinds of solicitations and claims, but however faint the prospect and hope were, I could but try and look out for some other berth at the same time.

Thus I did, remaining at my father's house and determined to await the result, with all the patience I could muster. After having up to that time led so exciting and active a life for a period of nearly five years.

In the mean time, I looked anxiously around me for an opening in any other profession, to enable me to live honourably and advantageously. But having left my home at the unusually early age of 15, educated for nothing but the profession which I had never doubted for a moment was permanent and thus being fit for no other pursuit, my difficulty was most disheartening. No amount of prospective labour, mental or otherwise, which afforded a fair glimpse of success, for which I could think myself fitted, could have deterred me. But I could see nothing in my favour.

When, lo! In the midst of these gloomy reflections, the newspapers announced the sudden escape of Napoleon from Elba;

that he had landed in France amidst the acclamations of almost the whole army, which had enthusiastically joined his banner and were then with him at their head, marching on Paris. And moreover that by the prompt energy of the Allied sovereigns, it was already, by treaty, decided on that an overwhelming army should, without delay, be assembled on the frontiers to oppose him under the command of the Duke of Wellington as generalissimo.

Here was at once, an apparent solution of my difficulty. A war arranged on the most extensive scale likely to last for some considerable time, perhaps for years, which would require all the zeal and energy which the country could supply.

I decided on joining this army, at any rate (as a volunteer if I could attain no higher and better position). True I was still on *sick* leave and had forwarded doctor's certificates and an application for a renewal of it only a few days before; which was really no deception, as I was suffering severely from the effect on my liver from the hard service and climate, the preceding winter. But in the impetuosity of youth and my previous invariable habit of volunteering whenever an opening of seeing active service presented itself, I shut my eyes to the *inconsistency* of making an attempt, when on sick leave, to be allowed to join the grand army and to the difficulties I must have to encounter in it. These difficulties on a short consideration appeared formidable enough. In the first place how could I *avoid* reporting myself to the Horse Guards, or to the officer commanding the depot of the 1st Battalion, to which I now properly belonged? Which would at once have knocked in the head all my attempts to join the 2nd Battalion, and thus to take part in the expected services which it might be presumed it would very soon, be actively engaged in? But I had made up my mind, at whatever cost or difficulty, to accomplish in some way, my being engaged in this great contest between the two first generals of the age, then immediately impending. Still I proceeded thoughtlessly in following up the irregular and inconsiderate disregard to discipline when anything of enterprise presented itself, to which I had been too long accustomed in the Adriatic and in Dalmatia.

I therefore decided on running the risk, avoiding reports to both the Horse Guards and depot and making my way to the Army in Belgium by the shortest way I could devise. The very next morning, I mounted the box of the mail and made for Newcastle, the nearest point affording promise of success, where my father had a clerical friend to aid my search if he could and in hope to find a ship about to sail without delay to some convenient port in the Netherlands. But not succeeding in this there, I went on to Sunderland where I was again disappointed from the same cause, viz the weather. I then went to Hull where I found a Dutch trader (probably in those days, a smuggler) in which I engaged a passage to Rotterdam; but with such wretched and repulsive accommodation, as would, had I less ardour have effectually cooled my zeal, and sent me back home.

But the *expected battle* and all its possible results and all such enthusiastic expectations, were too much for all difficulties and discouragements. So I persevered and faced the discomforts and at such a season [and] real dangers of such a voyage. We sailed (the skipper was in haste and urgent) the next day but were that night driven back by a tremendous storm. We tried again and were obliged to return again. The third time through a tempest we got to Rotterdam, when the skipper told me that two other vessels which left port with us, had gone down that night on the Goodwin Sands.

Here however, I was again disappointed in finding my regiment as I had expected; it had marched to Courtrai on the frontier and I had only to follow it as I could, which placed me in great difficulty. I had turned the little money I had left in England into gold as I had been advised, at the rate of 28 [francs?] a guinea which by so long [a] delay and hotels had reduced my stock very low. In fact, I had but a few shillings left to carry me to Bruges and thence to Courtrai; and only then with a mere chance of catching my regiment. But my usual good luck did not forsake me. I must have endeavoured to get some money from a bank or from some other means.

Although my situation appeared desperately unpromising to contemplate, I therefore resolved on going to the principal banker in Bruges (although having no letters of credit, nor anything else to show, further than that I was a British officer, left unexpectedly in a foreign country by the advance of my regiment to the frontier). And he nobly responded to my appeal notwithstanding the risk, the possible loss he might sustain by the result of the imminent approaching battle and campaign, but with all these pressing considerations he nobly ran the risk and advanced me fifteen pounds (I had asked for no more) on my simple note of hand. Being thus furnished with the means of proceeding I started next morning in the diligence to Courtrai. On our journey we were frequently stopped and delayed at successive village inns by the crowds of recruits then being collected and enrolled for the [Belgian] army and I witnessed a scene or two illustrative of the wide difference of habits and manners in our respective countries, not perhaps worth noticing now that travelling has become so familiar, but which in that day did not fail to impress me.

On arriving at the large and flourishing city of Courtrai, then occupied by the advanced posts of the army, I found at last, the 2nd Battalion of my regiment, of which I had been so long in search.

And here my next serious anxiety was how I could venture to present myself to Colonel Sir G. Berkley[3], the commanding officer of the battalion, [as] an unexpected interloper in fact. But when I found the regiment was under the immediate command of the benevolent and kind hearted Sir George, a brave and experienced soldier, I felt at least assured of a kind and courteous reception and every consideration of my case which could, in any reason be expected. Under such a commanding officer, from experience it was impossible to anticipate harshness, unless wantonly deserved and provoked. It was indeed at all times no easy matter to stir up the anger of this generous and honourable officer unless by unwarrantable conduct.

Learning that the hour of the battalion's parade was 9 o'clock and that Sir G.B[erkley] was sure to be there, I summoned up all the confidence I had at command and presented myself in front of the regiment as soon as it was dismissed. Sir G[eorge] was at first quite startled, but soon exclaimed, 'Well, Hildebrand, what brought you here, you belong to the 1st Battalion?' I stammered out my apologies as well as I could, and at last, Sir G[eorge] said 'Well I am very glad to have you, although I did not expect it and I hope you will be of use to us. But there is great irregularity in all of this and I must write and explain it to the Horse Guards. In the mean time you must consider yourself under arrest, but come to my quarters and stay with me and I have no doubt I will set all right in a short time'. And so it turned out, by Sir G[eorge]'s kindness, sanction was

---

[3] Lieutenant Colonel Sir George Berkeley served as Assistant Adjutant General to the Prince of Orange during the Waterloo Campaign.

given almost by return of post, to my being placed on the strength of the 2nd Battalion and that consequently, I should remain where I was.

And moreover I was in the furthest luck of being appointed (through the illness and absence of the captain) to the command of the light infantry company, to which I had always belonged and also through the illness and absence of the Adjutant to the acting Adjutancy, with the convenient addition of two excellent chargers to fulfil the necessary duties. Everything turned out most fortunately.

Courtrai was about 7 miles from Menin, a very strong and important fortress on the Western side of the small, but deep River Lys, on the opposite side of which the French had numerous pickets and sentries, we having corresponding guards on our side.

The river between us was so narrow that the soldiers on both sides could carry on uninterrupted conversation without restraint, which no degree of vigilance could have effectually checked had it been thought necessary and in time, from the habitually meeting the same faces, a considerable intimacy and good feeling had taken place, so much so that I was informed, although I never saw it, that friendly parties under due guard, had passed between the opposite parties and other civilities of civilised warfare. I as Adjutant, besides the visits of the field officers and captain of the day, made a daily visit to these our advanced pickets up to this time; and had always the usual sentries patrolling their respective beats in the most orderly manner, which from its mere tame sameness after a few days, induced from its mere monotony a kind of easy carelessness; although not relaxing a watchful look out and thus it went on for at least two months. In the mean time the garrison of Courtrai was kept alive and on the alert by constant parades and drills and a regular and undeviating parade every morning before daylight, which when these preceded the marches into the country every third day, were most trying to our olfactory nerves and disgusting in a high degree.

From the *then* (in the Netherlands) invariable habit of cultivating every inch of ground, by daily drenching it with liquid manure and this in the earliest morning, [which] with a dense fog settled over our heads, preventing evaporation until an hour after sun rise, it was indeed a most severe trial of our endurance. It is quite wonderful how the health of the men stood it; but after a good deal

171

of fever and ague in consequence of it, our doctors, from the observation of the habits and precautions of the natives, discovered that Dutch gin, taken neat and the first thing in the morning was the sovereign remedy and preventative of ague there; that it was their invariable custom to have recourse to it first thing; and our doctors, like sensible men who could take example and in spite of national prejudices adopted it, ordering a glass every morning to every man before he turned out, before light for parade. A prescription not very unwelcome to very many and I believe most beneficial in its effects; although it is to be lamented that in too many cases the habit thus acquired was not laid aside when there was no longer occasion for it. Nevertheless, for the time it answered an imperative purpose and no doubt averted much sickness, and not a few deaths.

I must now begin to give dates and whatever else may be required of our several marches and transactions from Courtrai to Waterloo and thence on to Paris, which I can do with a fair degree of accuracy from my campaigning map, which I always carried in my breast pocket and marked carefully daily, unless some unavoidable impediment intervened.

I shall begin with the 15th June (1815). I had ridden over as usual, but somewhat earlier, to visit the pickets before Menin when I was struck at once with the altered appearance of affairs on the part of the French. I saw no longer the smart trim sentinels on the Menin side of the river; they had been removed and replaced by most unseemly substitutes. The men left to undertake their duty were evidently peasants, some even without a little of the National Guard smartness but all quite a different set from those who had performed those duties up to the day before.

Startled at this, it was immediately apparent to me that the regulars had been removed for the purpose of collecting all that could be got together to concentrate the French army for an attack; which we had so long desired and expected. In no inconsiderable anxiety and full of the importance of imparting the first news of such an event, I hastened back to headquarters at Courtrai as fast as I could and reported the circumstance, but was astonished at the cool and apparently indifferent manner in which it was received by the officials. I could only conjecture that it was no news to the chiefs and as no bustle or move [took place] among the soldiers, such as one would have expected had any advance been in contemplation or attack expected, I was utterly at a loss what to think and so took my leave in some perplexity.

This was on the 15th June. The next morning being by no means satisfied with what I had seen the day before, notwithstanding that things went on in the usual tranquil way; [with] no bustle of preparation, I had only to fall back on the soldier's proper and habitual reliance on the sagacity, care and watchfulness of his general. I therefore without unnecessary anxiety, trotted back to Courtrai as usual, only making at our mess such casual and random remarks as the change in our pickets and my reliance that our Duke knew and was prepared for all about it.

The morning after this i.e. the 16th June, was our regular heavy marching order parade. Which took place as usual before daylight and the men were marched at least 5 miles into the country and returned at 9 o'clock thoroughly heated and tired and at once got rid of their clothes and accoutrements and went to breakfast. Hardly had the officer's breakfast ended, i.e. within a ½ or ¾ hour, when without the least previous warning or signal, the drums beat to arms all over the town with more than usual energy and vigour, the men were to resume their uniform and we were to march with all the haste we could. In short we were to march in half an hour!! And this after two months in quiet billets.

However, such was the zeal of the battalion, we were in the ranks almost instantly and did march at the time appointed, on such a march as I never had seen before or could have imagined.

I began this narrative with the determination (perhaps not a very prudent one) to relate all I saw as I thought worth notice, or could assure myself of on good authority in the course of my duties; without considering public opinion of them or looking to my right hand or my left with a consideration of personal consequences. So at this important period I must carry it out without even considering the prejudices and opinions of others, as to the much disputed question of whether or not we were surprised at Waterloo. After you have read the following narrative of what did take place and connect it with the quiet easy way in which the enemy was allowed to have his undisputed selection of the time and exact point of attack, you may form your own opinion on this head.

That we were hoodwinked by our spies, especially Fouche, the contriver and conductor of the whole egregious deception, of course all who can have but one opinion and are not to be moved (viz that *the Duke could* not have been deceived) will read with impatience my account of what really took place, but if I am to [have] credit for common veracity and a very small degree of common sense, I feel assured you will have no doubt that we were deceived; both as to the point of attack and its unexpected violence; and that under such circumstances, our triumphant success could be attributed to nothing else than to God's superintending Providence that we ever had the opportunity to fight the battle and should be brought off with such splendid and perfect success was almost miraculous, all things being fairly considered on both sides.

But to state things as they happened to us and our first march, after so long [a] sojourn at Courtrai. Nothing could have turned out more unfortunately for the 'esprit de corps' and its whole conduct. I have said before that the soldiers had been indulging in quiet billets for about 2 or 3 months, giving themselves up to all the luxuriance of Belgian hospitality, proverbially very great and the enticing good beer to any extent. In fact, they were stuffed to the throat with all these good things and were consequently, in the worst possible condition for even a fair march, exhausted as they were by their previous morning's march. Almost immediate and universal prostration of strength and energy, from sheer exhaustion, seized them all and they were thus soon absolutely beaten and totally unable to march with any regularity or obedience. As Adjutant and in charge of the rear guard I found it impossible to contend with this state of things, met with at every step. The men threw themselves down in every ditch they met with and exclaimed almost frantically 'There is no use in trying to drive me on. I could not move another yard. Shoot me, sir, shoot me at once, but do not drive me on'.

In this state of things I could only report and communicate with our rear, where there were two officers of the General Staff, stating the impossibility of keeping the men up; the answer to our lieutenant colonel was verbally (for we had no written orders sent to us on this or any other forced march, but orders were passed on from the rear) that we must persevere and to bring up even one man into the field if we could do no more, and to the commanding officer to take care to keep the battalion as close as possible as it was probable we should be attacked by separate regiments on the march. We were then and had been for some time separated from our *brigade* and marching on as an independent regiment. Now, I can conceive nothing like this excepting as a regular rout, and indeed such it appeared to all concerned in it only for the absence of all firing or anything like an enemy's presence or proximity. Thus we went on, as fast and as well as we could, bearing in our minds the urgent and peremptory order to bring up even to the last man into the field. After a considerable time, we were halted close to Oudenarde and from the summit of the hill and just close below us it then appeared (although it must have been four miles off) such a cannonade, such volleys of artillery as I had never heard before, or young soldier as I was could have imagined.

The fierce battle of Ligny[4] was then going on just below us and at its utmost height. I found on the pinnacle of this hill an old veteran captain[5], one who was supposed in those days what we called a fire eater, of all men the last I would have expected to meet with a very grave face on such an occasion, at any degree of firing. But he did look grave enough at the firing of this battle and shrugging up his shoulders, a peculiar and common habit with him, said in the most serious way, 'Mr H do you hear that? We shall have it tomorrow morning'. This I was too thoughtless and inexperienced to receive with all the seriousness he meant to impart and I ought to have felt. This happened about six in the evening of the 17th June[6]. It was a matter of very hard work and exertion, after our previous marching &c to sit up all night on the road to receive the straggling poor fellows who had been left behind, as they came up one by one, to make up as far as possible some small regimental force and at the peep of day set out again, for the field of Waterloo which we accomplished without knowing our destination or having another halt. It was a continuance of terrible marching through the same miserable, miry roads. Hence we were marched at once into line under the direction and guidance of a well mounted Staff officer and

---

[4] It is certain that he could see the fighting at Quatre Bras not Ligny.

[5] The most likely candidate for the very old captain with a strong fighting history would be Captain Thomas McNeil, who had joined the regiment in 1800 and became a captain in the Army in 1808 (regiment in 1813). He had served at Malta, Copenhagen, the Corunna campaign and at Bergen op Zoom.

[6] This is a mistake for the 16th June.

posted near the town or village of Enghien; to guard the wide and good military road leading to Hal and Brussels[7].

So fatigued and worn out were the men that in an instant after the halt, everyone glided down on the road on the spot nearest to his location and in a very few minutes, all excepting those told off for pickets and other duties were sound asleep, and so it continued for two or three hours disturbed only at intervals by distant firing and an occasional musket shot near at hand to keep the most sensitive of us alive. This was our night's bivouac and rest on this road for two or three hours. Here we remained without disturbance the whole of the remainder of the night, impatient as far as we were conscious beyond measure, and momentarily expecting to be ordered to move to our left, where all the fighting had been going on the whole day in and about the forest of Soignies, which was full of the enemies' troops.[8]

[7] They were actually in the vicinity of Enghien on the night of the 16th and Tubize on 17th. The Regimental History claims that the battalion was stationed at Braine l'Alleud on the 18th, but this cannot be correct. Having consulted Ferrari's maps, the most likely position for the woods in advance mentioned by Hildebrand would be in the vicinity of Lembeeck Wood at Glabecq, on the road from Braine le Chateau to Hal and much nearer the actual battlefield. Colville wrote the following day that he formed to the left of Prince Frederick's forces from Lembecke to Braine le Comte. This must be an error, Braine le Comte being many miles to the south, he must have meant Braine le Chateau. This position is less than three miles from the right flank of Wellington's army at Waterloo.

[8] He is confused here, particularly as his regiment did not participate in the Battle of Quatre Bras or the subsequent retreat by Wellington's army to the position at Mont St Jean, where it stood on the 18th of June in front of the Forest of Soignies.

Chapter 18

18th June 1815

The 35th was to spend the day of the Battle of Waterloo only ten kilometres from the battlefield, but because of the vagaries of the atmospheric conditions and the local terrain, it is claimed that they knew nothing of the battle at all, as they heard and saw nothing. This is difficult to believe and the evidence for this is very slight, as very few of the soldiers banished to Tubize and Hal seem to have recorded their memories, most being too upset that they had missed the greatest battle the British Army had ever known, being so close and yet so far.

Yet John strongly promotes his claim to have known of the battle and to have seen officers come from it. Major Slessor also states that he 'heard firing at intervals, but was ignorant of what was going on'.[1]

The added fact that John claims that his forward position was fired on by French skirmishers is also not completely unbelievable, for we know that small detachments of French cavalry were certainly probing around the wings of Wellington's army. It is therefore very believable that these cavalry pickets actually probed this small advanced guard to see if there were larger numbers of troops in the vicinity, which there surely were.

The battalion on this day numbered two field officers; five captains; twenty-three subalterns; thirty-one sergeants; sixteen drummers and 481 men. Why there were only five captains present when all ten companies were on campaign is not clear, leaving half the companies to be commanded by a subaltern. Ninety-four of all ranks were also recorded as sick which is a comparatively high figure, it is possible that

---

[1] *The Backbone*, p.300.

a number of these fell out on the rapid marches and had not returned in time.

At daybreak on the 19th, Major Slessor records 'Sir Charles Colville rode up and ordered us to give three cheers … Judge of our surprise, our chagrin, when he told us of yesterday's battle'. It was probably not much of a consolation, but the troops at Tubize were included in the numbers granted the Waterloo Medal a year later, the first campaign medal ever awarded to all ranks in the British Army. The division then marched to join the remnants of Wellington's army as they marched after the fleeing French and pursuing Prussians.

On 21 June, Major Slessor recorded that they had crossed the French border on their route to Paris. But there was the little matter of a number of fortresses which had to be dealt with on the way.

A Staff colonel came up in great haste, calling for a subaltern's picket immediately which was told off under the command of a very young chubby faced boy, who had only joined the regiment on our march the day before[2], he had made his way thus in advance from the aid of a very useful thickset pony, he never having been drilled or heard a shot fired until that day and I as Acting Adjutant was called upon to post this youth in his first command over about twenty men of the steadiest and most experienced and its proper proportion of non-commissioned officers. We were led down to the skirts of the wood and standing in a very small grass field the colonel called our attention to the situation of the post he had selected and said pointing to the wood on our right, 'that wood is full of the enemy's troops' and then, turning around and pointing in the opposite direction 'and that also. Keep a good look out, we are expecting to be attacked here directly' and [he] then rode off at a hard pace. I summoned the youngster and picket around me and endeavoured to enforce my orders on him and to impress on him the absolute necessity of vigilance and that he was there posted, and must not under any circumstances quit it until regularly relieved, however long that might be. While I was speaking to him four or five musket shots whistled over our heads from the said wood,

---

[2] This is most likely to refer to Ensign John Thomas who had only received his commission in December 1814.

when he turning to me with a bold face said 'You tell me to protect myself, what am I to do?' I replied briefly; 'dig a hole and this corporal who understands it well, will show you how to raise a defence against these fellows' and so I left him for that time, poor boy!

I heard, years after, that he turned out a gallant and good officer and died in honour, after many years of hard and good service.

We never moved out of the line, resting on our arms when we rested at all; every moment expecting our orders to advance. While in this state of anxious suspense and anxiety, a Staff colonel from the battlefield with a rather numerous and well-appointed Staff rode past us and addressed a few words as to what was going on in the other part of the field. I asked him how long we must remain in this inactive state. His reply was 'How can I tell? this is the post of your regiment in line and here you must maintain it until ordered away, or relieved. Never fear, you will probably have plenty to do before night. I have just brought you a reinforcement which you may need yet'. And he galloped off, leaving us to keep the field, in the same state of perplexity.

At peep of dawn the next day, 19th June, we were ordered, as being now well rested in our bivouacs, such as it was, to accompany the Prussians in pursuit of the routed French troops and it would be a difficult matter to describe accurately the details of the forced marches on which we entered that day. Of these I have little more than the dates, taken down from day to day on my campaigning map, carried in the pocket of my breast and now before me and from my memory to guide me from errors, but I think quite sufficient for the purpose in these respects.

We started from our road bivouac, as I have said, at peep of day and took the road through the midst of the field of battle, till we came to the intersection of the grand road leading from Brussels to Paris; and here at this junction it would be impossible to give the faintest idea of the scene before us, at this cross meeting of all the roads from every direction, tending towards the same point; with their choked up, crowded accumulation of baggage and all kinds of collections of that sort; accumulated in long cantonments; besides provision wagons under the commissariat, heavy luggage of all sorts, private carriages here and there crammed in and every imaginable kind of conveyance crowded together all striving to get beyond the vehicles preceding them.

This of course increased the confusion, which already extended as far as I could see (and I was told by some who being well mounted had had opportunity of forming an opinion, that it extended at least 7 miles before us). In fact, nothing could exceed the crowd, confusion and struggling irregularity of the line of march; until at last some dragoons by order of the commander in chief showed some force and determination and brought about better order and a *kind of line* for vehicles was formed, but not without much individual resistance and difficulty. In the bustle and confusion of the day before (i.e. the 18th) I had received a severe bruise in my right thigh (the effects of which I feel at times, and that with no trifling inconvenience and pain to this day) which for the time made me quite *unable* to move my leg, much less to make any exertion and I was thus laid aside from advancing with the army, I could not bear the idea for one moment of being left behind while they were going forward to future conflicts and perhaps future glory.

On this account I would not report myself [sick] so as to be left behind the army. An irrepressible impatience to get on seized me but I had no horse; the one I had for the campaign had disappeared the night before (I was told either stolen or strayed, certainly it had not been killed to my knowledge), therefore what was I to do? I could not walk a yard without breaking down. At that moment our good and gallant major (afterwards Colonel [Macalister][3]) hove in sight and I at once appealed to him. He seemed much amused at my impetuosity and impatience but replied at once, '*I cannot help you; I cannot lend you a horse*'; and pointing to the crowd of confused and choked, up carriages, horses and all sorts of things to impede, he said in a good-natured manner 'If you *must* get on, why do you not get a lift from one of these?'

Well knowing that there was no chance from any one of them at the rate then going on. Just at this moment I saw a brass field piece happening to pass, drawn by a pair of Wagon Train horses. But I still urged and asked his leave to mount astride on it. The major said 'Well if you must keep up with us I see no better plan, but it

---

[3] Major Charles Macalister commanded the regiment in Belgium, Lieutenant Colonel Berkeley being detached as Assistant Adjutant General to the Prince of Orange.

will be a rough conveyance'. With no little difficulty and the help of some soldiers near[by], I contrived to, *mount* and off we went at such a pace as the deeply ploughed up roads and crowded obstructions would permit, i.e. a snail's pace. But it is not easy to describe how painful it was from the rough heavy jolting. Yet I persevered, in my anxiety to get on for several hours and at last only gave in from the impossibility of penetrating the confused mass any further; but at last, spying my friend Major Mc A[lister], not far from us, he having advanced little or nothing quicker than ourselves, I once more appealed to him with no better success than before; but at last all of a sudden he exclaimed 'I think I have hit on the means of your at least keeping up with the battalion. I have just had sent to me, to be attached to the regiment, two vehicles on springs and each drawn by a pair of Wagon Train horses, driven by one of the corps, to convey the wounded who may require such aid. I will place them under your command, although I never before saw an officer so employed. You will at any rate, be able to ride and keep up'. Nothing could have rejoiced me more or removed my despair more effectually, so the driver was ordered to come near enough to take me up and off we set, but only to follow the line of baggage march which had by this time been established to keep all to their proper places with rigid discipline, not at all equal to my ardent aspirations.

So I immediately looked out for an opening or apparent break in the line determined to attempt, at least, taking advantage of it and soon hitting on what I considered a weak point, I instantly ordered the Wagon Train driver to make for it, but he pleaded 'orders' and was inflexible; when, lame as I was, I contrived to get down from my seat on which I was mounted in front and renewed my orders, with the presumed authority, then too much encouraged of combatants over non-combatants, and with all its accompanying youthful arrogance and haughtiness of manner (so utter groundless and for which I have been ever since ashamed when I thought of it) in the midst of this boiling impatience and determination to force my way and violate my orders, without consideration of the risk and consequences if I should encounter anyone who thought it his duty or felt inclined to oppose me.

A commissariat officer, who had charge of the provision wagons stepped forward, breasting our horses and *commanding* us in a firm tone to desist and wait our turn. I could not describe my rage, accustomed as I had for so long a time been to indulge my temper against the Italians and others who looked on the British officers as omnipotent in that country at that time, especially on the coasts; and in my exasperation in being thus stopped and set at nought by a young commissariat officer, I scrambled down from my carriage and in language far from courteous and of which I am now quite ashamed, while laying my hand on the hilt of my sword, an action which he immediately met and responded to, we advanced fiercely towards each other, when within a yard or two of meeting my opponent exclaimed 'What, H, is this you?' and simultaneously I called out 'What D is this you?'[4]. He had been my school and class fellow until the day I entered the army and placed in the commissariat, as many were in that day, from some accidental or physical objection that had prevented his entering the regular army, in which his father had been a general officer. I need not attempt to describe our joy at meeting thus after such a rough and unpromising beginning, and suffice it to say that it really was a joyous meeting, therefore we parted [&] not only gave me an excellent dinner as could be got in such a time, but filled my haversack with a fine leg of mutton and other good things, which could have been expected only from a commissariat officer, while I was utterly void of all but a small brandy bottle and some ration biscuits.

I must be pardoned for having digressed from my narrative to notice a matter so entirely touching myself; but it could not but have penetrated me on the spot, and has often since recurred to my memory from its strange circumstances and result. On we marched with all the speed and energy we could muster, but with hard work to keep up with the Prussians and with whom we were appointed to act.

Their cavalry was continually pressing and passing us. Of their infantry we saw little; I believe they with indefatigable zeal had pressed on during the evening and night before, clearing the way as

[4] There were five commissaries in Belgium during the campaign whose surname started with the letter D – Drake, Dumaresque, Daniel, Dallas and Dillon. The only one of these five who had a general of the same surname in the Army was Dillon. Major General Arthur Robert Dillon and therefore Commissary George Dillon. I have, however, been unable to establish a family link between these two individuals.

they did indeed of every appearance of the enemy, excepting the poor wounded straggling on the road side. And here the great general himself, the Duke of W[ellington], surrounded by his Staff, rode a few yards alongside and then passed us, the Duke in the highest of spirits and chatting with animation, excited no doubt by the result of the various successes and glorious victory so fresh and so exhilarating, speaking very fast and with much animation, the object of curiosity and admiration of us all while trudging along on foot. I in my ambulance and doing our best to keep order and restore the appearance of regularity; proud of our victor and not a little so, of whatever share we had had in the result.

I said we were accompanying the Prussians, each of whom was animated with deadly hatred and animosity of the French, urging them on far beyond the most zealous of ordinary exertions would require; and sure enough we could hardly advance a yard without witnessing this master passion of their hatred. Of these feelings we were almost, if not quite free, having only the ordinary feelings of a British soldier in pursuit of a thoroughly beaten and vanquished foe, but ready to stoop down and lift up and comfort as far as in our power every wounded or distressed victim of the disaster.

Not so the Prussians, when reminded of the calls of humanity. Their answer was always an enumeration of a long list of insults and atrocities of the French, to themselves or their relatives, when *they* were subdued, which they gloried in retaliating. We English were bad judges between them. We had not suffered or been so exasperated.

But it was indeed pitiable to witness the vengeance they had wreaked on every village, hamlet and house on the line of retreat. It is impossible to realise it, even at this time, although so long and often dwelt on and contemplated in one's mind. Some of the villages along the road (from Brussels and Paris side) were very long, perhaps for a mile long and from one end to the other it was one scene of indescribable desolation. Not a door, window frame, even a pane of glass, nor the least bit of woodwork of any kind left standing: all burned or smashed to pieces. Everything not absolutely demolished riddled with musket shots and black with the smoke which had been from the fires burning their dwellings. I will not dwell on this scene, a continued one for the whole line of march in pursuit, I could not describe it. But I may as an instance of wantonness accompanying it, too naturally.

As a matter of course we ransacked, although there never appeared a reason for it, the houses which the Prussians had taken such care to ransack before; and on entering one room, which struck me for its more than orderly appearance and much larger than usual, I saw as I supposed, a shoemaker of perhaps 50 years of age, sitting quite composedly and as if nothing had disturbed him and quite attentively employed at his work, but on going up to him I found he was dead; [he] had been shot through the head and (it must have been while he was warm) placed with great care and no little arrangement in barbarous mockery, in his usual chair and apparently at his usual work. The same sad scene continued for miles with little interruption, but personal sufferings, excepting from wounded French soldiers, who had been left often to their fate. were hardly ever met with; all the terrified inhabitants of the villages and farm houses had fled before our arrival. But for myself things began to look better the day after I abandoned my dreadful conveyance in ambulance, which was anything but agreeable.

I happened with my usual but really extraordinary luck, to meet with another old school fellow and dear friend, also in the commissariat department and one from whom I received immediate and permanent aid in furthering my views and help relieving my necessities. My friend not only supplied me with a horse to get on with, but left it with me during the whole time I passed afterwards encamped at Bois de Boulogne and at Paris and in fact till I left France at Calais to return to England. I was thus unexpectedly and effectually aided in every way, not to mention the constant supplies of provisions which I could have obtained in no other way or from any other person than a kind commissary, who had the whole range of the country to choose and purchase from. In the mean time I got on amazingly well with my lame leg; for my horse turned out useful and gentle in every way. We halted at Mons and were marched into a spacious and fine old church to bivouac for the night, but were detained there to meet some arrangement on the line of march the greater part of the next day.

During this time the men had free liberty over the church and from curiosity and in search of such articles as they could pilfer or plunder, made no slight use of it. The whole church was full of furniture and the altar end was heaped up with all kinds of precious articles and such matters as had been carried there, in terror of the

Prussians for safety; when, quite suddenly a crash of falling furniture, so loud as to startle everybody, about 3 or 4 o'clock in the afternoon fell down from around the altar and a poor miserable looking terrified man deprived of his concealment was exposed, standing with terrified countenance and without moving a muscle, or moving a limb. He must have been standing there in dreadful terror and afraid to move for at least 23 or 24 hours, when the Prussians vacated the church. I need not say how different [the] treatment he now received. We marched next day, at peep of day as usual, passing through Maubeuge and Landrecies and St Quentin, so to Cambrai on the 23rd.

Chapter 19

Cambrai and Péronne

The 35th was to be engaged in the siege and storming of Cambrai. John states that here he was put in a light company sent out to protect Lord Wellington whilst he observed the defences of the fortress, this reconnaissance is confirmed by General Colville. His further claim that this body of light infantry was commanded by Lieutenant Colonel Charles Napier, who certainly was in Belgium as a volunteer, may appear far-fetched, especially as according to Lieutenant General Colville's despatch from Cambrai, Brevet Colonel Neil Campbell, Major in the 54th Foot, commanded the light companies of Major General Johnstone's Brigade at the storming of Cambrai, and Campbell was senior to Lieutenant Colonel Napier in Army rank. However, Charles Napier wrote an account of himself accompanying Neil Campbell and three companies of light troops to Aubervilliers a few days later, which would seem to prove it.

Whilst his light troops continually fired through the embrasures to clear the ramparts of defenders, his skirmishers were taken aback by the exploits of one particular French artillery officer. Colville's artillery also sent a number of shells into the citadel, the town itself not being shelled as the populace was thought to be loyal to King Louis, and therefore opposed to Napoleon.

That night was a very wet one with both officers and their horses crowded into the tiniest of spaces desperately trying to get out of the rain in the few huts scattered around the area, leading to an exceedingly uncomfortable night and some laughter. This at least took their minds off the assault on the town planned for 18.00 hours that coming evening.

Roused before dawn, the soldiers were set to collecting any ladders that could be found in the farmhouses and agricultural sheds in the

186

vicinity. These ramshackle ladders were all they would have to get over the town walls.

The attack commenced exactly to plan, the ladders were soon in place and the men scrambled up them as fast as possible, although not a few of these rickety ladders gave way and propelled the men to the ground; certainly no joke for those stood below as they tried to dodge the bayonets fixed on the end of their muskets. But soon the town was in Allied hands.

The commander of the citadel, Baron Joseph Noos surrendered, but the terms agreed angered the soldiers who had begun the storming, who had anticipated a period of pillage after the successful storm. Colville states that only one officer was killed and about forty men were wounded in the escalade; a number probably from the breaking of ladders as described.

They now marched on to the more formidable fortress of Péronne which actually capitulated, almost without a shot being fired. The march for Paris then continued at a pace.

Sir Charles Colville[1] who commanded the 4th Division and to whom was committed the subjugation of Cambrai, which at first was expected to surrender at a simple summons, but it was too strong and well commanded to permit of such short work, was obliged to halt before the place. The Duke had so reckoned on its surrender that Sir Charles was at a loss what to do. He as a matter of course reported to the Duke and requested his immediate presence to inspect, who came up that day and immediately ordered a reconnoitring party as his protection during the reconnaissance. I was the oldest subaltern and also in command of a company of what had but recently been organized under the name of sharpshooters under the superintendence and arrangement of Colonel Napier[2].

Of course the command of this bodyguard of the great Duke was an intense object of my ambition and as I had the option I took the command and accompanied his Grace. We spent 3 or 4 hours in the

[1] Lieutenant General the Honourable Sir Charles Colville commanded the 4th Division.
[2] Lieutenant Colonel Charles Napier went to Ghent as a volunteer and was present at the assault on Cambrai, but I can find no other evidence to confirm that he actually commanded the light brigade there.

reconnaissance, when our Duke had indeed a most narrow escape but for his proverbial good luck in such matters. As our party's business was plainly to be seen and understood by the enemy on the ramparts and consequently by the aid of a spy glass, attracted the attention of all and excited their endeavours to pick off our chief; my special duty was to keep my party as watchful and active as I could to drive them from the ramparts whenever they appeared, and prevent their working their guns or using musketry against us. But a cannon ball from a brass field piece, esteemed at that period almost as certain in its aim as a rifle, while the Duke was dismounted with his arm holding his charger's bridle and his spy glass at his eye, struck the ground under his horse's belly and threw the sand all over him. I had the best possible opportunity of seeing what passed and I confess I was not at all surprised at the moment, that the occurrence produced no effect on him; he probably never observed it and merely shook off the sand and dust.

I had seen equal coolness in innumerable other cases. Turning to Sir C.C[olville] he only said as if in continuance to a previous remark or pursuing a course of reflection, 'Colville we must have this place tomorrow by escalade. It is essential to our advance'.[3] And after a *very* few words together, which I could not catch he mounted and galloped away.

But here I must take the liberty of relating an anecdote, a liberty I claim as my right, as I do not profess to follow strictly [the] history of the war, but I think remarkable enough to deserve recording as an instance of sang froid and cool daring. When my party was zealously firing their best and had actually driven *all* from the ramparts in front, a French officer of artillery in the midst of our hottest firing, sprang up on the exposed rampart as if in ungovernable indignation at his men's desertion and deliberately turning his posterior towards us and clapping his buttocks, opening his coat tails as a mark, stood in that indecent and contemptible attitude for some minutes exposed to the shots of my party. This

---

[3] Colville states that 'The Duke came up the next morning, and thinking it of most material consequence that so important a place should early be obtained as a place d'armes for the king, gave me the rest of my division'.

excited the coarse merriment of my men to such a degree that they all burst into rough laughter and made them incapable of even taking a wide range in their aim; and I ordered them to cease firing; but a very clever shot, a corporal, begged and entreated me more to allow him to have *one* more shot after all the merriment was over, promising me that he would certainly (and I was sure he would perform his promise) in the coarsest language do so and so towards the officer's future ability to offend either us or any others. This he proposed with a coarse joke most amusing to his comrades. But although the insult seemed unpardonable, yet he was a brave and daring fellow; so I thought his death after having braved it so long would have been little better than murder; and so I now think.

I now return to my narrative. Here was work to do and more than enough for the means then at our command. Cambrai was to be taken by escalade within a few hours but where were our ladders and other things necessary for such an attempt? Sir Charles and his Staff had to look to that and certainly lost no time. In the mean time we, the infantry, were marched into a small field to bivouack close to the fortress and thus to pass the night and do what we could to prepare ourselves for the event. It was awful wet weather and the ground in every direction saturated; the small ploughed field appointed for our bivouac, was deeper than I can describe and without even the shelter of tolerable hedges; but in one corner stood a small open hovel of brushwood and thatched in the way such contrivances are managed in the north of France; but pretty well supplied with straw inside.

On reconnoitring our bivouacs, this hovel did not escape the eye of the major's groom who as a matter of course, pounced at once on it and appropriated it to his master's horses &c. But the major was glad on such a night, to take advantage of it himself. In short we all, I mean the officers (the poor men had no such place of refuge) crept in one after another until the poor horses were turned out to the rain and the floor of the hovel as thickly occupied as possible by human beings, not an inch to be found into which one could penetrate and remain at rest. I had made my way earlier up to the furthest end and like most of the rest who could find room enough to lie down on, was fast asleep. Now it should be borne in mind that we were within a few yards of the strong fortress of Cambrai, which we were preparing to storm at any risk the next day and were consequently as fast asleep as fatigue and a place to lie on would allow us; but quite on the qui vive, when in utter darkness, the utter and pitch darkness of a rainy night, were all astounded by most extraordinary cries and exclamations from a strong Irish accent, with all the usual vehemence and not very patient or choice expressions. I sprang up to the rafters of the roof and awaited the denouement which had so surprised and if I may use the word, under such precarious circumstances, alarmed us. The cause was this. The poor horses had the same desire we ourselves had to seek shelter from the rain and one after another, sought the same refuge, when in creeping in with feeling their way with stealthy step, the major's large black charger made his first advance into the interior by placing his two fore feet on the chest of the young recently joined ensign who, modestly, had taken the *outside* spot of refuge at the extreme entrance of the opening: for there was no gate nor door and *stood for some time* on the spot on which he had planted his feet. All the time the youngster did not cease to vociferate exclamations, expressions of pain and alarmed surprise in a somewhat ludicrous phraseology. As soon as it was discovered what was the cause and extent of the alarm and the animals expelled, it would be difficult to describe the mirth and enjoyment in which the remainder of the night was spent in that hovel of straw on a very wet night.

Such are the joys and pleasures which visit on service men such as we were; men within and that only clandestinely, a very few yards of a large and well garrisoned fortress, which they were to assault and take by escalade or as the public despatch designates it, by surprise the next day. But it was real fun and enjoyment among us that night; so, war has its enjoyments as well as its hardships, the latter of which I always thought exaggerated as outbalancing its amusements and such pleasures at an early period of life have a zest, which nothing can equal or subdue.

The hour mentioned by the Duke to make the assault was 2 p.m.[4] and we had only that night to collect such ladders as would answer

---

[4] He is in error here; Colville clearly states that it was planned for 6 p.m., but was delayed until 8 p.m. because of a parley.

the occasion, as we could, for we had but a very few supplied us from our own resources. The fatigue parties under active officers were out the whole of that wet night to ransack and collect from every farm or country house all the ladders that could be collected, which when produced were a fair specimen of what could be gathered from a French neighbourhood under such circumstances and without previous notice, i.e. a motley assemblage of ladders of all lengths and sizes and very few in fair condition, such as they were. And with such frail and unsuitable materials the formidable fortress was to be assailed the next day: most of the ladders tied together the best way the time and opportunity allowed; but at all events, on these the men were to mount and attain the summit of walls of no diminutive height and moreover, with determined hard resistance of old veterans at the top.

The signal gun fired at the appointed 2 p.m. and the soldiers who had been sheltered under such buildings as they could find, of which too many had crept up in a long series of years, rushed on to the assault and it was impossible for the officers whose duty it was to keep order on the occasion and prevent them from rushing forwards beyond their battalions, as their speed and zeal would prompt, or in short to keep any order. When we came to the point of escalade, i.e. to the spot at the foot where the ladders were to be planted, nothing could describe the impetuosity and struggling of the men, to be the *first* on them and on the walls. It was *my* post of duty to regulate the ascent as orderly as possible and in so doing I was detained at the foot of the ladders longer than I liked, for I soon found that nothing could be more dangerous than that situation at the bottom; for the men crowded so fast and without order, on the old French ladders that they soon began to give way, rung after rung, and the men came tumbling down with their bayonets fixed on those below as fast as possible. But it is quite surprising how many of us got to the top in a few seconds and then all appeared settled, but for the result of a burst we were preparing for into the citadel. When suddenly, a powder magazine exploded in our rear but at some distance, in the fort behind us, there was at once a sudden pause and immediately after we had orders to retrace our steps and get down as fast as we had ascended and moreover that no soldier should be allowed to go into the town and that no one officer or private should be permitted to pass in or out without a written pass.

The soldiers thought this hard and even the officers did not like the written pass. It was one of the terms of the convention of surrender, agreed to no doubt, to save time and prevent the possibility of the detention of the army in its advance to Paris; but at the time it appeared hard on those who a few moments before had scaled the walls. It was however strictly obeyed, as all the orders of the Duke were without cavil or hesitation. We were marched back through the very gates which we had rushed through just before, in very different feelings of excitement, and back to our bivouac instead of to comfortable quarters in the town, to which after so long privation we had anxiously and confidently looked for a relief. We passed another night in the bivouac, which although not by any means so wet from above as the night before, was anything but desirable or comfortable from the saturated state of the ground. Our night passed somewhat sulkily, in consequence and without any such adventure as could create fun or enjoyment.

Observe that we were all, excepting perhaps two or three, under 35 years of age, the greater part little above half that age, thoughtless and ready for anything. The day break of the following day found us again on the march, not much refreshed by the way we had passed the two previous days and nights; but on we trudged, in the early part in no great spirits or communicative mood. As day advanced all this disappeared and things took their usual course of taking advantage of whatever might attract our attention and excite curiosity; but without knowing or caring to enquire about our destination or what we had to do. After a few miles we came close up to the strong fortress of Péronne distinguished as La Pucelle, because, in all the wars of France, civil or foreign, it had never been taken[5]. This charm we were about to break and marched straight on towards the gate. I suppose the garrison was in a panic, or some communication had previously taken place between Sir Charles and the governor, for there appeared on our part no expectation of

---

[5] The fortress of Péronne had been besieged in 1536 by the Comte de Nassau, but it had held out for over a month and the siege was then abandoned. For this success it gained the name of 'La Pucelle'.

resistance and when within a very few yards of the gate, the word was passed *from the rear* to halt (we were in open column of companies and were to open right and left, which of course was instantly obeyed) and the Guards marched through the open space, through the gates and thus it was as I more than once read in the public papers, that Péronne was taken *by them!* I did not hear a shot fired, nor witness the least resistance.[6]

We merely entered and passed on 27th June.

[6] The First Division captured a hornwork at Péronne and after a few shots were exchanged, the fortress capitulated. John is right in the sense that it was hardly 'stormed'.

Chapter 20

Paris

The march to Paris was relatively uneventful, although the British soldiers were generally horrified by the state of the villages through which they passed, the Prussians having already ransacked them in vengeance for all the sufferings they had endured in Germany under French rule.

John does not comment on this aspect of the war, but does remember being under heavy fire in a village near Paris. Although John calls it Montmartre, it was actually the village of Aubervilliers which lay just under those heights. As General Colville wrote of Aubervilliers 'The French still held two or three houses at the end of it under cover of their artillery on the canal … We … sent in only 400 men with strong supports outside, and as I have found the French perfectly soldierlike in that respect, I particularly constrained my people to avoid unnecessary fire … it turned out as I expected, one sentry being killed by the mechancete[1] of an individual, most probably, being my only casualty during the three days I occupied the village.

> Hard forced marching for the now much worn out strength and energies of our men; through Landrecies and St Quentin, 28th (after our delay by the taking of Cambrai) to St Just, 29th Chantilly, 30th St Denis, and to the heights of Montmartre where at first we met with some considerable resistance and were twice turned out to meet serious preparations by the French troops to dispute our possession. On both occasions we were drawn up in line to oppose the enemy

---

[1] French for malice.

194

in defiance to dispute our advance and the village of Montmartre temporarily fortified for resistance. Under Lieutenant Colonel Napier we searched every house and nook, which could shelter a soldier, which completely gutted it, and so close was the dispute of possession carried on that I had some sentries of my picket planted on one side of a brick wall only nine inches thick, while the enemy had their sentries posted on the other side to prevent our advance, but it led to no violent effort on either side to intrude on each other's territory and the next day the enemy withdrew. In fact, the Prussians were giving them enough to do all around, and the dispirited French were little disposed to prevent our possession.

But here we at once entered on most active measures on both sides shot and shell being poured in on us, from the Paris side of the river and counter-batteries at once commenced on our side; and, in one of these my military career was nearly brought to an end in the very termination of the great contest. I was sent to help in the construction of a battery, having for its object to silence and if possible destroy an opposing battery from Paris, and finding it necessary to keep a sharp look out for the firing pouring in on us in rather too quick succession, I had planted a man with a quick eye at either end of my battery to give notice of what kind of missile we might expect after each shot, the words of warning were 'shot' or 'shell', as the case might be; of the former (being protected by the ramparts as far as they were complete) little notice was taken, and the men went on with their work, then in fact, laying the platform of the battery, in which a director [of operations], I was so intently engaged that I took no heed to the cry 'shell', but continued in my stooping position quite bent down over the work, when hearing a shell approaching me with more than usual rapidity and starting up at almost my full height, I could perceive distinctly a shell descending as far as I could see, directly on my head. I cannot account for what followed but it was so near me and close to my eyes that I had lost all power to obey our directions to throw myself forward, flat on my face in such circumstances, but I involuntarily and without the least reflection or knowing what I was doing, keeping my eye steadily fixed on the shell, kept bending backwards to escape it until my head nearly touched the ground behind, when it just outside dropped over the battery wall and exploded on the ground beneath. This was not a pleasant hint

195

and therefore it rejoiced me much to hear, almost on the next moment 'There is a flag, Paris has surrendered'. And so it was, just in time to save my bacon, for they had got quite the range of our battery which was exposed enough. We had no more notice of 'shots' or 'shells'.

Although the war was not over, it was to *us*, as to all fighting and practical purpose as far as we knew and at the time believed. And I was in so short a time, ready to be again sent to the right about, to look for something to do to maintain myself.

At this point, John finished his memoir and I will simply add a few comments to round up events.

A Convention was signed on 4 July and on the 8th, after the French army had retired from the city to go beyond the Loire, the Allies entered Paris and the division encamped in the Bois de Boulogne, which became their quarters for the next two months.

After this period the regiment was moved twenty kilometres south of Paris, being quartered at Marcoussis and Linas on the road to Orleans, where it remained until December 1815. The battalion was then ordered home, being given a route to march to Boulogne over eighteen days. They passed through Bourg la Reine on the 5th; Beaumont sur Oise 7th; Naoilles 8th; Marseille en Beauvaisis 9th; Lahaye Saint Romain 12th; Airaines 13th; Abbeville 14th; Quin [Quend?] 16th; Nampont 17th; Montreuil 18th; Samer 19th; Boulogne 23rd; Marquise 24th; Wissant 25th; Calais 27th and sailed for Dover on 2 January 1816.

The battalion landed at Dover on 3 January and was immediately ordered to Ireland where it was stationed at Waterford and where the Waterloo Medal was issued to each man.

With the war reduction, it was only a matter of time before the 2nd Battalion disbanded, which it was ordered to do on 24 April 1817. Those men deemed still fit for service were transferred to the 1st Battalion, all unfit men in both battalions being pensioned off. The officers of the 2nd Battalion were placed on half pay.

It would seem that having joined the 2nd Battalion prior to Waterloo, that John was formally placed in that battalion and hence stayed with them both in France and Ireland. In 1817 John left the Army on half pay and joined Trinity College in Dublin to study for a degree in theology and as happened with many ex-soldiers at this time, he found God and joined the ranks of the clergy.

Whilst in Ireland John married Isabella Mary Hatton on 8 July 1817 at Wexford and the couple eventually had eleven children, Elizabeth; William; Henry; John; James; Henrietta; Ross; Edward; Henry; Charles and Frederick, all of whom except poor Elizabeth and the first Henry surviving beyond childhood. Unfortunately, Isabella died on 5 July 1838 and John married Frances Mary Patten on 12 January 1841 at St. James in Westminster and had another six children with her, Emily; Arthur; Godfrey; Edith; Algernon and Alice.

John held a number of clergy posts, but eventually he settled at the rectory at Kibworth, in Leicestershire; including becoming master of the prestigious local Grammar School.

John only began to write his memoirs in 1868 but he unfortunately died before he finished them on 23 August of that year and was buried in his own churchyard.

He is buried with his first wife at Kibworth Church. The simple angular marble stone tablet is engraved as follows:

On the Obverse
Sacred to the Memory of Isabella Mary the Beloved Wife of
Rev. J.B. Hildebrand who died 5th July 1840 aged 40 years.
Also of the Rev. J.B. Hildebrand who died 23 August 1868
in his 75th year.

On the Reverse is engraved
Sacred also to the memory of Frances Mary his 2nd Wife,
born May 1803 died 3rd Dec 1870.
Buried at Froxfield Wilts[2].

---

[2] Froxfield is a village which lies on the Wiltshire / West Berkshire border about three miles west of Hungerford. She is probably buried in the graveyard of All Saints Church there.

Appendix I

Forced Billet and Good Reception

22nd Landrecies

Here I had to wait in the wet and mud (very deep) for a long time after dark for my billet for the night, which I was to get from a country gentleman, I believe mayor of the commune, and who had been sent for many times to hasten his movements. At last he came and gave me a billet for the night on a chateau, which would give me every comfort and quite near at hand. As it was very wet, dark and muddy beyond description, excepting as a French country cross road, this assistance of its near proximity was most cheering; but we went riding on and on following our guide till certainly 5 or 6 miles must have past. At last our guide brought us to a fine looking large chateau and, tired to death and impatient of entrance we pulled up at the hall door, up some 6 or 10 fine stone steps, with an imposing appearance of grandeur and consequently comfort most encouraging and cheering. But after ringing peal after peal from the doorbell without any answer or notice I became impatient from the apparent designed disregard of our summons and turning to my servant (a soldier) said thrice [in a] distinct voice and loud 'Thompson, this will not do, they will neither give us a light excepting that one wax candle, make them hear or be civil to us, so do you take the horses to the stables which [I] have no doubt you will easily find and I will in the mean time keep the position and then I think we shall at least be sure of [a] more present civility'. I spoke these words in the hall (a fine one) at the foot of a large handsome flight of stairs and had hardly concluded the last word until which we had not been able to extract a sound, when with terrible exclamation from the top of the stairs, and between, a voice exclaimed 'What, are you

English?' and before giving me time to answer her question, a fine portly middle aged lady rushed down and cried out, 'Oh! we thought you were the Prussians again, and were afraid'.

And after being assured I was English, she threw herself rather over proportioned to my then tender age and to such a sudden demand on my muscular powers, into my arms, sobbing and asking in too much excitement to await replies, all kinds of questions. At last she calmed down, with two other younger ladies who accompanied her, to a more rational conference, while she in the exuberance of her Irish heart (for Irish she was the wife of a Dublin banker) was ordering and seeing to everything that could be extemporised for our outward comforts and to our accommodation for the night. This good lady told me much of her early history and loaded me with messages to her friends and relatives in Ireland which I executed as far as I could remember and accomplish. She had been married to a banker and lived in France for 25 years. This was their country chateau. The next morning before daylight, we according to our orders took leave and started to join my division, after very many more than common civilities and such a short acquaintance. But the remembrance of the Prussians made them cling to me at once.

Appendix II

Sleep in Water

Landrecy 22 June

The weather was so warm and showery that I must take leave to explain how the following circumstance, after marching without taking off their clothes from Courtrai or rather Waterloo and having tramped I may say for at least 30 or 40 hours and the last under the hot sun, towards evening we were halted on the bank of what appeared to me as the bank of an ancient river, long dried up and with a corresponding bank at about 50 or 60 yards opposite, the banks were quite green and with a gradual slope on either side and the interval between them, i.e. what I had conceived the ancient bed appeared also on our approaching it just as green and as it appeared to us a most inviting bed, accustomed as we had been to mud and dirt and the men consequently looked on it at once with the most ardent desire to pass the night in. Indeed, so weary and over-done were they that I do not think any amount of comfort or accommodation could have prevailed on them to prolong their advance a dozen yards. The sergeants had taken up and marked out the different distances of the bivouac and nothing could have persuaded them to have voluntarily enlarged the boundaries. The men literally rushed into the apparent luxury and we only discovered when we attempted to lie down, which the majority had on the moment of the halt involuntarily done, that the appearance of fresh and inviting grass was false and deceptive, it was in fact but a swamp with a sound bottom covered thickly and therefore most invitingly with a kind of grass, but really water reeds and the underneath bed corresponding.

As I had ridden all day, while the poor fellows had walked with their arms &c, I did not feel as tired as they were, but after trying to sleep lying down with a soldier's knapsack under my head, while the water really arose to almost meet my chest I found it impossible and got up. I found almost every one of that division of the army, 10,000 strong, fast asleep in the water and we marched the next day as usual at or before daylight, pursued our march and as far as I could ever learn as equal to work and free from the effect of such a night as if they had slept in down beds: for myself I never felt better. It has often occurred to me to mention this circumstance to medical men and I could never extract but one answer to account for it and that was 'excitement', under which we were all pre-eminently influenced at the time. And I think no doubt it was the true cause of its having been followed by no ill effects. Be it remarked that the same men, after they had settled down in good tents and had as many comforts as such a state of life affords, began to break down, one after another and go to the hospital from low fever.

Appendix III

In the Wood

We had started from Maubeuge as usual very early and consequently arrived at Landrecy by 10 or 11 a.m. and as was my custom wherever we halted my servant was ready with my gun dog without regarding the kind of country we were in. About 11 I started taking to me the most inviting path to a large wood such as are common in France which I entered from the nearest point, very close on our bivouac. It was very extensive and having no guide, not very safe to enter, especially after the late defeat of the French forces and the strong feeling of resentment &c naturally both general and intense. I very soon thought of these things finding myself as I proceeded onward, surrounded on all sides by large bodies of charcoal burners, wild looking enough and quite black, seeming ready for anything, which being dressed in an old regiment light infantry jacket a good deal the worse for the hard service it had seen, and an old forage cap not altogether calculated to inspire respect was I began to think not quite the costume with which to face such company. But as always I was thoughtless of fears and consequences and straight on I went without turning to the right or left until I came to the third centre I had met of guide posts to cross roads, which in utter ignorance of the vicinity I could not make out to any good purpose as to guidance or direction and on looking up to the direction of the setting sun, perceived that it must be getting late and that it was time for me to retrace my steps, but how? I had passed 3 of these centres without observation and if I had observed without understanding and trusting only to my recollection that I had been travelling from the sun towards the east, I set out at once for the w[est] and at an active and quick pace hoped soon to get out of the wood. But after going on at [the] double quick, for a considerable time and the darkness increasing without any prospect of escaping or having any correct idea of my direction I became somewhat alarmed and increased my pace until I began to feel inclined to give in, when all at once I fell over a ha-ha game fence, over which I fell neck and heels and without an idea of where I was; only that I had landed in the midst of the bivouac *somewhere*, and dark as it was by the watch fires and other lights I soon found out to my joy that I had hit close on my own tiny camp of two blankets but which had been for some nights my sleeping refuge.

These small tents were formed of two blankets, two muskets with fixed bayonets being the support at each end the blankets for support being penetrated by the bayonets and thus so tightly stretched that on creeping in at one end you had a sufficient protection from the weather and even a good deal of rain, and lying on the ground sufficient room to turn in and breathe, a paradise of a resting place to a weary soldier. So little is required by contrivance and a little trouble to make one comfortable under very discouraging circumstances.

My servant had here, also another luxury, viz a supper of 2 ammunition biscuits and a large onion and a canteen of rum, to which I immediately addressed myself and having nearly devoured at least half, was beginning to think of sleep when the bottom of my blanket tent was raised and a face now familiar to us when any work was to be done, Colonel Napier's, presented itself and asked if I could give him shelter as he had missed his way. He as a matter of course under such circumstances entered, shared my blanket and the biscuits, but would not taste the rum and we were soon asleep. Colonel N[apier] had taken the command, I could never tell how, of the temporary battalion of sharpshooters which our brigade General Johnson had formed and not appearing at parades or other duties was never absent when anything of consequence was expected.

And [not] until I read the life of the late Sir Charles Napier, the greatest and best general of his day, did I know it was the great man who was my bedfellow. I believe his independence of spirit perhaps occasionally carried a little too far, prevented his being in favour at that time at the Horse Guards or the government and that he joined our army in this irregular way as a volunteer – under favour of General Johnson of the 4th Division under Sir Charles Colville. His great and zealous spirit could not rest quietly and satisfied away from the army on such an occasion.

I have no doubt it was to such feelings I was indebted for an honour I can never forget.

St Denis and Paris

Our next march from Cambrai to Paris was through St Denis, at that time an extensive village and I may say a suburb of Paris, through which it was impossible to march without horror and utter astonishment at the destruction of everything that could be destroyed by our immediate predecessors the Prussians. I suppose its proximity to the capital and also because some serious resistance was expected.

There was a fine large and remarkable from its situation and imposing appearance house standing conspicuously outside of the town which attracted my immediate attention and I entered it not by opening a door or doors or any other usual expedient, for all doors windows &c &c had been utterly destroyed not leaving even a vestige to mark where they ever were, by the Prussians into which … [This was never finished].

Appendix V

The Garrison of Lissa

From various records it has been possible to establish with reasonable accuracy the initial garrison of Lissa in May 1812. In the Monthly Returns for the 35th Foot[1] the following are stated to be on Lissa:

Major John Herries
Captains Francis May & Thomas King, Lieutenants Archibald McDonald & Richard Webb, Ensign John Hildebrand, Assistant Surgeon John Ludlow. 8 Sergeants, 2 Drummers, 200 Rank & File.

Royal Artillery
1st Lieutenant William Rains with a detachment of 30 men.

In the Monthly Returns for the Corsican Rangers[2] the following are stated to be on Lissa:

Captains P Gerolame & Pearce Lowen, Lieutenant Cosmo Gugliano, Ensigns D Perette & Luigi Rigo with 200 Rank & File.

De Roll's Regiment
Captain Joseph Barbier, Lieutenant Otto Salinger with 200 Rank & File.

Calabrian Free Corps
Captain Roncus with 100 Rank & File.

---

[1] The National Archives WO17/145.
[2] The National Archives WO380/5.

Bibliography

In the course of this book, a great many books were consulted, but these are the primary ones:

Anon., *Army Lists,* various dates

Anon., *The Battle of Waterloo, by a Near Observer. 2 Vols.* (London, 1917).

Anon., *The Waterloo Medal Roll* (Dallington, 1992).

Anon., *The Royal Military Calendar* (London 1820).

Bromley, D. & J., *Wellington's Men Remembered* (Barnsley, 2012).

Burnham, R. and McGuigan, R. *The British Army Against Napoleon* (Barnsley, 2010).

Cannon, R., *Historical Record of the Twenty First Regiment* (London, 1849).

Colville J., *The Portrait of a General* (Salisbury, 1980).

Dalton, C., *The Waterloo Roll Call* (London, 1904).

Dietz P., *The British in the Mediterranean* (London, 1994).

Hardy M., *The British and Vis, War in the Adriatic 1805-15* (Oxford, 2009).

Hayter, A., *The Backbone; The Diaries of a Military Family in the Napoleonic Wars* (Durham, 1993).

Martin, R., *History of the British Possessions in the Mediterranean: Comprising Gibraltar, Malta, Gozo and the Ionian Islands* (London, 1837).

Mullen, A. *The Military General Service Roll 1793-1814* (London, 1990).

Pocock, T., *Remember Nelson; The Life of Captain Sir William Hoste* (London, 1977).

_____, *Stopping Napoleon* (London, 2004).

Siborne, Captain W., *History of the Waterloo Campaign* (London, 1990).

Syrett, D. and DiNardo, R., *The Commissioned Sea Officers of the Royal Navy 1660-1815* (Aldershot, 1994).

Trimen, R., *An Historical Memoir of the 35th Royal Sussex Regiment of Foot* (Southampton, 1873).

Index